Wertheim Publications in Industrial Relations

Wertheim Publications in Industrial Relations

J. D. Houser, *What the Employer Thinks*, 1927

Wertheim Lectures on Industrial Relations, 1929

William Haber, *Industrial Relations in the Building Industry*, 1930

Johnson O'Connor, *Psychometrics*, 1934

Paul H. Norgren, *The Swedish Collective Bargaining System*, 1941

Leo C. Brown, S.J., *Union Policies in the Leather Industry*, 1947

Walter Galenson, *Labor in Norway*, 1949

Dorothea de Schweinitz, *Labor and Management in a Common Enterprise*, 1949

Ralph Altman, *Availability for Work: A Study in Unemployment Compensation*, 1950

John T. Dunlop and Arthur D. Hill, *The Wage Adjustment Board: Wartime Stabilization in the Building and Construction Industry*, 1950

Walter Galenson, *The Danish System of Labor Relations: A Study in Industrial Peace*, 1952

Lloyd H. Fisher, *The Harvest Labor Market in California*, 1953

Theodore V. Purcell, S. J., *The Worker Speaks His Mind on Company and Union*, 1953

Donald J. White, *The New England Fishing Industry*, 1954

Val R. Lorwin, *The French Labor Movement*, 1954

Philip Taft, *The Structure and Government of Labor Unions*, 1954

George B. Baldwin, *Beyond Nationalization: The Labor Problems of British Coal*, 1955

Kenneth F. Walker, *Industrial Relations in Australia*, 1956

Charles A. Myers, *Labor Problems in the Industrialization of India*, 1958

Herbert J. Spiro, *The Politics of German Codetermination*, 1958

Mark W. Leiserson, *Wages and Economic Control in Norway, 1945–1957*, 1959

Studies in Labor-Management History

Lloyd Ulman, *The Rise of the National Trade Union: the Development and Significance of its Structure, Governing Institutions, and Economic Policies*, 1955

Joseph P. Goldberg, *The Maritime Story: A Study in Labor-Management Relations*, 1957, 1958

Wages and Economic Control in NORWAY

1945-1957

by

Mark W. Leiserson

HARVARD UNIVERSITY PRESS
Cambridge, Massachusetts
1959

Distributed in Great Britain by
Oxford University Press
London

The Library of Congress catalog entry for this book appears on page 174

Printed in the United States of America

To the memory of
William M. Leiserson
1883–1957

Foreword

The postwar years have seen throughout the world one of the greatest expansions of production in economic history. Virtually all countries, both Communist and non-Communist, have shared in this production boom. But the demands on the economies of the world have grown even faster than their capacity to produce. As a result, the production boom has been accompanied quite generally by inflation. In virtually every country of Europe the cost of living by 1957 was from 40 per cent to more than 65 per cent above 1948. Contrary to the predictions of many economists, the rise in prices has not tended to accelerate. Indeed, in nearly all countries of Europe the rise in prices between 1953 and 1957 was between 10 and 15 per cent — considerably less than the rise between 1948 and 1953.

The ways in which the rapid gains in production have been achieved and the devices by which inflation has either been held to a creep or reduced to a creep have varied from country to country, depending upon the distribution of political and economic power and the institutions and traditions of the country. Norway, more than any other country outside the iron curtain, has relied upon central planning. Dr. Leiserson's study sets forth in fascinating detail the devices that have been used in Norway in executing the plan, the principal problems that have been encountered, and the results that have been achieved. He gives a lucid analysis of how the methods of executing the plan have changed as circumstances have changed — though the basic goals have remained unchanged. Dr. Leiserson's objective has been an ambitious one, and he has accomplished it with conspicuous success. He has examined the fundamentals of the Norwegian economy and has sought to explain just why the economy has behaved as it has. His study is one of the most careful and most sophisticated examinations of the operations of an economy that has ever been made.

The basic character of the Norwegian plan was derived from the fact that the country was controlled by the Labor Party. Hence the purpose of Norwegian planning has been, as Dr. Leiserson points out, "to produce results more or less in conformity with the ideas of social justice prevalent in the labor movement." Two principal but closely related problems confronted the Norwegian planners. One was to prevent the rapid expansion of the economy from producing runaway inflation — since runaway inflation would have caused a host of problems as well as severe injustice. The other was to prevent collective bargaining from interfering with the high rate of capital formation required by the objectives of the national plan. These two objectives have been achieved. The rise in prices has been substantial and it has not been stopped, but it has not been runaway, and the rate of rise, on the whole, has shown a tendency to diminish. The rate of capital formation, in spite of the strong trade unions, has been higher relative to the gross national product than in any other country outside the iron curtain.

Prices have been controlled by a variety of devices that have varied with circumstances and with the immediate objectives of price policies — because, while the fundamental objective of price policy at all times has been to prevent runaway inflation, the immediate objective has sometimes been to check the rise in prices and at other times to absorb gains in purchasing power by assisting a rise in prices. The arsenal of instruments used to deal with prices has included rationing, excise taxes, licenses, subsidies, planned changes in the rate of government saving, and wage restraint.

Achievement of a high rate of investment has been mainly accomplished by wage policy and price policy. The peculiar collective bargaining institutions of Norway have been favorable to a policy of wage restraint. The great centralization of bargaining has made it natural for trade unions to consider the effect of wage changes upon prices — an effect which the individual union can ordinarily not afford to consider under decentralized bargaining. Consequently, Norwegian trade unions in the postwar period appear to have been an influence for holding down money wages rather than raising them. The government has attempted at various times to limit the pressure for wage increases by influencing the cost-of-living index — "manipulating" the index is perhaps not too strong an expression. But the efforts of some of the national trade union leaders and the government to limit the rise of money wages have not been sufficient to permit the high rate of investment required by the national plan. Controlled inflation has been the device used to divert resources into investment on the scale required by the national plan. By permitting prices to rise at more or less controlled rates, profits were kept high. At the same time, dividend payments were limited and other devices were used to stimulate corporate saving. Thus, inflation has been a device for encouraging both savings and investment. It has also been a device for reconciling national planning with the institution of collective bargaining.

The Norwegian experience sheds light on many interesting issues that Dr. Leiserson ably discusses. A widely discussed question is whether it is possible to maintain a stable price level under full employment when trade unions are strong. The Norwegian experience reminds one that the answer to this question depends, among other things, upon the nature of the particular institutions of collective bargaining. There are great differences in collective bargaining institutions, and different institutions produce different results. The Norwegian experience characteristically shows the effect of trade union structure upon union policies. With highly centralized bargaining, as in Norway, unions have good reason to take account of the effects of wage bargains upon prices. When bargaining is in small units, individual unions cannot afford to practice wage restraint. But even when the bargaining is virtually on a nation-wide basis, the unions may be optimistic in their estimates of future productivity increases and thus may push up wages too fast for productivity. At any rate, in Norway the price level has continued to rise at about the same rate as in other countries in Europe. To some extent, the rise of prices in Norway reflects the unusual dependence of the country upon foreign trade.

Of considerable interest is Dr. Leiserson's discussion of the relative importance of collective bargaining and market influences as determinants of the hourly earnings of workers. Again the results of the Norwegian experience reflect the special circumstances of Norway. The Norwegian unions were not seeking to reenforce market trends, but to hold them in check and, in some cases, to divert them — the unions were trying to retard the rise of money wages and to change the structure of wages through raising low paid workers and low paid industries relative to high paying workers and industries. An important circumstance was the fact that unions in Norway are strongest in the high paying industries.

The attempts of unions to limit the rise in wages and to alter the structure of wages has been the principal reason for the "wage drift" — a substantial rise in hourly earnings that cannot be accounted for by contractual wage settlements. The wage drift seems to have been greatest where the opposition of unions to market influences has been most pronounced. Thus the net effect of collective bargaining upon money wages has been considerably less than the unions intended it to be.

Of unusual interest are the compromises that have been worked out in Norway between national planning on the one hand and collective bargaining on the other. Sometimes it is said that the two are incompatible, but the Norwegians have succeeded in combining national planning with considerable autonomy on the part of trade unions. The trade unions temporarily permitted bargaining to be subordinated to state controls, but the unions have insisted on their independence, and compulsory arbitration, accepted as a necessary expedient for a few years, has been terminated. But the victory of the trade unions has been far from complete. The planners, as I have indicated, have used inflation to control the allocation of resources. In spite of the increased autonomy of the trade unions, the share of private consumption in the net national product has gone down and is, indeed, one of the lowest in Europe.

Dr. Leiserson's able study is an examination of economic issues. He does not undertake to deal with the important and interesting political issues raised by national planning, such as the problems faced by the Labor Party in deciding what values the plan should implement and the difficulties of reconciling different ideas within the party. There are hints of conflicts of view and of cabinet changes as a result, but examination of these events and their philosophical implications lie outside the scope of the study.

When one compares the experience of Norway with the experience of other European countries, one wonders whether Norway would have done just as well or better with considerably less central planning. Unfortunately, one can only speculate about the answer. No two countries have the same conditions, and the differences in policies between countries have been great. But the differences in results are surprisingly small. Norway has done better than some countries in increasing production and in keeping inflation fairly moderate, but it has not done as well as other countries. Norway has, however, as I have pointed out, had the highest rate of capital formation of any country outside the iron curtain. Is this high rate of capital formation a virtue or a waste? Would less central planning or a different kind of central planning have permitted Norway to have gained an equally large increase in output with less capital formation and with release of a larger share of current output for current consumption? Undoubtedly, the nature of Norwegian industry, the importance of shipping, of electric power and of pulp and paper, explain in large measure the need for a high rate of capital formation, although the record of France, which has achieved a very rapid gain in output with a low rate of capital formation, must be enviable to many countries.

Sumner H. Slichter

Contents

Tables

Author's Preface

The importance of wage determination processes in any system of economic control needs no emphasis in these times of strenuous, even bitter controversy over union power, cost inflation, and employment policy. A principal assumption of this book is that an analysis of wage determination in the relatively highly controlled Norwegian economy will have value in considering the problems of any economy where the government makes a conscious effort to preserve full employment, price stability, and free but organized labor markets.

In undertaking this analysis, I have not attempted to provide an "inside story" of collective bargaining and economic policy in postwar Norway. I have deliberately emphasized economic factors, seeking explanations in terms of avowed economic goals and relatively distinct features of the economic environment rather than attempting to unravel the complex web of personal, organizational, and political motivations which underlies economic behavior. Nevertheless, any valid insights into Norwegian economic problems and the interaction between the system of collective bargaining and economic control are primarily the result of the patience and kindness of those Norwegians who in one way or another helped me to some understanding of the Norwegian economy in this deeper sense.

Of the many in government and private life with whom I worked as an economist in the U.S. Special Mission to Norway for Economic Cooperation from 1951 to 1953 or who were gracious enough to discuss my problems during a return visit in the summer of 1956 on a Wertheim Fellowship, I can here mention only a few: Petter Jakob Bjerve, Director, and Odd Aukrust, Chief of the Research Division of the Central Bureau of Statistics; Konrad Nordahl, Chairman, and Kjell Holler, chief economist of the Norwegian Federation of Labor; Lars Aarvig, chief economist of the Norwegian Employers' Association; Governor Erik Brofoss and Mr. Gabriel Kielland of the Bank of Norway; Messrs. Eivind Ericksen, Trul Glesne, and Hermod Skånland of the Norwegian Finance Ministry; Mr. Dagfin Juel of the Prime Minister's Office; Mr. Haakon Lie, general secretary of the Norwegian Labor Party and his wife Minnie; Per Krog of the Federation of Agricultural Cooperative Associations, and Per Gustavsen, presently of the NATO Secretariat. There is no adequate way for me to express my deep appreciation for the help and friendly hospitality they extended to me.

On this side of the Atlantic I count it more an honor than an obligation to acknowledge the aid and encouragement of Professors Sumner H. Slichter and John T. Dunlop. Both, at one time or another, have paid me the high compliment of taking my work seriously enough to subject it to searching criticism.

My debt to all of these and others is immeasurable but none can be held in any way responsible for errors of fact or vagary of interpretation.

The bulk of the statistical material in this study derives from three main sources of data prepared by the Norwegian Central Bureau of Statistics: (1) production statistics from surveys of mining and manufacturing establishments issued annually under the title *Norges Industri: Produksjonsstatistikk;* (2) national accounts figures for the years through 1951 appearing under the title *Nasjonalregnskap* in two volumes of the official Norwegian statistical series — Norges Offisielle Statistikk XI. 109 (1952) and XI. 185 (1954) — for the years since 1952 published in the Annual Economic Survey for 1957 (*Økonomisk Utsyn over Aret 1957.* N.O.S. XI. 285); (3) the annual survey of wages published in the official statistical series under the title *Lønnsstatistikk.* For purposes of brevity these sources have been cited simply as *Produksjonsstatistikk, Nasjonalregnskap,* and *Lønnsstatistikk* respectively, without referring to individual volumes. All national accounts figures for the years since 1951 are preliminary and subject to revision. Moreover, the data on man years of employment and wages and salaries by sector for 1952–1955 (Tables 14–17) are early, unpublished estimates which the Central Bureau of Statistics very kindly supplied. They undoubtedly will be changed before appearing in final published form.

Without the financial assistance of a Jacob Wertheim Fellowship in Industrial Relations the study would never have been completed. And I am further indebted to the Wertheim Committee for providing the services of Mrs. Ruth Whitman. She has my profound gratitude and admiration for her work in preparing the manuscript for the press and her valiant, if vain, struggle to bring light and air into my English. Grateful acknowledgment is due as well to Mrs. Anne Granger for typing the final manuscript and to Mr. Hans Hylin of Oslo for assistance in some of the statistical calculations. My wife Jean, in addition to typing early drafts and preparing statistical tables, has cheerfully borne all the burdens which both the research and the writing indirectly inflicted upon her.

The dedication of this book is a poor expression of the debt to my father. Although he died before the completion of the manuscript, the good humor and gentle irony of his comments at earlier stages were at once humbling and inspiring. I would like to think that at least a shadow of his wisdom and spirit found its way into these pages.

Mark W. Leiserson
New Haven, Connecticut
September, 1958

Wages and Economic Control in Norway
1 9 4 5 – 1 9 5 7

CHAPTER 1

Wages in a System of Economic Control

If pressed to identify the central economic problems confronting the present generation, most economists would almost certainly give prominent place to the difficulties of simultaneously achieving and maintaining "full employment," stable prices, and relatively rapid rates of economic growth. And high on the list of associated controversial issues would be the question of the degree and character of governmental intervention if the objectives of stability and growth are to be realized.

Much discussion has been focused upon the question of whether the processes of wage determination in an economy with powerful and independent collective bargaining institutions will tend to frustrate any general governmental measures to foster high and stable levels of economic activity. Of necessity this discussion usually takes place on an abstract level. Differences of opinion are usually based on differing judgments regarding the behavior of trade unions and the operation of collective bargaining. It should be possible to cast some light on the relative validity of these judgments by an analysis of the wage determination process in a system where the government assumes a high degree of responsibility for the operation and growth of the economy, yet where private collective bargaining institutions are still accorded a powerful and independent status. The present study is an attempt to present such an analysis, utilizing the more than ten years' experience in Norway with the establishment, operation, and continual adaptation of a highly integrated system of economic policy measures and their interaction with the structure and behavior of private economic organizations.

The Philosophy of Economic Control in Norway

The Labor Party which has enjoyed an absolute parliamentary majority in Norway since October 1945 is socialist both in origins and avowed objectives. But one of the most distinguishing features of Norwegian socialism has been its nondogmatic and pragmatic character, or as Professor Galenson has put it "its ability to synthesize different shades of opinion by concentrating on immediate objectives." [1] This is not to say that the Labor government has lacked fairly well-defined socio-economic objectives; rather, that the evolution of economic policy in postwar Norway cannot be viewed simply as a process of establishing a "socialist" state in accordance with some rigid blueprint of Norwegian design.

In the first years after the war the immediate problems of economic reconstruction dominated economic policy decisions. Still it is not too much to say
that throughout the whole postwar period economic policy was shaped to
conform with what the Labor government consistently cited as its fundamental economic objectives:

To insure full and efficient employment.

To establish the necessary conditions for a steady increase in production and
productivity.

To ensure a reasonable distribution of the available supply of goods and
services between the various economic sectors, social groups, and parts of the
country.[2]

Taken simply as statements of desirable ends, these basic goals are general
enough to be applicable to almost any Western democracy. Their true
significance, however, rests on the conviction of the Labor government that
they are attainable (and only attainable) under a system of "economic
democracy." At the base of this concept lies the fact that capital must be
employed to serve socio-economic ends and that uncontrolled private administration of capital cannot be relied upon as a means to these ends.

Labour's views on economic democracy are based upon what can be called the
"social concept of capital." The owner of a private enterprise does not merely
exercise exclusive private legal rights and does not administrate his private
property only. He is entrusted with the productive capital of our society upon
which economic progress, social prosperity, and the economic future of the
workers depend.[3]

Such a concept of economic democracy has led away from the idea that
nationalization of all industry is essential in a socialist society.

It is . . . important not to consider socialism as equivalent to public ownership
of all enterprises. It was an idea that once was considered fundamental, but it has
been modified into a much more complex and advanced concept of socialist
economics in a Welfare State: full employment, fair shares, social security and
the responsibility for economic policies vested in Parliamentary organs.[4]

In brief, the objectives of the Labor government may perhaps best be
described as that of establishing a socially controlled economy where the
government does not hesitate to wield its authority in economic affairs to
achieve its goals as determined and controlled under a democratic and representative form of government. A salient feature of this type of socially controlled economy, as developed in Norway, is the existence of central economic
planning in the sense of an explicit and conscientious effort to make any
governmental program internally consistent and to make possible a rational

evaluation of the appropriate policy measures to be adopted in carrying out that program.

Vesting the state with prime responsibility and authority for the economic well being and social welfare of the Norwegian people has inevitably had an impact on the degree of individual freedom in the society. Indeed, Labor Party spokesmen are wont to cite the elimination of the unrestricted exercise of economic freedom (characteristic, as they see it, of "economic liberalism") as an important advantage of the controlled economy. Nevertheless, in most respects, devotion to the traditional ideals of individual liberty is as strong in Norway as in any other country in the world. The focal point of the system has been to establish control over the use of productive resources. The greatest impact has been on the exercise of property rights in the use of natural resources and the instruments of production. The liberal tenets of consumer sovereignty and free labor, on the other hand, are accorded a prominent, but not entirely inviolate, place in the Norwegian socialist credo.

The Economic Achievements of the Postwar Period

A superficial survey of the performance of the Norwegian economy since the war yields impressive evidence that the system of economic planning and control has been apparently successful in attaining its short-run policy objectives. At the end of the war Norway found herself with almost one fifth of her capital equipment destroyed (including the loss of around 50 per cent of the merchant fleet, her greatest source of foreign exchange earnings), with industrial production less than two thirds and commodity exports less than one quarter of their 1938 levels. In addition, the occupation authorities' method of financing their expenditures had created a vastly inflated supply of money and bank reserves. Yet within two years from the date of liberation, real gross national product and industrial production were back to prewar levels and in 1956 exceeded those levels by some 70 per cent and 100 per cent respectively. The volume of commodity exports in the latter year was over 50 per cent above 1938 and the merchant fleet at over eight million gross registered tons, was 75 per cent larger than the maximum prewar size. Throughout the ten-year period a gross investment rate in the neighborhood of 30 per cent of gross national product was maintained. The rate of growth in output per man-year averaged over 4.5 per cent a year from 1946 to 1950 and around 3.0 per cent from 1950 to 1956. The level of real wages had risen by 1956 to 40–45 per cent over 1938; private consumption per capita had increased to a level of 40 per cent above the prewar standard.

Unemployment during the postwar years has been extremely low; by virtually any criteria a state of full employment (if not "over-full employment") has existed. Production losses due to strikes and industrial disputes have been negligible in the aggregate. The rise in prices that has taken place, while substantial, is about the same order of magnitude as the postwar price increases in the United States over the same period, nor does the increase stand out as extreme compared with other Western European countries. While still liable to substantial fluctuation, the balance of payments deficit in 1956 was small. Even in 1954 and 1955, when the deficit was roughly equal in absolute magnitude to the 1946 deficit, it amounted at the most to 5 per cent of gross national product with total export earnings covering almost 95 per cent of current expenditures for the import of goods and services. In the first postwar years the latter ratio ranged between 75 and 85 per cent. Finally, there has been the gradual but imposing reduction in the monetary potential of the financial system. Bank reserves at the end of 1955 were less than one-quarter what they had been ten years previously. The ratio of the total money supply to gross national product dropped from a level of almost 85 percent in 1946 to about 52 per cent in 1956.

To the Labor government, of course, the economic achievements of the period gain significance from the fact that they were accomplished within the framework of a democratic Welfare State. The benefits of various types of social legislation have been increased in size and coverage as the economic situation of the country has improved. Equally fundamental, in terms of the underlying social philosophy of the Labor Party has been the equalization (relative to prewar) in the size distribution of personal incomes and in the distribution of income between the major economic sectors of the country — particularly between agriculture and industry.

The Relevance of the Norwegian Experience

The intrinsic interest in the Norwegian experience of a controlled economy would perhaps be sufficient justification for a descriptive treatment of postwar economic developments in Norway. The Norwegian experience, however, is not merely interesting, but is relevant to economic policy in other countries — the United States in particular — and raises questions as to the possibility of generalizing from that experience. Such generalizations inevitably involve the assumption that the fundamental elements — the criteria for decisions and the "environmental" constraints on these decisions — in terms of which individual or collective behavior is to be explained — exhibit enough similarity to permit valid comparisons between Norway and other countries. The claim that study of trade union behavior in the Norwegian economy will be useful in the analysis of trade union behavior in the United States implies that the determinants of trade union decisions are sufficiently analogous in the two situations to endow comparisons with some analytic significance. Clearly such an implication is subject to empirical evidence, even though in large part the evidence necessarily must involve comparisons of what are essentially subjective goals and value-orientations. It is hoped that enough of this evidence will be found in the analysis that follows to justify the generalizations ventured at the end.

The logic of this approach is not altered when governmental, rather than union or worker, behavior is the subject of analysis. Just as the decisions of individual or organized economic units may be explained in terms of the goal toward which action is directed relative to the constraints which the "environment" places upon that action, the explanation of governmental policy decisions may be approached in similar fashion. In the latter case, however, it may become more difficult and, hence, more important not to confuse analysis of governmental behavior in terms of its own criteria for action as justification for that action in any broader sense. The proposition that the evolution of Norwegian economic policy, in general, and wage policy, in particular, has a general relevance is not, so far as the present study is concerned, based on the normative judgment that governmental decisions in other countries ought to follow goals similar to those which guide economic policy in Norway, but rather on the refutable hypothesis that such a similarity either already exists or is likely to develop in the future. Further, this presumption of "similarity" need not, and in the present instances is not intended to, extend to all the goals toward which the behavior of government, unions, and other institutions, is oriented.

With regard to the role of "environmental" influences, it would, of course, be absurd to ignore those unique characteristics of the Norwegian social, economic, and political environment which have obviously been of extreme importance in shaping economic developments. In this case there can be no stress on "similarity" as a basis for generalization. Instead, particular care must be taken to elucidate the manner in which these idiosyncratic factors have in fact affected economic behavior in order to permit some judgment of the significance of abstracting from these factors. In other words, the now commonplace view of Scandinavian countries as the "social laboratories" for the Western world must be recognized for the metaphor it is and not be permitted to obscure the fact that experience in those countries has no more the character of "laboratory" results than empirical observations of economic development in any other countries.

The point of these preliminary remarks on the possible significance which may be derived from a study of the postwar Norwegian economy is to illuminate certain of the basic principles which underlie the organization and emphasis of this analysis of Norwegian wages and wage policy. Specifically, in order to derive some general results from the study, the focus of the analysis has been on three sets of "wage problems" as they affect the achievement of stable full employment and the rate of economic growth. First is the problem of price stability and balance of payments equilibrium connected with wages as a cost element, as well as a primary determinant of consumer incomes and, hence, demand. Secondly, there are the closely related problems of the effects the relative wage share exercises upon the rate of capital accumulation the economy is able to undertake and maintain. Thirdly, another range of problems involves the efficiency and relative rates of growth among economic activities within the economy and is connected with the allocative function which wages perform in directing manpower to various economic sectors, occupations, and locations. It is perhaps unnecessary to emphasize that these problems cannot be dealt with entirely separately from one another.

The next two chapters undertake to establish the "initial conditions" and basic "structural constraints" which have been of importance in shaping the actual course of wages during the period under consideration. Chapter 2 gives a brief survey of the general social and economic landscape, covering generally, but perforce somewhat superficially, economic structure, socio-economic organization, including the impact of the war and occupation. In the succeeding chapter the rationale and instruments of postwar Norwegian economic policy are examined in order to bring out as clearly as possible the nature of wage policy problems as a part of the general structure of economic policy and control.

Against this background, Chapters 4 and 5 provide a more or less straightforward description of the implementation of wage policy as carried out in compulsory arbitration awards or in centrally negotiated settlements between union and employer federations. This description of the centralized process of wage decision-making is supplemented by the analysis in Chapter 6 of the actual course of development in money wage levels and the relation which that development bore to wage policy decisions.

The remainder of the volume is devoted to detailed analysis, in turn, of the relation between wage developments and the general level of prices, labor's share in national income, the rate of capital formation and the allocation of labor within the economy. The final chapter attempts to draw together the threads of the analysis and to provide an evaluation of Norwegian experience in handling the wage problems of a controlled economy.

CHAPTER 2

The Institutional and Economic Framework
of Wage Determination

Analytically, the degree of complexity of the Norwegian economy probably is close to that of the larger industrial nations. The importance of natural resource endowment, location, topography, particular social institutions, and so on, in shaping the course of economic development is as great as if not greater than in larger countries. Consequently, both for an adequate understanding of Norwegian experience and as a basis for relevant generalization, it is necessary to have continually in mind certain of the distinguishing characteristics of the Norwegian economic, institutional, and political structure. The present chapter is designed to give an impressionistic sketch of certain features of the socio-economic environment which appear to have been of particularly crucial significance in the evolution of Norwegian economic policy in general, and wage policy in particular.

The Structure of the Norwegian Economy

With a population of only 3.5 million and a total area of 324,000 square kilometers (about 126,000 square miles), Norway is the least densely populated country in Western Europe. But almost three-quarters of this area consists of barren land, lakes, and other uninhabitable terrain. About 23 per cent can be used for productive forest operations and only 3 per cent is suitable for farming or grazing. Furthermore, the population is concentrated in the southern and southeastern parts of the country, almost 30 per cent of the population living in the districts immediately adjacent to the Oslo fjord. The four northernmost provinces account for over 40 per cent of the total area of the country and contain less than 16 per cent of the inhabitants.

Having neither sufficient cultivable land to provide food nor an abundant variety of natural resources, Norway has been forced to develop export production through intensive exploitation of those resources it does have in order to obtain in world markets the products it needs for economic survival and growth. Her dependence on foreign trade is extreme: imports of goods and services amount to close to one-half of net national product. The importance of foreign trade to the economy is so large that considerations of the external economic situation are always present, and very likely dominant, in the minds of those concerned with economic policy.

This "external" orientation of the Norwegian economy is, of course, reflected in the economic structure of the country. Quite naturally Norway has turned to the mountains, the sea, and the forests as the resources upon which to base her export industries. Forestry, fishing and whaling, mining, and ocean shipping account for between one-sixth and one-seventh of total factor income. The merchant fleet of approximately eight million gross registered tons (the third largest in the world) directly furnishes net foreign exchange earnings sufficient to pay for one-quarter to a third of total imports. The other sectors not only supply directly a significant quantity of export products in the form of ores, fish, and whale oil, but also are the raw material sources for the most important export industries in the manufacturing sector. About 25 per cent of the net product (at factor cost) of the manufacturing sector originates in the export industries of fish canning and freezing, pulp and paper chemicals, fats and oils, ferro-alloys, aluminum, and other metals.

As important as raw materials resources in shaping the character of the Norwegian economy has been the availability of hydro-electric power. Hydro-electric power production now is around 25 billion kilowatt hours per year, of which almost half is used in the electro-chemical, electro-metallurgical, and pulp and paper industries. Moreover, as the major undeveloped natural resource of the country, hydro-electric power inevitably has been and will undoubtedly continue to be the principal foundation for industrialization of the economy. Forestry, whaling, and, to a lesser extent, fishing, have already been expanded to close to the maximum limit, while exploitation of mineral wealth has inherent limits and in any case depends upon the use of power in the reduction and processing of ore. The hydro-electric power potential of the country has been estimated as sufficient to provide an annual production of 120 billion kilowatt hours, so that generating capacity is presently only about one-fifth developed.

In terms of a ratio between actual and "potential" resource exploitation, Norway, even at the current level of technology, must be judged to have relatively large opportunities for further economic development. Those sectors upon which economic development is dependent, however, impose relatively heavy capital requirements per capita on the economy. Prime examples are, of course, shipping and hydro-electric power development, as well as the electro-chemical and electro-metallurgical industries and further expansion of mineral and forest resources. The situation is aggravated by climatic and topographical factors which make necessary relatively large capital outlays on the construction and maintenance of roads, communication facilities, and other forms of "public" capital. As a consequence, rapid economic progress not only involves a high rate of domestic capital accumulation, but also is likely to generate a need for long term capital imports.

Norwegian industry is concentrated on light manufactured products with a substantial portion of production carried out in extremely small units. Firms of less than 100 workers employ over half of those engaged in mining and manufacturing and account for about 45 per cent of the net value added in this sector. In 1952 there were only 43 firms in mining and manufacturing with 500 or more workers. Nevertheless, in relative terms, there is still a fairly high degree of concentration of production in the larger firms, with 3 per cent of the mining and manufacturing establishments holding half of the total value of fixed assets and producing 40 per cent of the net product.[2]

In summary, all these structural characteristics of the Norwegian economy — the dependence on foreign trade, the large capital requirements for economic development, the substantial importance of small firms, with, nevertheless, a significant concentration of production in the larger units — these not only exercise a direct effect upon economic developments but also are primary considerations in the formulation and execution of economic policy.

Economic Organization in the Norwegian Economy

Like other European countries, Norway has developed a relatively highly organized economy in the sense that individual economic units have tended to band together into various types of associations. The history of coöperative activity on the part of producers, workers, and consumers extends back into the nineteenth century. Trade and industry associations among whose purposes were regulation of prices, competitive practices, and control of entry began to be formed with increasing frequency around the turn of the century and grew increasingly important throughout the interwar period.[3] Governmental policy toward these private arrangements to regulate competition, as expressed in trust control legislation shortly after the first World War and subsequently revised and expanded has been one of supervision and control rather than "trustbusting."

The greatest degree of joint production and marketing arrangements have been developed in agriculture, forestry, and fishing. Producer coöperatives in fishing are legally accorded exclusive rights to the sale of fish in Norway. Virtually all dairy production and about 70 per cent of meat and egg production is sold through coöperatives. A substantial percentage of private forest owners (holding over 60 per cent of the total forest acreage) market their timber through the Forest Owners' Association. Because of the high dependence upon grain imports, the marketing of grain is carried out by a government monopoly which sets domestic grain prices. By law, too, all sales of potato starch must be made through the Potato Starch Factories' Sales Association controlled by the potato farmers. There are also various kinds of agriculture coöperatives,[4] and in addition there are two farm union organizations, Norges Bondelag and Norsk Bonde-og Smaabrukarlag — the latter being primarily an organization of small farmers. These two organizations are particularly important in negotiations with the government on agricultural price and subsidy policy; in a sense they act as the farmer trade unions. Finally, consumer coöperatives in Norway, as in the other Scandinavian countries, have attained considerable importance in retail trade.

The Development of Collective Bargaining Institutions

It is against this background of a high degree of organization and coöperative activity in all aspects of Norwegian economic life, that the institutions of industrial relations and collective bargaining must be viewed. The organized labor movement in Norway,[5] although it originated in the middle of the nineteenth century, began to attain sizable proportions only in the two final decades of that century. It was not until 1899 that the Norwegian Federation of Labor (Arbeidernes Faglige Landsorganisasjon i Norge, colloquially referred to as the LO) was formed with an affiliated membership of less than 5,000 in six craft unions and the Oslo City Central. The extent of union organization was considerably higher than this, unions with a membership of some 15,000 having been represented at the founding convention, but dissatisfaction over constitutional provisions kept most of the unions from affiliating immediately.

Membership in the LO grew steadily and rapidly over the next twenty years, reaching a membership of 143,000 in 1919. Unemployment and considerable industrial strife during the twenties brought a halt to this rapid growth. From 1919 to 1923 LO membership dropped by over 40 per cent and it was not until 1931 that this loss was fully recovered. Between 1930 and 1939, however, membership increased by two and one-half times to over 350,000. A slight decline during the occupation period was rapidly made up after liberation with the onset of another period of rapid organization. By the end of 1956 over 550,000 workers were in unions affiliated with the LO, but the rate of growth had slackened considerably. While this represented only about one-third of the total labor force, approximately 90 per cent of all workers in shipping and mining and manufacturing were organized, and about 50 per cent in building and construction.

Paralleling the growth in union organization since the turn of the century has been the development of employer associations. In 1900, the year after the founding of the LO, the national federation of employers' associations — The Norsk Arbeidsgiverforening (NAF) — was formed. Its growth has been fairly steady (with the exception of the period 1920–30) but in terms of employees working for member firms less rapid than that of the LO.

Moreover, the NAF has never attained the exclusive position in the organization of employers which the LO achieved in the organization of workers. Not only has a considerable fraction of the employers remained outside the NAF, but several large employer associations (most importantly in the shipping sectors) continue to maintain their independence of the central association. Nevertheless, by virtue of its size and "inclusion within its ranks of most of the important enterprises, the association's policies have ramifications which spread far beyond its actual membership." [6]

Both the LO and the NAF from their inception tended to concentrate authority in the hands of the central organizations. Although at the time of the founding of their association, trade unions were by no means extensively or powerfully organized, the preceding decades had seen a substantial amount of union activity, industrial strife, and general social ferment. The immediate motivation in the minds of the NAF founders was to strengthen their position vis-a-vis organized labor. In the words of the official historian of the NAF:

The main trend in this whole [early] period had a defensive character. . . . Through a steadily more widespread organization of workers, the strategic balance of power in the [labor] market began to shift. Judged according to modern conditions, the real power of the trade unions in this period was, truly enough, not immediately great. It was also rather restricted to particular trades. But far-sighted employers could easily imagine the situation when they would come to face, alone, a completely monopolistic combination of workers. One can perhaps say that the *possibilities* played as great, not to say a greater, role here than actual registered events. One saw what the development would reasonably lead to and was interested in taking corresponding measures in time. [7]

Not without considerable internal difficulty, the NAF has continued to increase the degree of concentration of authority. While individual contracts may be negotiated by the constituent associations, the central board of the NAF can veto decisions running counter to national policy and must approve in advance any collective agreement entered into by an affiliate or individual member. To enforce adherence to the policies of the central organization, the NAF may levy substantial fines, invoke an economic boycott against members breaking the common front in a strike, or withhold strike insurance benefits (the latter being of relatively minor significance). Members forego recourse to the courts when joining the organization and cannot resign for two years after affiliation and then only upon twenty-seven months' notice. [8]

But, as Galenson remarks, "The real strength of the Employers' Association lies not so much in formal constitutional provisions as in the attitude of Norwegian employers toward their collective bargaining organization, and in the strong solidarity that exists when industrial relations are at issue." [9]

This employer "solidarity" principle has been embodied in the constitution of the NAF since its founding in the form of a clause prohibiting members from taking competitive advantage in any way of another member whose operations have been stopped by a strike.[10] In this adherence to the principle of solidarity, the development of the Employers' Association has also paralleled that of the trade unions.

Both the centralism and the solidarity of the Employers' Association are associated with the Norwegian employers' conception of their organization as an instrument of defense (and sometimes offense) in the struggle with organized labor. In Petersen's words, the association "from its first hour was intended to be a fighting organization (*kamporganisasjon*)." [11] Nevertheless, the NAF has throughout its history accepted the institution of collective bargaining. What attacks there have been on the collective bargaining process *per se* have been made by independent employers' associations and radical movements within the labor movement itself.

The problems of centralization of authority and worker solidarity were even more difficult and more important to the LO than to the NAF. Not the least important source of the dissatisfaction alienating the strongest unions represented at the constitutional convention of the LO was the degree of central authority accorded the LO secretariat in the original constitution. The original motivation for this centralism is ascribable to the weakness of the unions at the time of federation.[12]

A certain amount of retreat from the extreme centralization of authority took place after the affiliation of the stronger national unions. Probably more decentralization would have developed as the national union grew in power and stability were it not for certain offsetting factors. Most important were the growth of worker class consciousness and the close relationship between the trade unions and the political labor movement.[13] The decade 1910–1920 saw the growth and eventual triumph of radical socialist and semisyndicalist principles within the labor movement. The 1920 Congress of the LO decided to erect regional trade union councils rather than national unions as its basic structural unit. At the same time, national unions were to be reorganized along strictly industrial lines. However, the renunciation of collective bargaining as the principal function of union organization which had been implicit in the original program of the socialist-syndicalist group never took place. Throughout the following twenty years of considerable internal struggle, traditional trade union principles grew in strength. At the end of the 1930's, when the more conservative forces became dominant, it "appeared that Norwegian labor was approaching the tempo of social change exemplified by the Swedish and Danish movements. . . ." [14]

The radicalism of the early 1920's left its mark on the Norwegian labor movement and is, even now, by no means dead. First of all, the emphasis on vertical organization had the effect of making industrial unions the basic organizational form. Over 80 per cent of the total LO membership in 43 unions is concentrated in 13 industrial unions and one general workers' union ranging in size from 10,000 to 55,000 members. Membership in the nine unions organized on a relatively narrow craft basis amounted to less than 6 per cent of the total union membership and half of this was divided about equally between the Printers', Masons', and Maritime Engineers' unions.

Secondly, the social-political orientation of the radical wing, combined with the centralized organization of employers in the NAF, encouraged centralization of authority in the LO against the growing power of the national unions to the point where the federation assumed the leading role in the formulation of wage demands and negotiation of agreements. A major development in this centralization process was the negotiation in 1935 of a master agreement between the LO and NAF. This basic agreement, revised but not basically altered since, covers many of the nonwage aspects of industrial relations. These clauses are automatically included in agreements between any of the affiliates of the two organizations and moreover, serve as models for other agreements with firms not associated with the NAF. This basic agreement provides that the "central organizations or their subordinate bodies may not contact their opposite members with respect to wage and working conditions without the permission of the other organization." [15] In effect, negotiated agreements between the LO and the NAF take on the character of a super "key bargain," setting the pattern to which other agreements tend to conform. It was not until 1949, however, that the LO constitution was amended to provide explicit authority for the LO secretariat to demand conformance by constituent unions to a centrally determined wage policy. Until that time, the power of the LO, aside from general adherence to the principle of labor solidarity, was based principally on control of a central strike fund and, in the postwar period, upon the role conferred upon the federation by the compulsory arbitration legislation.

Finally, the radical political philosophy of those elements within the labor movement which attained a position of dominance in the early 1920's served to bind the trade unions to the Labor Party, even though the effort to transform the trade unions into a thoroughgoing political movement was unsuccessful. The resulting political orientation has meant that Norwegian trade unions have tended to give a rather broad interpretation to their goal of furthering the economic interests of their members. It has, therefore, been more or less natural for larger social objectives and interests of other groups in society to be accorded important consideration in the formulation of trade union objectives and policies.

The Trade Unions and the Labor Party

From its founding, the LO has maintained a generally socialist philosophy and a basic policy of close association with the Labor Party. Point 4 in the objectives listed in its original constitution was: "In coöperation with the political labor movement, to work for the socialization of production and commerce." [16] Until 1933, when the Communist Party split off from the Labor Party, two members of the LO Secretariat were appointed by the Labor Party executive board, two members of which, in turn, were appointed by the LO Secretariat. Although the radical elements which gained ascendancy in the LO in the early twenties failed to direct trade union activity exclusively into political channels (and a conservative trend set in thereafter), this did not destroy the closeness of the relationship. In part, this was possible because of the decline in radicalism which took place within the Labor Party itself during the same period.

At present the only formal tie between the two is a joint advisory committee of coöperation consisting of two members of the LO Secretariat and two members of the Labor Party's executive council. However, there are usually several (at present, three) members of the LO Secretariat elected to the executive council of the party. The party is also dependent on the affiliation of local trade unions for a goodly portion of its membership (national unions and the LO do not affiliate as such); any union member who does not wish to join in his local union's affiliation with the Labor Party must apply for exemption from membership and party dues.

The strength of the tie between the LO and the Labor Party, however, rests, not in these formal arrangements but on basic agreement as to sociopolitical objectives and the intangibles of mutual respect and confidence.[17]

The center of the "mutuality of ideals" between the trade unions and the Labor Party has been the goal of establishing a "socialized" economy. But since the period of extremism through which both organizations passed during the twenties, the socialistic ideal has undergone considerable modification. The LO in 1949 dropped from its constitution the provision calling for the socialization of production. In its place there was substituted a statement that a basic objective of the organization was "to work for the achievement of economic democracy through: (a) transfer of enterprises and activities to government ownership where that can contribute to increased production, better conditions for wage earners, and the general social welfare; (b) securing wage earners a satisfactory position of influence in the economy." [18]

The retreat from the traditional doctrine of nationalization of production is not looked upon by either the Labor Party or the unions as a shift in fundamental "socialist" ideals. Rather it is interpreted as merely a change in the means by which social democracy is to be achieved. Both the unions and the Labor Party are firmly committed to the general proposition that the state should assume primary responsibility for the economic welfare of the country and should be prepared to take whatever measures are deemed most appropriate to exercise that responsibility, subject only to the limitations imposed by a political democracy including, the trade unions emphasize, maintenance of a "free and independent" trade union movement.

Before this abbreviated sketch of the political connection of the trade union movement and the Labor Party is concluded, a word must be devoted to the influence on their relationship by two other organized interest groups — the Communist Party and the agricultural organizations. The existence of an active and well-financed Communist Party in Norway, especially in the early postwar years, was, naturally enough, a matter of particular concern to both the unions and the Labor Party. By providing a continuing challenge to the trade union leadership and standing ever ready to exploit any dissatisfaction among the rank and file, the Communists were able to pose serious and occasionally acute difficulties for the execution of union wage policy. Furthermore, the fact that since the war the Labor Party's parliamentary majority has been measured by three votes or less (with the exception of the years 1949 to 1953 when the margin was 10), has tended to give strategic importance to Communist influence. Since Communist votes were likely to be a direct subtraction from Labor Party electoral strength, the potential impact on the position of the Communists was a continuing consideration in the formulation of policy.

This sensitivity to the Communist problem and the strenuous, unremitting efforts by both union and Labor Party leadership to render the Communists impotent made the issue of Communist influence loom large in policy determination particularly in the earlier years. Still, the impact of the Communist threat on wage developments and the general course of economic policy must be accorded only minor importance. Not that that threat has not been real and serious. But the fact is that the Communists in Norwegian trade unions never seem to have risen to a position above that of capitalizing upon and providing a focus for rank-and-file discontent. Their role was that of a peculiarly vociferous barometer of membership opinion; the response of the union leadership to the pressures which their activity registered would very likely have been of the same character even in the absence of organized Communist efforts, although it might very well have been less prompt. Even a *disloyal* opposition may sometimes serve the function of increasing leadership alertness to rank-and-file sentiments.

In this study, in order to emphasize the underlying character of the constraints which rank-and-file attitudes and desires placed upon trade union leadership, relatively little attention will be devoted to the actual political processes through which membership wishes were translated into policy decisions of union leadership. The relative neglect of Communist activity in the analysis of postwar wage policy which results from such an approach rests on the judgment that the Communists were able to exercise little *independent* influence on the course of wage developments, that the sources of their power during this period were rooted in economic factors which would have made themselves felt even in the absence of a Communist Party.

As for the importance of the agricultural interests, while the bulk of the Labor Party's political strength is concentrated in the worker population in general and organized labor in particular, it is only by virtue of its influence in rural areas that it has been able to achieve and maintain its position of a majority party. In the main, this influence among rural voters is associated with the deliberate policy of the Labor Party favoring improvements in the conditions among small farmers and encouraging the development of agricultural coöperatives. In part, too, the dominance of the larger landowners in the Agrarian Party has served to swell the ranks of the small holders who vote Labor.

This dependence of the Labor Party upon the rural vote for majority powers tends to give the agricultural interests disproportionate influence in the determination of economic policy in the Labor government. It has probably also been a factor in trade union acquiescence to policies which are relatively advantageous to income recipients in the agricultural sector. However, the conflict of interest between the income objectives of the farmer and the industrial worker is still present and, as we shall see, is a source of difficulties for the formulation of economic policy by the Labor government.

The Goals and "Internal Logic" of Norwegian Economic Planning

The nature of the immediate economic problem which Norway faced upon liberation — and their importance in shaping basic economic policy — will be one of our major concerns in the following chapters. Even though the tasks of reconstruction probably would have led even a non-Labor government to extensive employment of direct regulations and control, the character and scope of the control system actually developed inevitably reflected the economic philosophy and longer run social and economic aims of the Labor government.

One of the features of the Norwegian system of social control and national economic planning has been the emphasis on achieving "democracy" through institutions created for the purpose of obtaining the advice and coöperation of various interest groups in the economic programs. For example, one of the most important was the Economic Coördination Council (*Samordningsraad*), which included representatives from industrial, agricultural, commercial, financial, labor, and consumers' organizations. Its function until its dissolution in 1955 was to act as an advisory body to the government on economic policy. Also several Industrial Development Committees (Bransjeraad) to advise the government on economic problems within particular economic sectors have been established.

The focus of the work of these consultative bodies and the central tool of Norwegian economic planning, has been the national economic budget. The budgeting process on both a long term and annual basis has provided the framework within which the attempt was made to achieve some reconciliation of conflicting economic interests in the formulation of government economic policy. The former head of the National Budget Office once described the process of preparing the national budget as consisting of meeting and conferring with representatives of the various government ministries and private economic organizations until a program was developed that dissatisfied everybody.

The budgeting process was designed to take into account explicitly the interrelationships between the various economic sectors and to do so quantitatively. The requirements of both completeness and quantification in the planning process meant that national budgets, although containing a considerable amount of detail, inevitably had to be constructed in rather aggregative terms. Policy decisions, therefore, were made and implemented on the basis of judgments as to their impact on the economic aggregates of the national accounting system. A clear statement of the process of economic planning in terms of national accounts aggregates has been provided by the Norwegian planning authorities in an early exposition of the principles of national economic planning:

In the circumstances where one restricts oneself to objective, measurable magnitudes, *it can be said . . . that the "general economic situation" (konjunktur situasjonen) at any given moment from a real economic standpoint, is nothing else but the magnitude and composition of national accounts figures at that point of time.*

As a starting point (for a national economic policy) one could imagine being confronted with having to choose, for a given period, the size and composition of the items in the current national accounts. Many alternatives could be considered, with only the condition that figures be mutually consistent in a purely accounting sense. To each of these imagined alternatives — if there was thought of bringing the alternative to reality — one could apply a social evaluation. One could order various alternatives in series, evaluated on the basis of social-economic welfare criteria. If the intention were to put the best of these alternatives into practice, one would immediately be confronted with the natural obstacles which rest in the fact that productive capacity and the total supply of manpower available to the country are limited. It would be necessary to choose within the framework of such capacity limits. It would also be necessary to take account of the fact that many of the economic aggregates depend directly or indirectly on relations with other countries so that we ourselves are not solely decisive, no matter how strong domestic regulations may be. Next it would appear that certain alternatives must be eliminated because their implementation would create conflicts with certain recognized institutional arrangements and with principles of individual economic freedom and freedom of choice in a number of areas. But within this practical framework one can see that the ideal regulation of the total economy (*konjunktur regulering*) on the part of the state is an economic policy where the state arranges its own economic activities and the indirect politico-economic instruments in such a way that *the current national accounts come to represent the highest possible level of social-economic welfare.*[19]

It is important to emphasize the aggregative character of the Norwegian economic plans, since it had a decisive influence on the means employed in achieving planned objectives. With basic economic objectives cast into the form of quantifiable economic aggregates — total output, consumption, balance of payments position, and so on — the first line of economic policy was composed of measures designed to affect the over-all aggregate totals — what might be called macro-economic policies. Such policies may be distinguished in the first instance by their generality and secondarily by their tendency to operate indirectly. Examples, of course, are general fiscal and monetary measures, exchange rate determination, banking and interest rate policy, and general price controls insofar as they specify price-making rules rather than decreeing individual prices. Wage policy also fits into this category both because of its generality and the indirect nature of its effects. Within this framework of macro-economic policies and controls, there was a whole range of more detailed regulations and controls of varying degrees of specificity which can be distinguished by their particular or differential character, on the one hand, and their tendency to operate directly, on the other. Examples which may be cited are quantitative import restrictions, construction licensing, rationing, detailed price regulations, special taxes on particular industries, direct subsidies, and so on.[20]

With the continuing effort of the Norwegian planning authorities to integrate plans, policies, and programs in the context of the national economic budget so that explicit consideration could be given to interrelations between economic objectives and economic sectors, it has been, in a very real sense, the macro-economic policies of the government — that is, those policies distinguished by their generality — which have formed the foundation of the Norwegian system of economic control by providing a structure of economic instruments broad enough in scope to correspond to the comprehensive and integrated national economic programs. The more limited direct micro-economic policies and regulations, in this sense, supplemented the macro-economic, being instituted to achieve desired results not attainable through aggregative policies alone or to avoid undesired differential effects of such policies.

In this perspective the elaborate system of detailed direct controls which existed in postwar Norway, and which might appear as the most striking characteristic of Norwegian planning is seen to have no necessary connection with the avowed objective of establishing and maintaining a planned and regulated "social economy." Conceivably direct controls could disappear without upsetting that objective if macro-economic measures were capable by themselves of achieving socio-economic objectives. From the standpoint of efficiency and optimum use of economic resources, the simpler and less manpower-consuming the system of economic controls could be, while still maintaining effectiveness and comprehensiveness, the better. In fact, there has been a pronounced tendency toward the elimination of direct and detailed controls over the postwar period; moreover, there has been a continuing positive effort to create those conditions which make aggregative policies sufficiently effective to eliminate the need for detailed regulations.

Another general characteristic of Norwegian planning of importance for understanding postwar developments is the sharp distinction built into the conceptual scheme of Norwegian national accounting and budgeting, between flows of "real" and "financial objects." [21] In maintaining this axiomatic distinction, real objects are given a certain priority over financial objects in the sense that financial objects (defined broadly as economic claims and counter claims) are essentially dependent on particular institutional and legal relationships.

One of the main characteristics of real objects is that they would be of economic importance even if no property rights existed. In such a case there would be no financial objects at all. A real object may be defined without taking regard to ownership, while a financial object can only be defined *in relation* to a certain creditor and certain debtor.[22]

On the assumption that property relationships between persons within the country can be traced (on the most abstract level) as a variable, subject to manipulation by society (as represented by the government), and that no economic value is placed on such relations in themselves, it follows that the economic welfare of the country is primarily dependent on the stock of real capital within the country and the net claims of the country on real resources of other countries. (The latter are included since utilization of the services of real objects abroad for domestic benefit involves relations between persons or governments which must be taken as relatively fixed by the home country.)

The sum of real capital at home and the (external) financial capital of the country is its *national wealth*. It may also be called its *essential* capital, because it is this capital — together with its labor force which represents the essential condition for the maintenance and development of its standard of living.[23]

This explicit and systematically pursued distinction between real and financial quantities is directly related to the tendency to separate sharply means and ends in economic policy. As a result, basic policy goals have been formulated in real terms with monetary and fiscal policies assigned the role of economic instruments, purely and simply, to be decided upon in view of the real program objectives. The Minister of Finance forcefully expressed this position in a speech to the Storting on the occasion of the first budget presentation of the postwar Labor government:

It (the real economic situation) is determinative for the supply of goods which current production can provide as the basis for our standard of living. When evaluating propositions of *monetary policy,* one must, therefore, always inquire as to what real economic purpose the monetary policy proposal is intended to serve. Monetary policy must not, under any circumstances, be set up as an end in itself. Monetary policy is an instrument for real economic policy and must be appropriate to the latter. Only in this way can one secure full and rational utilization of our productive resources and contribute to a just distribution.[24]

This more or less purely "instrumental" attitude toward economic policy pervaded the whole structure of Norwegian postwar economic planning, giving it a uniquely "enlightened," "unorthodox," or "radical" character (whatever term is most appropriate depending on one's evaluation of comprehensive national economic planning). The resulting process of national planning and control can be schematically described as an attempt to formulate economic objectives (as quantitatively as possible) in real terms and then to adapt and employ from the whole range of direct and indirect, physical and financial controls available, those which a pragmatic and objective evaluation indicated to be the most effective in achieving the basic economic objectives.

Needless to say, the actual planning process only approximated any such austere logical ideal. Numerous other considerations did enter into policy formation as is inevitable in a democratic country with healthy political institutions. In fact, noneconomic and institutional limitational factors were accorded explicit recognition — witness, in the passage quoted earlier, the possibility of the exclusion of certain alternative economic policies where they would "conflict with certain recognized institutional arrangements and with principles of individual economic freedom. . . ."[25] Nevertheless, Norwegian economic planning seems to maintain a clear separation of the real and financial, along with a systematic adherence to the separation of means and ends, thus enabling an approximation to a quantitative measure of social and economic welfare for planning purposes.

CHAPTER 3

The Strategy and Structure of Postwar
Economic Policy

The tendencies toward centralization of economic decision making, stemming from the extreme dependence upon external markets, the solidaristic attitudes of both workers and employers, and the relatively high degree of concentration and organization in the economy, has meant that general economic and financial considerations have been and are given greater weight in the wage determination process in Norway than is usual in other countries. The system of comprehensive economic planning developed during the postwar years relied upon and strengthened these tendencies. The high level of economic sophistication which characterized the planning authorities meant that governmental attitudes toward appropriate wage policies tended to have a derivative character. That is, once the fundamental economic objectives had been determined and the means selected by which these objectives were to be achieved, the implications for the wage policy were rigorously drawn and efforts directed toward ensuring wage settlements consistent with the basic decisions. And, as we shall see as we follow postwar wage developments, a great deal of the government's activity with respect to wages consisted of attempting to persuade the trade unions precisely how wage objectives were constrained by over-all economic objectives and the general economic situation. An analysis of Norwegian wage policy, therefore, must necessarily begin with some consideration of the more general economic policy objectives and the manner in which policy decisions and controls with respect to the labor market have been related to goals and techniques of national economic planning.

The Problem of Postwar Reconstruction

As the Norwegians once again became masters of their own economic destiny, they found themselves faced with three basic economic problems.[1] First, there was the problem of reconstruction arising out of the great capital destruction during the war and the resultant low level of production. Secondly, there was the problem of maintaining a high level of employment, which was made more difficult by the substantial growth in the labor force immediately prior to and during the war and by the internal shifts in manpower which had taken place under the occupation authorities. Finally, there was the problem of inflation posed by the tremendous accumulation of liquid assets and purchasing power in the hands of both consumers and businesses, coupled with the pent-up desires of both groups to reëstablish and exceed their prewar economic position as rapidly as possible. The manner in which these problems were handled determined the governmental attitude toward general wage developments during the first postwar years and have been of basic importance in the formulation of economic policy even in recent years.

In the first postwar years, the rate of capital accumulation was considered primarily in terms of replacement of war losses. The magnitude of these losses of real capital were estimated to represent an over-all reduction of 18.5 per cent in the total real capital stock of the country from 1939 to 1945. But, equally significant was the manner in which this reduction was distributed among industries and types of capital. The losses in the equipment categories (excluding land, buildings, and inventories) averaged about 45 per cent of prewar levels and together accounted for over one-third of the total reduction. Doubly serious, was the wartime destruction of the merchant fleet — over 50 per cent — because of the importance of shipping earnings to Norwegian foreign exchange revenues.

Reductions in manufacturing and commercial inventories alone accounted for about one quarter of the total reduction of capital; inventory levels in these sectors were only 27 per cent of prewar. This reduction in stocks should be viewed in connection with the great decrease in the stocks of durable goods in the hands of consumers. While these are not generally considered capital goods, quite obviously part of the available resources during the reconstruction period would have to be devoted to restocking of this "consumer capital." Furthermore, to take account of the increase in population during the war years, the estimated reduction in consumer durables could be increased by roughly 15 per cent.

The destruction of buildings, while small relative to total prewar capital, loomed large in absolute magnitude. Here too, the actual problem was even greater than indicated by the bare statistics of estimated capital loss. Not only had there been a 5 per cent increase in population during the war, but the rate of family formation in the same period was reaching a peak. From 1940 to 1945 there was an estimated net decrease in dwelling of some 11,000 units and a net increase of almost 72,000 married couples.[2] This meant that the "housing shortage" had increased almost six-fold during the war — from somewhat under 19,000 units in 1939 to over 111,000 units at the end of 1945. In addition, the expected rate of family increase was such that even with optimistic estimates about the possible rate of construction, the shortage could be expected to continue to increase for some years after the war.

Although the effects of war and occupation were a dominant concern in evaluating investment needs, it was recognized from the outset that the program for reconstruction could not be set up simply in terms of replacement of capital losses. Shifts in the structure of world trade, particularly the loss of Germany as both customer and supplier, implied the necessity for corresponding shifts in the structure of both domestic and export industries if an approach to equilibrium in the external economy was to be achieved. Such adjustments implied a need for an increased flow of investment into the import saving and export industries, and, in the latter case, particularly those exporting to the dollar area. Moreover, the natural demands for increased living standards after the stagnation of the thirties and the privation of the occupation period could not be ignored and meant pressure for an investment rate sufficiently high to provide a basis for consumption standards above prewar levels within the near future.

It is perhaps belaboring the obvious to note that the objectives of replacing wartime capital losses and raising the level of production, to encourage higher living standards as well as stability in the external economy, were sufficient in themselves to produce policy decisions directed toward achieving an extraordinarily high rate of capital formation. But even immediately after the liberation (and to an increasing degree since), concern over the problem of achieving and maintaining full employment may be said to have been of equal importance.

The world depression of the early thirties affected Norway severely, perhaps more severely than necessary because of her adherence to a deflationary governmental policy. In addition, the labor force was increasing rapidly during those very years when the economy was least able to absorb more workers.[3] During the thirties the number of persons over fifteen years of age increased by over 315,000 — a rate of 1.5 per cent a year. This increase in the adult age groups meant an addition to the labor force of 15,000 to 20,000 a year — a total increase of 13 to 15 per cent over the decade.[4]

The prewar Norwegian economy seems to have displayed what has been called a "structural" incapacity to absorb this increased supply of workers.[5] Even in 1938 and 1939, 60 to 65 thousand were unemployed, and it is quite certain that a great deal of "disguised unemployment" existed in agriculture and fishing.

Most of this unemployment disappeared during the occupation, as a result of withdrawals from the labor force and the impact of German demands on the economy. From 1939 to the first half of 1944, employment in building and construction increased by some 54,000, in industry by 12,000. In the same period employment in agriculture, forestry, and fishing declined by over 35,000.[6] By the end of 1945, unemployment had increased in construction and manufacturing, while many persons had returned to agricultural and fishing activities. Thus, the net shifts in the distribution of manpower between 1939 and 1945 are not so striking. The problem remained of effecting transfers of manpower out of the less productive areas such as agriculture and fishing. After the occupation there was the additional problem of the substantial reserves of idle manpower in the form of collaborators excluded from work, Norwegians gradually returning home from abroad, and military forces which later would be released to civilian employment.[7]

The employment problem at liberation, therefore, was a compound of the transitional difficulty of readjusting to a peacetime economy, the more fundamental task of bringing about changes in the economy to eliminate the recurrence of "structural" unemployment which had characterized the late thirties, and reducing "disguised unemployment." Solutions to these problems were intimately connected with the general problem of reconstruction and rehabilitation.

The pressures for a high rate of investment, of course, did not arise simply from a hypothetical evaluation of capital requirements for the rehabilitation of the Norwegian economy. The state of the Norwegian monetary and financial system at the end of the occupation was such that the financial resources available to the business and banking sectors, and, to a lesser extent, in the hands of the consumers, threatened a potentially explosive inflationary situation.

During the occupation there was a large accumulation of liquid assets in the hands of both the public and the banks. The Germans had financed their occupation costs, in the main, by the simple expedient of drawing on the Norges Bank. Total advances to the occupying authorities amounted to over 11 billion kroner. Over half of this tremendous increase in central bank credit was offset by repayments by the government to the occupation account and by the accumulation of government deposits in the Norges Bank. But this still permitted over a billion kroner to accrue to the banking system in the form of deposits with the Norges Bank and almost two and a half billion kroner to accumulate in the hands of the public in the form of currency. This represented a twenty-fold increase in bank deposits in the Norges Bank and a ten-fold increase in the amount of money in circulation. Not only had the banks accumulated deposits in the Norges Bank, but they had reduced their mortgage and commercial loans by 1.2 billion kroner, while investing 2.8 billion kroner in short term treasury bills and another billion kroner in other government securities. Although demand and time deposits had risen by almost five billion kroner by the end of the war, the ratio of liquid reserves to total deposits (demand and savings) had increased from less than 5 per cent to almost 60 per cent. Consequently, the money supply (defined as money in circulation plus demand and savings deposits) had been swollen to three times its prewar size, and the credit potential had been built up to even greater heights.

Programs for Economic Rehabilitation and Development

Before the end of the war, preparations to deal with the threat of inflation upon liberation were undertaken by the Norwegian government in London. The comprehensive system of price controls which had developed during the occupation was extended by provisional decree immediately upon liberation. Wage increases, in compensation for real wage declines during the war, were also negotiated prior to liberation, but were coupled with a general freeze of nonwage provisions in collective contracts. The LO and NAF were placed in control of any wage changes, irrespective of membership of the parties concerned. By the end of the summer of 1945 a series of emergency financial measures had been introduced to institute some degree of control over the monetary situation. These included a general exchange of Norges Bank notes associated with registration of bank accounts and a partial blocking of the larger bank deposits. These immediate sanctions were undertaken to permit the orderly development of more permanent measures after elections had been held.

But even before these elections could take place, the temporary stabilization measures began to be accorded a more enduring status by the decision to maintain the postwar exchange rate at the level of 20 kroner to one pound (4.97 kroner = $1.00). The issue was brought to a head by the wage demands the unions raised shortly after liberation and which had resulted in an arbitration award of 20 øre per hour.[8] The Coördination Council (Samordningsraad), in its recommendations to the government, asked for an immediate statement of government intentions regarding stabilization and an early decision on the future exchange rate. A committee appointed in August 1945 to make recommendations as to the future rate of exchange unanimously agreed in favor of a depreciation of the kroner to $24 = £1$. The coalition government, however, decided against depreciation, primarily because of the necessity of maintaining stable prices at their current level in order to avoid any real wage deterioration with its resulting labor unrest and strong upward pressure on the whole cost structure.[9]

After the elections in October 1945 which brought the Labor Party to power with, for the first time, an absolute majority in the *Storting* (the Norwegian parliament), the problems of reconstruction, employment, and inflation were the focus of a comprehensive and coordinated program of attack.

To the Norwegian planning authorities, the last of these problems was "financial" in character and had "real" significance only indirectly because of concern over the distribution of wealth and the influence exerted by holdings of liquid assets on the current flow of expenditures, and hence on the use and allocation of real resources. The first two problems, however, were considered more fundamental, since as they constituted basic questions of the use and allocation of real resources.

Hence, there was never any question but that logical priority would be accorded to the problem of directing a flow of resources into investment adequate to achieve high levels of real output and eventual stability in the external economy. Production and employment goals were controlling. The determination of financial policy was a matter of evaluating the significance of various monetary measures on the use and allocation of real resources.

Shortly after assuming office, the new government presented a tentative program for reconstruction.[10] In terms of admittedly rough figures, the government sketched the principal alternatives confronting the country in the distribution of its available resources over the coming five-year period. The magnitude of net investment in plant, equipment, and inventories necessary to raise production to the 1939 level, was estimated at about 2500 million kroner (1939 prices) or roughly four billion kroner at 1946 prices.[11] Some new investment was inevitable along with replacement, and the total investment volume during reconstruction was estimated at some six to eight billion kroner.[12] Other investment demands had to be expected, particularly for housing. In his budget speech of February 1946, the finance minister outlined the problem as follows:

Taking into account that, simultaneously with reconstruction, a substantial amount of new investment must be expected, one arrives at a probable total volume of investment of between 4,000 and 5,000 million in 1939 kroner or 6,000–8,000 million at today's prices. Assuming it would be possible to maintain the same yearly investment volume as in 1939, it might well require eight to ten years for reconstruction, if that were to be accomplished out of our resources without an import surplus. It would bring considerably lower levels of consumption and mean such unfavorable conditions for the great portion of the population that it would never be possible.

Under these circumstances, the policy decided upon was to limit private consumption to an average for the period 1946–1950 somewhat below the 1939 level and incur an import surplus for the five years of four to five billion kroner. On the basis of an estimated 19 per cent growth in output during the period and a possible range of average annual public consumption between one and one-half billion kroner per year, the expectation was that reconstruction could be accomplished within five years.

While this program was originally set up in terms of reconstruction objectives, it was not restricted to reattainment of the prewar position. By 1948, when Norway drafted a second long-term program in connection with the institution of the Marshall Plan and the establishment of the Organization for European Economic Coöperation, greater emphasis was placed on the fact, already recognized in 1946, that mere restoration of prewar capital would not be sufficient. Demands for higher levels of consumption were, of course, always present. But with Norway's extreme dependence on foreign trade, more pressing difficulties centered on reëstablishing her external economic position. Total production was already some 25 to 30 per cent higher in 1948 than prewar, but the volume of exports, though substantially increased over 1946, was still 15 to 20 per cent below the 1938 level. In spite of the emphasis on reconstruction of the merchant fleet, the contribution of net shipping receipts to total foreign exchange revenues was still relatively smaller than before the war.

The long-term program which Norway submitted to the OEEC in 1948 [13] set forth an outline of an expanded investment program which, with economic aid from the United States, was intended to achieve a stable foreign balance along with higher standards of living by 1952. Net investments for the period 1949–1952 were projected at some nine billion kroner compared to approximately five billion kroner estimated for the years 1946–1948,[14] an increase in the annual rate of investment of one-third to one-half. Principal emphasis was on the expansion of export- or import-saving industries. Such an expanded program was made possible only by the expectation of considerable external assistance from the United States which would provide additional resources to permit a more rapid rate of capital accumulation without impinging on consumption levels.

Stabilization and the Theory of Suppressed Inflation

The demands placed upon the economy by the planned investment program posed a resource mobilization problem similar to that imposed by the demands of war. The task of ensuring a flow of resources into investment involved maintaining a high level of investment demand, limiting consumption sufficiently to allow for an adequate supply of resources for investment purposes, and, at the same time, avoiding the interruptions and losses which strikes and labor unrest would entail. In view of the logical priority given by Norwegian economists to current real flows of goods and services, it is not surprising that the solution of these problems was sought in the deliberate adoption of a policy of suppressed inflation.

The single most important financial decision on the part of the postwar government — the one that did most to shape the course of economic development — was undoubtedly the decision not to attempt a drastic monetary reform in order to eliminate war-induced inflationary pressures nor to permit those pressures to result in a certain degree of open inflation, but rather to establish by means of direct controls and subsidies a "stabilization line" to limit price and cost increases, while waiting for inflationary pressures to be worked off by an increasing volume of production, on the one hand, and a continuing import surplus on the other. A general policy line was fully worked out very soon after liberation and was adhered to successfully until the general devaluation of European currencies in the fall of 1949. Because of its obvious importance for wage policy, it will be worthwhile to look rather closely into the origins and rationale of this stabilization policy.

The government's reluctance to abandon the "stabilization line" which had been first introduced as a temporary holding operation had its roots in four basic and interrelated considerations: namely, the reductions of income inequalities and avoidance of labor unrest, control over the internal level of costs relative to the rest of the world, the maintenance of a high level of investment demand, and the need for major structural shifts in the allocation of the labor force.

We have already noted how the objective of avoiding a deterioration in the workers' real income was a major factor leading the coalition government to reject any depreciation of the kroner. The finance minister, in presenting the first budget of the postwar Labor Government in February, 1946, reëmphasized the point.

The Government views this stabilization and equalization line as vitally important as a means of securing the workers' living standards and thereby preserving peace in the labor market. It needs to be clear to everybody that nothing, today, can contribute more to lowering the standard of living than labor strife. A labor dispute has, of course, other effects besides that of reducing total national product, but it is not so dangerous when there are sufficient stocks to rely upon. When we, as today, must live from hand to mouth, the situation is entirely different.[15]

But this in itself probably would not have been sufficient to forestall devaluation if other factors in the situation had not been judged to indicate that the benefits to be derived from exchange rate adjustment were limited. The general view was that in the immediate postwar situation, the supply of major exports was so inelastic that relatively little or nothing was to be gained by depreciation. Moreover, there seems to be little doubt that a major consideration supplementary to those already mentioned was the Norwegian expectation that the future course of world markets was principally dependent upon the level of economic activity in the United States. Briefly stated, the apparent belief was that for a few years world prices would continue to rise under the influence of a high employment and even inflationary situation in the United States. Once this postwar boom had run its course, however, it seemed most probable that the United States would lead the world into another depression.

This expectation of a postwar boom followed by depression in world markets quite naturally strengthened adherence to a policy of stabilizing internal costs at their existing level and leaving the exchange rate unchanged. With increases in world prices expected to continue in the immediate future, Norway could expect, by keeping a stable cost-price structure, to improve her relative cost position without undertaking a difficult (if not impossible) cost deflation, nor incurring the great risk of setting off an inflationary spiral by depreciating her currency in a situation of tremendous excess demand. On the other hand, it was imperative, because of Norway's vulnerability to external cyclical influences, that she not be saddled with an inflated cost level when the expected deflationary movements eventually began in the United States and the rest of the world.

If the maintenance of industrial peace and the conserving of Norway's competitive position vis-a-vis external markets were sufficient reasons for avoiding even a limited degree of open inflation, there remained (logically) the possibility of a drastic monetary reform and a generally deflationary policy designed to bring about an approach to monetary equilibrium. Such a course was given slight consideration by the Norwegian authorities. In connection with legislation on a proposed extraordinary levy on capital gains accrued during the occupation period, the government registered its opposition to the idea of drastic deflationary measures, citing the experience after the first World War.

There is . . . reason to recall that after the first World War it was sought to decrease the level of demand in the face of a somewhat similar situation of a greatly expanded volume of purchasing power. The results of the financial policy which was carried out at that time should be sufficiently well known — and appreciated — so that it is not necessary to review them again. Certainly it can be said that no one this time has any thought of striking out on a deflationary course with falling prices and wages and other incomes in the society . . . what happens to the monetary condition of enterprises can be of real importance to the utilization of the firms' production possibilities and the country's manpower.[16]

Rather than accept any drastic purging of the monetary system to reduce aggregate demand, the government felt that the problem should be attacked primarily from the supply side.

In the opinion of the [Finance] Ministry, the problem of inflationary pressure is, first and foremost, a question of supplying the goods to cover the extraordinary large demand which now is making itself felt. If this demand can be satisfied by an especially large import surplus in the next 2–3 years and by utilizing to the fullest our productive potential and our manpower for productive purposes, there is reason to believe that inflationary pressure will be essentially eliminated.[17]

In part this position stemmed from a general skepticism toward the effectiveness of drastically reducing the amount of liquid assets held by the public.

Inflationary pressure depends . . . not only on purchasing power alone but equally importantly on all the motives leading to a desire to purchase. Purchasing power expressed in currency and liquid assets is certainly greater now than any time previously. But it does not follow on this account alone that this power to buy will be exercised in actual purchases. Purchasing power is a prerequisite for any purchase, but whether the purchase takes place depends, for the consumers concerned, essentially on the desires they feel. As far as businesses are concerned, profit expectations are controlling. . . . It must be expected in the extraordinary situation we now find ourselves, with commodity shortages in most areas, that bank deposits will probably be used to buy clothes and other consumer durables, the purchase of which cannot be covered by the current income of those concerned. But it does not follow from this that one can immediately assume that the public will continue to activate past savings even after the most urgent demands for replacement of lost consumer durables are met. The public will in the future still seek to live within their incomes and adjust their consumption expenditures to current money incomes. The Ministry therefore considers it to be of far greater importance to the dampening of inflationary pressure that a way is found to prevent the abundance of money from making itself felt in a strong increase in money incomes which is not matched by a corresponding increase in production.[18]

Another important factor affecting fundamental financial policy was the judgment that directing the major weight of the attack on inflationary pressure against the level of liquid assets would directly interfere with efforts to solve the other two fundamental problems of full employment and reconstruction. These latter problems required the maintenance of a high level of aggregate demand and in particular a high level of investment expenditure. Because of the behavior relationships assumed to exist between liquidity and expenditure, there was reason to believe that a reduction in holdings of financial assets of a magnitude sufficient to reduce inflationary pressure significantly would have its greatest impact on investment decisions and might easily lead to a situation where investment expenditures fell short of the level necessary to achieve the desired rate of reconstruction or even to maintain full employment.

In addition there seems to have been an implicit assumption that structural changes and shifts in employment are most easily brought about in a climate of labor shortage — that a general excess of employment opportunities was more conducive to a reallocation of manpower with a minimum waste of resources than a more balanced situation in the labor market would be.[19]

In order, therefore, to insure an adequate flow of investment expenditure, the government refrained from any large-scale, immediate attempt to reduce the level of liquid assets in the economy but instead deliberately embarked upon a "permissive" monetary policy — that is, stabilizing interest rates at a low level and permitting banks to expand credit at a rapid rate. The resulting investment pressure, coupled with the level of pent-up consumer demand, quite obviously necessitated the imposition of a whole system of direct and indirect controls, if attainment of the real economic objectives of the planning authorities was not to disappear in the flames of hyper-inflation. The problem was to impound the swollen supply of liquid assets so that the pressures tending to increase the flow of expenditure in the economy were kept in check and released only as they served the purposes of the planning authorities.

In basic outline, the Norwegian system of mobilizing resources for reconstruction in the first postwar years resembles what Professor Galbraith has called "the disequilibrium system" [20] employed by the United States during the war. But an integral part of the system as it was developed in postwar Norway was the intention that the inflationary pressures be harnessed not only to force rapid reconstruction but also to bring about their own eventual diminution and disappearance. Of primary significance, therefore, in the Norwegian postwar experience, was the deliberate and systematic effort to supplement the policy of suppressed inflation with policies designed to bring the system eventually back into equilibrium at a higher level of real output. In other words, even though inflationary pressure was to be permitted to persist for some time, continuing efforts were made to reduce the magnitude of this pressure until it finally would be reduced to a negligible proportion.

Vital to this general line of attack was a fiscal and financial policy designed to reduce inflationary pressure from the demand side. Consequently, at the same time that the government was avoiding stringent monetary reforms and maintaining a low interest rate, it was deliberately arranging the financing of import surpluses so as to have the greatest impact on the level of bank reserves and also maintaining tax rates at a level which led to the accumulation of large budget surpluses.

The details of this twin-pronged drive to achieve greater balance in the economy in a relatively short period of time cannot be dealt with here. What is of importance for our present purposes is the central point that Norway's economic policy immediately after the war was developed as a powerful instrument to eliminate inflationary pressure quickly without jeopardizing full employment and, at the same time, protecting and improving the country's external position by avoiding a rise in internal costs relative to the rest of the world.

Economic Controls and Wage Policy Instruments

The success of the strategy of suppressed inflation obviously was in large part dependent upon the effectiveness of the instruments of "suppression" and the skill with which they were employed. On the one hand, direct quantitative controls were necessary to ensure a use of resources which more or less conformed to the "social optimum" embodied in the annual national economic budgets and the longer-run programs; more general controls over prices and incomes were required not only to assist in bringing about the desired use of resources, but also to bring about a gradual reduction of inflationary pressure by reducing liquidity and by limiting the rate of increase in money incomes sufficiently to allow improvements in output and supply to be effective in cutting down the inflationary gap. The importance of the direct quantitative regulation was, of course, greatest in the earlier postwar years when inflationary pressure was the greatest.

The backbone of the direct control system was a complex of licensing and rationing regulations. The dependence of the economy on imports made import licensing a particularly strategic instrument. With strict control over investment goods imports and comprehensive regulation over construction through an elaborate system of building licenses and construction materials allocations, it was possible for the government to maintain detailed supervision over not only the level but also the composition of investment activity. Similar supervision over consumption was exercised via import licensing and rationing. The effectiveness of these quantitative regulations depended, in part, on the existence of a certain degree of excess demand in those markets where they were applicable. Consequently, it was to be expected that reliance upon and the significance of these direct regulations would diminish if the disinflationary aspect of Norwegian economic strategy proved sufficiently successful to bring about an approach to equilibrium. Such an erosion of the system of direct quantitative regulations has in fact taken place.

In spite of the fact that these quantitative regulations have been and (though to a much lesser extent) still are more important instruments of economic policy in Norway than in most other Western economies, it is the more general measures designed to influence general price and income developments that are of particular significance in the present context. Central to any effort to establish some degree of control over the level of internal costs and disposable incomes is the problem of limiting wage increases. A striking feature of the Norwegian version of the controlled economy, however, has been the absence (with minor exceptions) of direct governmental regulation of the labor market. Governmental influence in the wage determination process has been more a matter of bringing indirect pressure to bear on the parties in collective bargaining than attempting to assert control over the results of bargaining.

This pattern was established even before the end of the occupation when preparations were made for an orderly resumption of collective bargaining relationships as soon as the liberation took place. In spite of the German attempts to nazify both the Federation of Labor and the Employers' Association, both organizations managed to survive the occupation through a combination of overt and underground activities in Norway and maintenance of representatives in Stockholm and London.[21] Upon the request of the Norwegian government in exile, representatives of the LO and NAF in Stockholm and London undertook to prepare recommendations on wages, working conditions, and legislation to be instituted when Norway became free. The recommendations of this committee, arrived at after consultation with union and employer representatives in occupied Norway, were incorporated with some change into a Provisional Ordinance Concerning Temporary Adjustment of Wage and Working Conditions in Liberated Districts, dated September 15, 1944.

In this emergency legislation, the wage provisions of which are discussed in Chapter 4, all nonwage provisions of collective agreements were frozen. But it was provided that any change in wages desired by individual employers, employer associations, or trade unions were to be negotiated by the two central organizations, irrespective of whether the firms or unions concerned were members of those associations. In case of disagreement between the two organizations, compulsory mediation and arbitration procedures could be invoked. The compulsory arbitration features of the provisional ordinance were continued in subsequent legislation until the end of 1952, when they were allowed to expire. And, although the control by the NAF and LO over wage conditions of nonmembers was deleted in mid-1946, the general effect of the compulsory arbitration legislation was to place initial responsibility for the determination of wages upon the two central organizations.

The procedure which led to the final step of compulsory arbitration was: If the parties in wage negotiations were unable to reach agreement, mediation proceedings were opened under the auspices of the state mediator. In the event mediation did not produce agreement, the state mediator could either (1) refer the dispute directly to the ministry of labor which could then submit the dispute to a wage board for an arbitration award which would be binding on both parties, or (2) issue a proposal with or without the prior "consent" of both parties. Consent of the parties to the issuance of a mediator's proposal, in effect, constituted agreement to arbitration by the mediator because such a proposal, when made, was referred directly to the employers and workers for ratification or rejection. In case of rejection, the mediator in his discretion could refer the proposal to a wage board which could approve or disapprove, but not, in any way, modify the proposal. If the wage board disapproved, the dispute was then to be referred to the ministry of labor for further disposition. Lacking the consent of the parties, the mediator could, nevertheless, submit a proposal to the parties and even require its submission to referendum by the respective memberships of the organizations concerned. But if the proposal was rejected, the dispute could not be certified by the mediator directly to the wage board but only to the ministry of labor. The ministry of labor, when it received a report of a failure of mediation, had three (later four) days to decide whether to refer the dispute to a wage board for decision. Only if the ministry did not decide to invoke compulsory arbitration by a wage board could a legal strike or lockout take place. Throughout the period when these compulsory arbitration provisions were in effect, virtually all disputes were, in fact, referred to a wage board for settlement. Illegal strikes, nevertheless, did occur, but penal sanctions provided in the law were not used.

The only basic revision in these compulsory arbitration procedures, prior to their expiration in December 1952, occurred in 1949. At that time an amendment was introduced which made only those disputes arising out of demands which had not been approved by the executive bodies of the LO or NAF subject to compulsory arbitration. This amendment meant that collective bargaining between the central organizations could take place without any restrictions, the effect of compulsory arbitration being to force conformity, on the part of the affiliated members, with centrally determined policies.

Thus, even during the period of compulsory arbitration, the wage determination process was left primarily in the hands of the central organizations. Except for a period of a few months in the latter part of 1947 when a temporary wage-stop law was in effect, the government has instituted no direct control over wages. The wage boards, although governmental tribunals, were tripartite in character and not formally bound by considerations of general economic policy although, in fact, such considerations weighed heavily in their decisions.

Under this system, wage policy became, in the first instance, a matter of joint trade union-government formulation. Typically, the ministry of finance or the prime minister presented the government's views on the general economic situation to the representative council of the LO when the question of contract revision and wage demands was up for discussion. Sometimes the presentations contained explicit recommendations as to the character of the LO wage demands, but often the representative council was simply left to frame its decisions in accordance with general economic considerations.

Compulsory arbitration in this process provided a means whereby an approximation to the wage decisions of the LO could be imposed, if need be, upon employers and individual unions without risking the disruption of strikes. While the wage boards were formally independent bodies, it was quite natural for them, in the absence of any other criteria, to base their decisions upon an assessment of the general economic situation and current government economic policy and, once having rendered a "key" decision, to pattern all other awards on that basic settlement. This does not mean that the wage boards merely rubber stamped the wage demands of the LO. The awards inevitably contained an element of compromise between the positions of the two central organizations.

The centralization of power in those two organizations made it possible for the government to rely upon them heavily to develop and police (without serious work stoppages) general wage settlements which would not interfere with the fulfillment of planned economic objectives. On the employers' side, if the NAF had not been in a position to enforce conformity on the part of its members to the wage provisions of centrally negotiated or arbitrated agreements, it is almost certain that the extreme tightness in the labor market during the postwar period, associated with the high investment goals of the government, would have led to competitive wage bidding by employers and wage increases in excess of what was considered desirable from the point of view of general economic policy. As a matter of fact, as will be discussed in greater detail in the following chapters, throughout the postwar period there was actually a continuing upward drift of wages above the increases negotiated in the central agreements or awarded by the wage board, part of which is undoubtedly attributable to the desire of employers to hold on to their labor supply and to attract additional workers.

On the union side, it is also quite certain that the central authority of the LO was exercised over the wage demands of the affiliated national unions to keep the pressure for wage increases within bounds. The need for central control in framing union wage demands was given explicit recognition in a 1948 amendment to the labor disputes law which provided that "affiliates and members of the Norwegian Employers' Association of the Norwegian Federation of Labor cannot terminate their collective agreements without permission of those central organizations." [22] As far as the NAF was concerned, this provision merely confirmed authority already contained in its constitution. But for the LO, authority which had previously been exercised over contract termination was based principally upon a constitutional provision requiring prior LO approval of wage demands, if the national union desired the economic support of the federation, or if more than one union was involved.

The final step in consolidation of the central authority of the LO was taken in 1949. In anticipation of the eventual expiration of the compulsory arbitration legislation, the 1949 LO congress adopted constitutional amendments requiring, without qualification, prior approval of the LO secretariat before any union could enter into negotiations for new contracts or give notice of contract termination. Moreover, while strike notices may be issued once the secretariat has approved the original contract demands, no strike action can take place without separate approval of the secretariat. The justification put forth by the constitutional committee which drafted these amendments was solely in terms of the necessity for the continuance of a rational wage policy in a controlled economy.

The proposal in Point 1, Paragraph 14 [requiring secretariat approval of new contract negotiations and contract termination], in the opinion of the committee, is necessary if the Wage Board should be dissolved and if society should continue to seek to operate a regulated economy. It is immediately obvious and should not require any detailed proof that the economic policy which assumes full employment, price control and general control over the economy, with the objective of creating an equal distribution of income in society, cannot be carried out unless wage policy also fits into the system. It goes without saying that the labor movement will be best served if conformity to social policy is achieved by the labor movement itself.[23]

Control of Nonwage Incomes

While efforts to control the level of internal costs and individual incomes found their primary focus in wage policy, the corollary problems of controlling nonwage incomes were equally important. Rental incomes were controlled directly. Incomes from interest were limited by consistent adherence to a low interest rate policy. The net result was to reduce drastically the ratio of these types of income to total factor income. Of greater quantitative importance were controls over independent incomes in agriculture, forestry, fishing, and business profits.

With regard to the former, government policy was carried out in negotiated settlements on prices with the major producer organizations. To a certain extent the national wage settlements were a leading factor in these price negotiations. It was a policy of the government to work toward a greater equality in income between the agricultural and nonagricultural sectors. Consequently, much weight in negotiations on agricultural prices and subsidies was given to estimates of farm income calculated on the basis of current costs of farm operations. Partly as a result of conscious policy, but probably more because of other factors to be discussed later, incomes in these areas rose substantially more than in other economic sectors. In fact, control over agricultural incomes and prices came to be of crucial importance to the whole issue of wage-price stability.

Control over profits (before taxes) was also administered via the price control system. Suppression rather than immediate elimination of internal inflationary pressures seems to have produced a tendency toward significant increases in the volume of profits (before taxes). Even the existence of a comprehensive system of price control apparently could not overcome all the well-known forces leading to an increase of profits relative to wages in an inflationary situation. The administration of the price control system was based in large part on the control of profit margins in the manufacturing sectors rather than on price ceilings. There was no systematic effort to reduce profit margins during the postwar period in order to permit an increase in wages at the expense of profits, although after some of the wage settlements, the burden of proof was placed upon the manufacturers forcing them to apply for price relief because of increased wage costs. To a considerable degree, businesses seemed to have been left adequate room to take advantage of the increased profit opportunities presented by high and rapidly expanding levels of demand.

That a labor government could pursue policies which permitted and perhaps even encouraged a high volume of profits in the private business sector is not so anomalous as might appear on the surface. A system of comprehensive economic control gave the government much greater opportunity to maintain the position vis-a-vis the labor unions, for example, that evaluation of economic policies should take into account the total operation of the whole policy and planning structure rather than being restricted to the immediate impact of a particular line of policy in a single area. Specifically, high profits could be viewed with equanimity because other controls and regulations were in force to insure that they would in fact contribute to the social and economic goals of the government.

Included in the price control legislation was authority to maintain a general limitation of dividends. Set at 5 per cent of the value of the paid-in capital stock, the dividend limitation was an effective stimulant to corporate saving. In addition, there were certain direct legal requirements forcing corporate saving until corporate surplus reached a certain minimum level, as well as a provision that, if permission was granted to distribute dividends in excess of 5 per cent of capital plus reserves, an amount equal to this excess had to be appropriated to surplus.[24] A large amount of internal financing of investment was made possible, too, by provision for so-called "excess price" depreciation which permitted higher allowances because of the increases in the level of prices. This provision was suspended in 1950 in an effort to reduce investment demands after devaluation, but the government then made provisions for tax-free appropriations to surplus on conditions that future expenditures of such funds be subject to governmental approval.[25] All in all, it seems clear that the system of quantitative controls over imports and construction, together with price control, dividend limitations, and other regulations promoting internal business saving provided the government with considerable authority over the use of profit incomes, and in particular, the authority to assure the use of such incomes for "social-economic purposes" — that is, investment in accordance with the economic development programs.

These controls over the flow and use of private incomes were, of course, only part of the total governmental influence on the use of resources by the private sector. In a sense they can be characterized as supplementary to general fiscal policies and measures affecting private disposable incomes. The character and course of fiscal policy during the postwar period is a subject for a later chapter. Nevertheless, mention should perhaps be made here of some of the characteristics of the Norwegian tax structure, which tended to have a differential influence on the flow of private incomes (particularly profit incomes), more or less independently of the absolute size of government revenues and expenditures.

Although it is impossible to delineate precisely the impact of business taxation in Norway, there seems to be some evidence that the tax system produces substantial incentives for internal business saving (in spite of a tax on undistributed profits). The cumulative effects of profit and capital taxes in conjunction with various direct regulations concerning capital structure tend to make dividend disbursement extremely expensive.[26]

Aside from ordinary direct taxation of business, the authority to levy extraordinary indirect taxes has been of particular importance in regulating the flow of profit incomes. This authority, which in the original emergency price control legislation could be invoked by administrative decree, was continued in the permanent price control legislation, but only after *Storting* action "in the case of indirect taxes deemed of great significance to the country's economy." [27] These special levies are the principal means by which the government is able to regulate the flow of incomes into the private hands in the face of fluctuations in export prices. Since their use is generally restricted to export industries, they are probaly best considered as a form of profit taxation rather than as ordinary indirect taxes. They serve to limit the cost raising impact of high profits in export industries enjoying a temporary boom. At the same time, the government is provided the opportunity to impound inflated export earnings, thus generating internal saving to offset the inflationary pressures which would otherwise develop with any substantial drop in or elimination of the import surplus. The actual importance these measures have had will be seen when we consider the effect of the Korean war on Norway's external position and its consequent internal impact.

Finally, the relatively heavy reliance on indirect taxation should be mentioned as an important structural element in the control of private incomes. Under circumstances of inflationary pressure resulting from high investment demand and upward pressures on the wage level, increases in indirect taxes may be considered as a means of permitting prices to rise and still maintain or increase pressure on profit margins. Precisely just such a mechanism has been proposed by the Swedish economist Gøsta Rehn as part of a program to achieve stability under full employment conditions.[28] The efficiency of such a policy cannot be explored here; the Norwegians, in fact, have never pretended to employ indirect taxation, as Rehn suggests as the primary instrument of economic control. The fact remains, nevertheless, that changes in the level of indirect taxes during the postwar period were influential in determining the relative share of profits, particularly as prices increased after the devaluation of 1949.

Wage Policy and the Control of Labor Income and Costs

In a very real sense the successful operation of the whole planning and control structure outlined above depended upon the adaptation of wage movements to the requirements of the national economic program. Merely to list the economic objectives of the government — full employment, rapid reconstruction and economic development, and eventual achievement of internal financial stability and balance of payments equilibrium — suggests the problems which confronted the government in the area of wage policy. From the viewpoint of costs, wage increases had to be kept within limits that would not lead to a deterioration in the competitive position of Norwegian exports in world markets. From the viewpoint of incomes, increases in wage incomes had to be restricted sufficiently to generate a level of domestic saving high enough to make possible a rapid rate of capital formation without increasing internal inflationary pressure and the aggravation of the balance of payments deficit such pressure would entail.

The problem was, of course, to accomplish the restriction of wage movements as deemed appropriate in the light of planned objectives and general economic conditions without, in the attempt, raising worker dissatisfaction to a point where strikes and work stoppages jeopardized the very objectives being sought. The necessity for industrial peace cannot be overemphasized as a factor in wage decisions. It was, so to say, the anvil upon which wage policy decisions were hammered out. Neither the government nor the LO leadership could afford, in any given situation, to ignore the demands of the union membership for improvement in wages and working conditions. Consequently, any particular wage settlement usually had the character of a delicate judgment as to how much wage restraint could be practiced without producing widespread dissatisfaction with centrally negotiated wage settlements.

In view of the nature of this process, it is not surprising that the trade unions could, and did, successfully insist on the primacy of their authority over wages and working conditions of the workers. The government, therefore, was precluded from instituting direct regulations of wages and manpower in a manner comparable to its control over prices, profits, and materials.

Such a system had both its advantages and disadvantages from the point of view of economic control. A clear advantage, and one that it is difficult to overestimate, was the incorporation of the organized labor movement into the planning and administrative process. The possibility of conflict between the government and the unions over wage questions was minimized, since it was up to the central leadership of the trade unions to secure conformance on the part of the national unions to the national wage policy. On the other hand, the fact remains that the government had to operate with only an indirect control over both wage rates and wage incomes. In spite of the centralization of wage negotiations between the LO and the NAF, some room existed for variations among individual wage settlements by the national unions. Moreover, the process of incorporating the terms of the general settlements into individual contracts, as well as the administration of those contracts, permitted some leeway for divergence of actual wage increases from the centrally determined pattern. Finally, even under conditions of full employment, the connection between changes in contract wage rates and changes in wage incomes is far from being completely rigid. For these and other reasons, which are discussed at greater length in Chapter 6, increases in employee incomes tended to exceed contractual wage changes by a significant margin. Without doubt, however, the centrally negotiated and administered wage settlements have been the principal proximate determinants of actual changes in the incomes of wage earners.

CHAPTER 4

Wage Stabilization and Controlled Inflation, 1939–1952

Since wage policy decisions were focused on centrally negotiated wage settlements between the trade union and employer federations, a logical first step in the analysis of postwar developments would be to survey the course of those negotiations during the postwar years.[1] There are four distinct periods in the development of wage policy, associated with the changing economic circumstances and shifts in general economic policy. The first covers the period of immediate postwar adjustments when wage developments prior to and during the occupation and the effort to achieve a tenable stabilization line were the dominating factors. The second period is that of "stabilization" and suppressed inflation maintained until devaluation at the end of 1949 led to revision of subsidy policy in early 1950. The third period is that of the upward inflationary movement during 1950–51 resulting from the abandonment of a rigid "stabilization line." Finally, the fourth period, extending from 1952 to the present, is one in which negotiations have taken place under conditions of considerably reduced internal inflationary pressure and relative stability in world price levels, with, moreover, a substantial relaxation of direct governmental controls. The first two periods are dealt with in the present chapter, the latter two in the following chapter.

Wage Developments Before and During the Occupation, 1930–1945

"Wage policy after the war is, indeed, in many ways a continuation of the work which was stopped in 1940."[2] Wage movements during the thirties exhibited considerable stability compared to the fluctuations of the preceding decade. Contrasted to the trend of falling money wages with rising real wages which characterized the years 1920–30, wage and price movements moved more or less in unison, both falling until 1935 and rising thereafter. Real wages were relatively stable, but tended to fall after the cost of living turned upward in 1935. It was only in 1938 and 1939 that substantial real wage gains began to be made. In general, the years from 1930 to 1939 cannot be said to have brought more than extremely modest gains in workers' standards of living.

The outbreak of war brought the immediate expectation of rising world prices which could not fail to have their impact on the Norwegian price level. The LO opened negotiations with the Employers' Association in early November for the purpose of protecting the real wage level through an automatic cost-of-living-index provision. On January 4, 1940, the state mediator made a proposal, later accepted by both parties, awarding full compensation for the increase in the cost of living from September 15 to December 15, 1939, and providing for future adjustments on March 15 and June 15, 1950, if the cost-of-living index moved by at least five points. The mediator's proposal, however, included two innovations which were to be of considerable significance: any cost of living supplements after December 1939 were (1) to provide only "three-quarters compensation" for movements in the price index and (2), to be distributed generally as an equal absolute amount to workers, irrespective of their hourly rate (but keeping a distinction between men and women).

The first of these stipulations was based on the theory that war-induced price rises would stem primarily from real shortages, the burden of which in lower consumption levels should be distributed among all social groups. Acceptance of this position speaks well for the trade unions' sense of social responsibility. But, as the chief economist of the federation pointed out, "that the trade unions were guaranteed index adjustments every three months also played a role since too great a lag in wages behind prices was thereby prevented." [3] The issue of "full" or "three-quarters compensation" was to be raised again after the war. The award of a flat øre per hour cost-of-living supplement, presumably in conformance with the "solidaristic" wage policy of the trade unions, was to become standard practice in the postwar adjustments.

April 9, 1940, brought the Germans to Norway and collective bargaining relationships no longer existed as they had in the past. The day prior to the invasion the cost-of-living index for March 15 was published, showing a rise of some 6 per cent from December 1939; which meant an upward wage adjustment of eight øre for men, five øre for women. In May, 1940, a general wage stop as of April 9 was instituted, and in early June, presumably under the pressure of the occupation authorities, the Employers' Association and the Federation of Labor agreed on the cancellation of the cost-of-living increase of 12 øre (eight øre for women) which had been granted as of December 1939.

Subsequently, no general changes in contracted wage rates took place until the liberation on May 8, 1945 (see Table 1).[4] The substantial increases

Table 1. General wage settlements, 1940–1951

Date	Hourly paid workers		Salaried workers[a]		Percentage supplement[b]
	Men	Women	Men	Women	
	(øre/hr)	(øre/hr)	(kroner/mo)	(kroner/mo)	(per cent)
April 8, 1940	8	5	17.38	13.75	4.5
May 8, 1945	30	20	63.28	49.84	17.5
Sept. 10, 1945	20	14	42.00	33.00	15.0
Sept. 1, 1946	5	5	10.55	10.55	3.5
March 1, 1947	5	5	10.55	10.55	3.5
Sept. 1, 1947	5	5	10.55	10.55	3.5
April 15, 1948	(10 øre and 5 øre supplements to lower paid workers)				
June 16, 1949					
Oct. 14, 1950	18	18	38.00	38.00	11.0
April 14, 1951	17	17	36.78	36.78	10.7
Oct. 13, 1951	21	21	44.47	44.47	12.9

Source: Gøthe, *Lonnspolitikken etter Krigen* and Statistisk Sentralbyrå, *Okonomisk Utsyn*.

[a] Salaried workers at or over sixth-year wage classification.

[b] Calculated on base rates stipulated in the contracts which, in general, remained unchanged during the period.

in average earnings which nevertheless occurred during the occupation were the result of a general shift to incentive wage systems combined with non-contractual wage increases in individual firms suffering most acutely from the labor shortage. The money wage increases were still not sufficient in the manufacturing sector to offset increases in the cost of living. By the time of liberation real wages in manufacturing were some 15 to 25 per cent below prewar. This is undoubtedly a minimum estimate of the decline, since it is impossible to take into account the deterioration of quality, restriction of choice and variety, and so on. In addition, the only cost-of-living index available for the war period suffers from certain defects, not the least of which is that it was calculated on the basis of worker expenditure patterns in 1927–8. Perhaps a better indication of the decline in living standards during the occupation is the estimated reduction in real per capita consumption in excess of 40 per cent.[5]

Important as the magnitude of the reduction in real wages was for the development of wages after the war, the manner in which this reduction was distributed among different groups of workers was of equal and, perhaps, of more lasting significance. Daily earnings of men in agriculture (a relatively low wage sector) more than doubled, while in the higher wage manufacturing sectors, the percentage increase for male workers was only slightly over 30 per cent. This was a general pattern; the phenomenon of narrowing earnings differentials was pronounced and pervasive throughout the economy. Later chapters will deal with this aspect of the problem in greater detail. Here we will discuss three particularly significant features of these relative wage changes.

First, the narrowing of differentials was virtually universal, affecting not only occupational rates but also earnings differentials among and within major economic sectors, as well as sex differentials. Secondly, there seems to be evidence that the greatest increases in earnings took place in the smaller firms not covered by nationally bargained wage contracts. The increase in average hourly earnings for men in manufacturing firms associated with employers associations was about 60 per cent of the total average increase for male workers in manufacturing. A plausible case can be made that under conditions of a general contract rate freeze, there was a tendency for increases to accumulate faster in nonunion firms where no formal contract rate structure existed. The experience in the construction industry in Norway during the occupation would seem to substantiate this (although certain special circumstances were present).

The total increase [in earnings of construction workers] from the first quarter of 1940 [to 1944] is 10.2 per cent, less than one would expect in view of the role German construction activities should have played. But . . . the statistics include only firms who are members of the Employers' Association. In these years, a great number of new firms were expanded on the basis of the large German contracts. One can be certain that wages in these wholly or partly German undertakings were on a higher level than shown in the statistics.[6]

Finally, it should be kept in mind that (with the minor exceptions already noted above) the substantial increases in earnings (even in those firms working with union contracts) took place without any change in contract rates. The upward movement in earnings through personal increases and more widespread use of incentive rate systems rather than negotiated rate increases is a phenomenon that has continued throughout the postwar period under the label of *lønnsglidning* or "wage drift."

Certain features of the wage movements prior to and during the occupation certainly aggravated the problem of preventing inflationary pressures from breaking out into an explosive inflation. The depressed conditions of the thirties, followed by the deprivations of the occupation period, quite naturally tended to increase the urgency of workers' demands for compensation for wartime losses.

That the losses inflicted upon trade union workers . . . should be compensated for, runs like a red thread through the union activity in London and Stockholm during the war as well as at home in Norway in the first years of peace. This was the first and last commandment; it has nearly been the completely dominating goal of post war wage policy.[7]

Also, shifts in relative wages during the war period inevitably produced situations where demands were raised for the elimination of "inequities" between various groups of laborers.

But there were two important factors more favorable to the establishment of stability in the labor market. Most important was the centralized organization and "solidaristic" tradition of the trade unions which provided the means and the rationale for avoiding a scramble for economic gains at the expense of other groups of workers, organized or unorganized. Coupled with this was the trend toward equalization of wage incomes during the occupation, in spite of distortions, which had resulted in a wage structure more in accord with the equalitarian attitude of the Norwegian union movement. As a result, pressure from the lower wage groups for increases based on grounds of "equity" was considerably lessened.

Immediate Postwar Wage Adjustments

The Provisional Ordinance Concerning Wages and Working Conditions in Liberated Districts, dated September 15, 1944,[8] which had been worked out during the war in accordance with recommendations of the LO and NAF representatives in Stockholm and London was the basis upon which collective bargaining relationships were resumed. Supplementing this provisional ordinance was an agreement between the Federation of Labor and the Employers' Association — the so-called Stockholm protocol — on a cost-of-living supplement to be effective immediately upon liberation. These two documents were designed to form satisfactory interim arrangements pending the development of more permanent legislation and the normal functioning of collective bargaining. The Stockholm agreement was to be in force for only three months after liberation and the temporary decree was to expire within one year after cessation of hostilities, unless extended by the government.

The major wage provisions of the agreement and ordinance can be briefly stated. The ordinance reëstablished the provisions of all contracts valid on April 9, 1940, as well as the terms of any State Mediator's proposal made in connection with disputes not yet settled as of that date.[9] This provision meant that the cost-of-living supplements of December 1939 (12 øre for men, eight øre for women) were to be reëstablished. Wage control was established by provisions in the ordinance making it illegal for alterations in contracted wage terms to take place except by agreements between the central organizations of unions and employers (irrespective of whether union or employer was associated with the LO or NAF [10]) and by instituting compulsory arbitration if there was failure to reach agreement.[11]

The Stockholm Protocol supplemented the ordinance's effect on the cost of living adjustment by providing that a total cost-of-living increase (including the restoration of the prewar adjustment) should take effect immediately upon liberation as follows: (1) Adult male workers, 30 øre per hour; (2) Adult female workers, 20 øre per hour; (3) Workers receiving percentage supplements, 17.5 per cent; (4) Salaried workers, 63.28 kroner and 49.84 kroner per month for males and females respectively.

This increase was viewed by the trade unions as only a preliminary payment toward a more satisfactory cost-of-living adjustment when the Stockholm agreement expired. Already in June 1945, the representative council of the LO had adopted a resolution calling for the opening of negotiations on wages and authorizing the secretariat to terminate the wage agreement with the Employers' Association. But, significantly enough, as much emphasis was put on lower and stable prices as upon increased wages. The recommendation for the use of subsidies on consumer goods to raise real wages, first made to the London government in 1943, was renewed. Willingness to practice wage restraint was expressed, but with certain reservations:

The union movement will make a positive contribution to the solution of the reconstruction problem by being content with moderate compensation for price increases. But the absolute pre-condition for this position on the part of the union movement is that all other groups in the nation, in industry, commerce, agriculture, and fishing, also show the same willingness to forego otherwise justifiable demands, so that any increase in the price level is avoided.[12]

This did not prevent the Federation, however, from demanding "full compensation" for price increases since 1939 when wage negotiations were begun in August. The demand for "full compensation" was justified in the federation's view by the fact that

workers and employers who stayed in regular work are without doubt the part of the population who bore the heaviest burden and had their living standards reduced severely during the war years.[13]

In the face of employer opposition based on the dangers of inflation, the issue was rapidly placed before the newly constituted Wage Board for arbitration. The Wage Board's decision in September rejected the demand for full compensation but awarded a 20 øre increase for men, 14 øre for women and 15 per cent for those receiving percentage supplements with corresponding supplements for salaried employees. These increases were calculated to provide three-quarters compensation for the cost-of-living increases from September 1939 to July 1945, when the "wage drift" (calculated at 15 øre per hour for male workers) was included.[14] The Wage Board thus continued the "three-quarters" principle which had been established in the 1939 settlement.

The board's decision was intended to form the general basis for wage policy during the stabilization period. The coalition government, upon the advice of the Economic Coördination Council, had announced before the decision the intention of stabilizing the cost of living (with the aid of subsidies) at the then existing level. It was hoped that the magnitude of the two postwar cost-of-living supplements, amounting to about a 30 per cent increase in wages, would be sufficient to allay pressure for further wage increases in the near future, so long as the cost of living did not rise.

The election of the Labor government in October and the general adherence of the trade union leadership to the stabilization policy permitted the September award to be accepted without serious incident, even though there was considerable dissatisfaction within the unions. This dissatisfaction was aggravated by the decision of the Labor Court in December 1945, refusing to grant back pay for the 12 øre cost-of-living increase which had been eliminated by agreement between the LO and the NAF in June, 1940.[15]

All the collective agreements which had been extended for one year under the terms of the Provisional Ordinance of 1944 were to expire during 1946, and the trade unions undertook a comprehensive revision of all contracts beginning in January of 1946. During these negotiations, both the LO and the NAF took the position that a general wage increase should be avoided, except perhaps, for low wage groups. The trade union leadership was under considerable pressure from the government not to permit any general wage increase because of the danger to the stabilization policy. In a strong speech before the Trade Union Congress in May of 1946 the finance minister explained in great detail the importance of maintaining the stabilization policy and the dangers that would be faced if another wage increase took place.

It must be clearly understood that when the supplements of 30 øre and 20 øre were granted, the conditions for an immediate increase in wages did not exist. One can say that wage increases which would come eventually [from increased labor efficiency] were anticipated or discounted.

When I, therefore, hold generally to the position that there ought not today to be a general increase in wages or agricultural prices, it is because I believe that it is correct to maintain the stabilization line which, in my opinion, would be broken if one went through with such increases.[16]

Nevertheless, when workers' demands for a general wage increase caused difficulties in reaching agreement on the first contracts up for revision, the issue eventually came before the Wage Board with LO support and approval.

In view of the position which had been taken by the government and the strong recommendations from the Economic Coördination Council stressing the importance of holding the stabilization line, the board was placed in an awkward dilemma. It chose to give in to the workers' demands rather than risk the prospect of strikes and unrest which would, under the strained circumstances of the time, probably have jeopardized the whole reconstruction problem. The award announced on June 7, 1946, provided for a 15 øre increase for both men and women for all contracts in the mediation stage or which had not been renewed by July 1. To soften the impact of the increase, it was to be granted in three steps of five øre each as of September 1, 1946, March 1, 1947, and September 1, 1947. The award was rationalized as a further anticipation of increases in productivity, which, the board said, would to some extent be stimulated by the wage increase. In any event, this decision broke with the principle of three-quarters compensation previously enunciated by the Wage Board and provided the workers with a real wage increase, not a cost-of-living adjustment.

The index regulation in the agreement concluded between the two central organizations was shifted to the new cost-of-living index (1938 = 100) and based upon the July 1945 level of 155.8. Most important, it provided for a wholly automatic adjustment every six months, beginning in August, 1946, of 1.5 øre for every point change in the index, provided the index had moved five points from the base level of the level at the last adjustment. Thus, the so-called "red line" was 160.8, five points above the level July 15, 1945.

In addition to the general supplement of 15 øre, upward wage adjustments were widespread in the individual contract revisions throughout 1946 and into 1947. These changes amounted to as much as 20 to 30 øre in the low wage industries, such as pulp and paper and textiles, and were estimated to add about 15 øre more to average contract wage rates. By the first quarter of 1947 upward revisions in contract wage rates had increased average hourly earnings by almost 35 per cent over the average level of the second half of 1944.

The Period of Stabilization, 1946–1950

With most contracts running for two years, it was hoped that the June 1946 settlement represented an acceptable compromise on the wage front which would permit orderly execution of the stabilization policy. Difficulties, however, arose almost immediately. The cost-of-living index rose over the "red line" of 160.8 in November and December, 1946, but was pressed downward by increased subsidies in January in order to avoid the automatic wage increase which otherwise would have had to be granted as of March 1. However, upward pressure on the domestic price level continued with increases in agricultural and import prices. By June the index had again crossed the "red line," reaching a level of 162.1. By reducing the general sales tax from 10 per cent to 6¼ per cent, the Government was again able to avoid the scheduled index adjustment in August. Thus, the government found itself having to increase subsidies, in spite of its position against such increases announced in conjunction with the wage negotiations of June 1946. At the same time it was forced to reduce the sales tax at a

time when financial and monetary conditions made such a reduction unde-
sirable. The situation was aggravated by the fact that wages continued
to rise not only as a result of contract wage changes, but because of supplements granted above the stipulated rates.

By mid-summer 1947, the government considered the situation so serious
that it instituted a whole series of special measures designed to maintain
the stabilization line.[17] Included in these was a proposal for a temporary
wage stop prohibiting all increases in wages, except those provided for by
index regulations contained in collective agreements. The intent of this
measure was to eliminate the practice of granting wage increases above
the contract rates which had "grown so considerably during 1947 that the
condition can be described with some justification as a black market in
manpower." [18] The government pointed out, however, that such a wage
stop was not a complete answer to the problem.

This [wage-stop] law will be an important instrument not only in halting the
upward drift which already has occurred, but also in normalizing wage conditions. The Government wishes, however, to emphasize very strongly that this
is not simply a question of imposing prohibitive regulations. That black market
wages have occurred is, in part, due to the fact that the workers themselves
demand higher wages, and, still more frequently, that employers offer rates
higher than provided in the collective agreement. From the discussions that have
taken place, it seems reasonable to expect that the two central federations through
their organizational apparatus are willing to cooperate in making these regulations
effective in relation to their members.[19]

The Representative Council of the LO endorsed the wage stop in late
August 1947 with some misgivings, and the law became effective October
10. Because of the opposition of the unions, the law was allowed to expire
at the end of 1947 and, hence, had little or no direct effect on actual wage
movements. Psychologically, however, it may have been important in im-
pressing upon the workers how seriously the government viewed threats
to the stabilization line stemming from increased wages.[20]

With most contracts expiring in 1948, the Representative Council of the
LO met again in November to decide on the general position to be taken
in negotiations. The result was a strong recommendation against any general increase in wages and any widespread reopening of contracts during
1948. The council summed up the reasons for this position as follows:

In order to preserve the position which has been won, to safeguard the country's
economic independence, and to avoid the disaster of inflation, the principal task
of the trade unions today must be to help to increase production and to force
living costs down through more rigorous price control, thereby further improving
conditions for the wage earner.[21]

The wage negotiations of 1948 in a sense represented a turning point. *"We can say that with the contract revisions of 1948, trade union policy was more and more characterized by restraint in order to conserve what had been achieved."* [22]

This restraint on the part of the trade unions in foregoing demands for general wage increases during 1948 and 1949 did not mean complete inactivity on the wage front, however. Along with the LO Secretariat recommendation in the fall of 1947 that contracts be extended without any general increase went the proviso that contracts in the low wage industries could be reopened with the permission of the secretariat. During the winter months, LO leadership was active in obtaining the reactions of the individual union membership to the "freeze" on general wage demands and in assessing the particular desires of the various unions as a preliminary to working out the process whereby the Secretariat would grant permission for contract reopening in particular cases. Although the unions were, by and large, willing to accept the policy of no general wage increase, still "the question of wages was regarded as the most important by the unions concerned." [23] Rather than leave the formulation of special demands for low-range workers to the individual unions, the secretariat decided to formulate a general demand to cover all low wage workers.

When negotiations with the Employers' Association on the general demands broke down, the Ministry of Social Affairs lent its support to the LO's position by requesting the parties to reconvene in an effort to reach an agreement settling the wage problem for the rest of the year. Subsequent negotiations with the Employers' Association led to the adoption of an agreement on substantially the unions' terms. It provided for a 10 øre extraordinary supplement for men averaging less than 2.50 kroner per hour (2.60 kr. in Oslo) and women averaging less than 1.60 kroner per hour (1.70 kroner in Oslo) where manhours worked under incentive systems averaged less than 25 per cent of total hours worked. Thus the unions hoped to allay general wage pressure from the membership through continuation of wage equalization and through restricting the increase to workers whose earnings were least likely to increase without contract rate changes.

The impact of this settlement on the general wage level is impossible to estimate quantitatively with any degree of precision, but based on the LO chairman's estimates of the workers affected, it is likely that it represented about a 2 per cent increase in average contracted wage rates.

Economic developments in the latter part of 1948 and early 1949 strengthened adherence on the part of the unions to a policy of money wage stability. The cessation in the postwar upward movement of world prices began to be felt in Norway as prices of certain imported consumer commodities and of important export items showed a tendency to fall. These signs of the long-expected postwar recession tended to dominate trade union attitudes on the wage question when the second postwar LO convention convened in May of 1949.

The opinion was that there would be a downward adjustment of prices to a more reasonable level. Increased competition would appear again and marketing difficulties would have to be expected. The problem of unemployment which had caused anxiety in the period before and after the liberation again came to the fore. It was particularly the export industries which felt to be in danger. . . .

Another side of the stabilization policy presented itself. The outlook for the cost of living was no longer the completely overshadowing problem. Concern shifted from consumers to business enterprises. Now it was the prospect for the firms' cost level which had to receive the greatest weight.

This was the background which led to the trade unions' continuation of the cautions and restrained line which had found expression in the contract revisions of 1949.[24]

The pattern of 1949 wage changes, therefore, developed as a continuation and extension of the type of adjustments instituted in the 1948 negotiations. The determining settlement was the adoption in June 1949 of the state mediator's proposal after the LO and NAF had failed to reach any agreement on any general extension of substandard wage adjustments. The conditions for the 10 øre supplement introduced in the 1948 agreement were altered to give adult males receiving under 2.65 kroner per hour (2.75 in Oslo) an increase of 10 øre per hour or a lesser amount up to that limit, but at least 5 øre per hour. For men earning over these limits there was to be a supplement of 5 øre up to 2.80 kroner per hour (2.90 in Oslo). For women the corresponding limits were 1.70 and 1.85 kroner per hour (1.80 and 1.95 in Oslo). Workers wholly or partly under incentive systems were to receive these supplements only for hourly paid work.

The complicated character of the 1948 and 1949 agreements undoubtedly was a reflection of the effort to mitigate the ban on general wage increases imposed by the stabilization policy in face of the continuing pressure from the workers for higher money wages. It is likely that the restrictions and limitations surrounding the 10 øre and 5 øre supplements were, in fact, unable to prevent a general diffusion of the wage increase throughout industry.[25]

With the wage supplements of 1949 went a revision of the cost-of-living contract clauses which eliminated the automatic cost of living adjustment. The state mediator's proposal in June provided for a "semi-automatic" index adjustment; if the cost-of-living index on February 15, 1950, showed a rise or fall of seven points (previously five points) relative to the index for May 1949, the LO or NAF could reopen negotiations for a corresponding wage change. In case no agreement could be reached, contracts could be canceled on one month's notice. This revision widened the "red lines" somewhat — seven points on a base of 158.6 — giving the government a bit more flexibility in its manipulation of prices entering the index. The semi-automatic feature of avoiding stipulation of the size of the adjustment had been sought by the unions since 1948, when the weakening tendency of prices had begun to be observed. With the expectation of falling prices, the unions were seeking to prevent automatic wasting away of the money wage gains of the past years. At best, however, this provision was only a somewhat perilous substitute for actual incorporation of the cost-of-living supplements into basic wage rates, which had been one of the LO's demands in negotiations.

From the government's point of view, the 1949 settlement seemed to represent a considerable gain in the struggle to maintain control over the wage level. With most contracts renewed for a period of two years and with the loosening of the extremely sensitive built-in link between wage and price movements, it appeared that wage stability was at hand, at least for a time.

Devaluation and Controlled Inflation, 1950–1951

September of 1949, however, brought the devaluation of the pound sterling and most other European currencies including the Norwegian kroner. A 30 per cent currency devaluation obviously required a thorough reappraisal and readjustment of the stabilization policy which from the beginning had been predicated on a stable external value of the kroner. With the continuation of the Labor government in power after the general elections of October 1949, the future of the whole stabilization policy was submitted to reëxamination. After consultation with the Economic Coördination Council in December, the government announced its intention of restricting subsidies and permitting a rise in the internal price level.[26] The increase in subsidies from around 700 million kroner a year to over a billion kroner, which it was estimated would have been necessary to offset the effects of the devaluation on the cost of living raised "such great difficulties of monetary transfers that the Government . . . felt unable to put forward proposals for such an increase in appropriations for subsidization of prices."[27] The decision was not based merely on practical grounds, however; there was explicit recognition of the desirability of eliminating subsidies on the scale theretofore maintained by permitting cost and income adjustments to establish reasonable balance both externally and internally without extensive subsidization. The majority of the Economic Coördination Council stated:

A revision of the subsidy system must be regarded principally as a link in the effort to improve the economic position of the nation. Equilibrium must be attained in our external economy in the course of a few years and it is therefore necessary to take steps in good time to preserve a high level of employment and production [lest] . . . balance be forced via a reduction of imports when foreign aid ceases. . . . Today we have greater possibilities of avoiding this than we shall have later. In the Board's opinion these possibilities lie in increased production, a cut in investment, and some reduction in demand for consumer goods. The reduction in subsidies is an important and necessary link in this work. . . .

The council went on to point out that the subsidy arrangements were established as temporary measures immediately after the war when rationing and import regulations were essential. Since many of those controls had already been or were about to be terminated, the subsidy system lost much of its justification. And, finally, in the opinion of the council majority, "equally important is the need for creating more rational price relations between various groups of commodities."

The revision of the subsidy policy did not mean that the government intended to relinquish control over the price level. The problem now became one of controlling an increase in the domestic price level without setting off an excessive wage-price spiral and without permitting the price increases to lead to undesired shifts in the income distribution. This meant that the instruments of the postwar stabilization policy — price control, regulation of profits, and dividends, rent control, low interest rates, extraordinary duties on certain exports and imports, as well as subsidies — would continue to be administered as before but without attempting to achieve absolute price stability.

Since the price increases were bound to impose greater burdens on some groups than on others, the government was forced to consider ameliorative measures such as increased subsidies to agriculture, a rise in pensions for the aged and handicapped, and increased children's allowances. Most important, however, was the necessity for working out a new agreement on wage adjustments.

The terms of the June 1949 settlement, which had been introduced into most collective agreements, provided only one reopening date — February 15, 1950 — for the semi-automatic cost-of-living adjustment. Although the government had announced its intentions of revising its subsidy policy prior to that date, actual reductions in subsidies were not undertaken until April 1950. Since the February deadline had been passed without the cost-of-living index exceeding the "red line," no contractual basis existed for any upward wage adjustments to compensate for the sharp rise in the cost of living which began in April. In its recommendations to the government in March 1950, the Economic Coördination Council had noted the desirability of effecting the withdrawal of subsidies prior to any wage readjustments and emphasized its opinion that "if the reduction in subsidies is to attain its purpose — that of decreasing consumption — it will not be possible to give full compensation for the rise in prices." Nevertheless, the council majority recognized the reasonableness of the trade unions' desire for a cost-of-living adjustment under the extraordinary circumstances, and it pointed out that the recommendation for subsidy reduction was predicated on the assumption that it could be carried out without incurring labor strife.

If a revision of the subsidy system were to be effected under such circumstances that it involved disturbance in the workshops, this would constitute a risk of such dimensions that the Council could not then recommend the withdrawal of subsidies to the extent actually called for on economic grounds. The Council, therefore, recommends that the Government take steps to bring the organizations [LO and NAF] together with a view to agreement on this matter.[28]

It was under government auspices, therefore, that discussions between the employers and the unions were concluded in March, with an agreement calling for a reopening of negotiations in the fall, upon the invitation of the government, if the cost-of-living index as of September 15, 1950, exceeded 165.6 (1938 = 100) "as a result of the new subsidy regulations." It further provided that if no agreement was reached, a tripartite board would be constituted to determine whether a provisional wage adjustment should be effected for the remainder of the contract period.

This extraordinary cost-of-living agreement represented significant departure from previous practice in that not only was the agreement reached through the direct intervention of the government, but it named the government as a third party to any negotiations that might take place pursuant to the terms of settlement. Moreover, the parties agreed in advance to governmental arbitration of any dispute over a cost of living adjustment in the fall of 1950. Thus, governmental arbitration of disputes over wage demands, even though approved by the central organizations, was reintroduced in this instance after having been eliminated in the revision of the Labor Disputes Law in early 1949.

By this direct intervention the government sought to establish a degree of control over the cost-increasing influence of devaluation and external price rises. By entering as a third party to the wage negotiations, it proposed to broaden the scope of the wage bargain to include governmental action which would be accepted by the unions as satisfactory substitutes for money wage increases without the cost-rising impact of the latter.

From April 1950 the cost-of-living index rose rapidly, reaching 179.5 (1938 = 100) on September 15, some 12 per cent over the March level and 13.9 points over the "red line."

In accordance with the March agreement, the government on October 23 called upon both parties to take up the question of compensation for the rise in the cost of living. By the terms of the earlier agreement the maximum demand the trade unions could make was full compensation for the price increases resulting from the reduction of subsidies. After a week of negotiation the LO and NAF agreed to a general cost-of-living increase of 18 øre as of October 14, 1950, for both men and women (11 per cent for those receiving percentage supplements and corresponding increases for salaried workers).

The increase was calculated to provide full compensation for the estimated increase in expenditures of the "index family" resulting from the reduction in subsidies alone. In terms of the total price rise, it was estimated that the settlement provided the "index family" somewhat less than two-thirds compensation for the increase in prices since May of 1949. On the average, the cost of living supplement of 18 øre represented a 5 to 6 per cent increase in wages from the first quarter of the year, whereas the cost-of-living index on the old basis (the one specified in the previous agreement) showed an increase of over 12 per cent during the same period, and even the revised index indicated an increase of over 7 per cent. That the extraordinary degree of restraint exhibited by the unions was motivated by the fear of inflation is apparent in the rather blunt statement of the Chairman of the LO after the agreement had been ratified:

the wage supplement which has been given does not completely make up for the reduction in the standard of living which has occurred because of the price increase since the contract revision in 1949.

This reduction in living standards is the wage earners' contribution to avoiding an inflationary development in the coming period.[20]

A further contribution to the avoidance of uncontrolled inflation was the extension to 1952 of collective agreements expiring in 1951. However, provisions were made for one automatic cost-of-living adjustment and possible semi-automatic increases or decreases thereafter. Specifically, if the (new) cost-of-living index by March 15, 1951, moved five points above or below the September 1950 level of 108.3 (1949 = 100), wages would automatically be adjusted by 2.6 øre for every point change in the index (1.3 øre for younger workers, 1.59 per cent for those with percentage supplements and 5.49 kroner per month for salaried workers). Unique features, however, were the provisions for extension of both the automatic and semi-automatic adjustments. If the "red line" was not crossed by March 15, 1951, an automatic adjustment would, nevertheless, take place as of the first month the index did push across it. Once this occurred, a further five-point rise or fall in the index would be the basis for new negotiations, provided at least six months had elapsed since the previous adjustment.

As a result of this arrangement, an automatic cost-of-living supplement became effective April 15, 1951. Hourly paid workers (both men and women) received an increase of 17 øre per hour (10.7 per cent for workers with percentage supplements) and salaried workers received a corresponding supplement. By September 15, 1951, the cost-of-living index under the impact of the post-Korean inflationary movement throughout the world had reached 125.8 (1949 = 100) almost 11 points over the March 15 level of 115.0.

The issues raised in the resulting negotiations, dispute and ultimate arbitrations, posed some of the most difficult problems of wage settlements theretofore faced in the postwar period. For the first time since the revision of the Labor Disputes Act in 1949, the employer and labor organizations confronted each other on a major issue in the context of completely free collective bargaining. It rapidly became apparent, however, that the two central organizations were unable to reach agreement regarding a general wage increase on their own initiative. Negotiations between the parties broke down after a short interval: the LO was not prepared to compromise its demand for "full compensation," while the NAF opposed a general wage increase of any magnitude. The state mediator found the positions of the two parties so irreconcilable and so divergent that he could find no basis for formulating a compromise proposal for submission to the parties. With the failure of mediation, the government was faced with the threat of a strike, set for early December, involving about 180,000 workers throughout all sectors of the economy. Not unexpectedly, therefore, the government proposed and the Storting passed legislation providing for compulsory arbitration of this particular dispute by a special wage board.

Both the LO and the NAF emphasized that the basic issues in the case could only be determined in light of the general economic situation. The question of achieving a new stabilization line and the development of a correspondingly appropriate wage policy had been a subject of active study since the automatic wage increase in March 1951. The Economic Coördination Council at the request of the government in July had advised against establishing a new stabilization line, taking the position that the uncertainties of the future economic situation made it impossible to foresee how effective such an attempt might be. During the summer, also, the question of increased family allowances as a means of ameliorating the undesired effects of the rising price level had been considered by the government, the Economic Coördination Council, the LO, and the NAF. The trade union position, however (which frustrated any such attempt), was that family allowances should in general be separate from the system of wage payment and that, in particular, if increased allowances were to be introduced as part of a wage settlement, the LO "could not accept an arrangement which benefited only some of the wage earners." [30]

In mid-October, simultaneously with publication of the September 15 index which touched off the first negotiations, the government obtained from another advisory body composed of economic experts, the Monetary and

Financial Council, an evaluation of the problem of wage compensation for cost-of-living increases, on the basis of as complete an analysis as possible of the total economic situation and the necessity for avoiding inflationary or other damage to the economy. This report's conclusions emphasized the contingent character of any judgment regarding "full compensation" for cost-of-living increases, listing the principal necessary conditions for such compensation: (1) no deterioration in the terms of trade; (2) continuing availability of the clearing and credit facilities of the European Payments Union; (3) a limitation on the level of defense expenditures and an assumption of an increase in production of 3 to 4 per cent; (4) increased imports of consumer goods; and (5) no increase in the volume of investment. In the face of the manifest uncertainties surrounding these conditions (particularly the terms of trade) the Council concluded with the recommendation that

In the wage settlement one should seek to obtain a margin of safety relative to the abovementioned conditions in the form of partial compensation. The magnitude of this safety margin will depend on the judgment one has as to the likelihood that the conditions which have been listed above will be fulfilled.[31]

Needless to say, the probabilities were evaluated differently by the opposing parties. The unions' view, briefly stated, was that while real wages had declined since 1949, productivity, production, and the general economic strength of the economy had increased; therefore, there was every justification for the "full compensation" of 28 øre per hour. In arriving at this figure for "full compensation," the unions did not take into account the "so-called wage drift," which, they maintained, was in large part a result of individual increases in efficiency leading to higher incentive earnings. Moreover, the LO claimed that the effect on the cost-of-living index of the increase in the general sales tax from 6¼ to 10 per cent in April, 1951, ought not to be eliminated in the compensation calculation, pointing out that the full effect of the previous reduction on the cost-of-living index had been taken into account in 1947 in order to avoid an automatic increase under the then existing contracts.

In rebuttal, the Employers' Association emphasized that: (1) the economic improvement varied from sector to sector; (2) a general wage increase would result in a general price increase and further demands for wage increases; (3) the foreign economic situation was liable to undergo serious reversal at any time; and (4) the extraordinary assistance from the United States was scheduled to cease in 1952 at the same time that the defense program would place an increasing burden on the economy. With regard to the sales tax, the NAF maintained that in any event it ought to be eliminated in calculating the increase in the cost-of-living for wage adjustment purposes, inasmuch as the tax had been raised for the express purpose of providing for the planned increase in defense expenditures which was a burden to be shared by all. Finally, the employers maintained the "wage drift" also ought to be taken into account in calculating any cost-of-living wage adjustment.

The majority of the Wage Board resolved the dispute by what might be called a compromise "in favor of the unions," namely a supplement of 21 øre for hourly paid adult workers, both men and women (11 øre for younger workers), and a 12.9 per cent increase for those with percentage supplements. (Corresponding increases were provided for salaried employees.) The basis for the majority's decision was stated only briefly and in general terms.

Recent price increases have resulted in a reduction in real wages for most wage earners. At the same time there has been a genuine improvement in the country's over-all economic position. . . . The majority is consequently of the opinion that there is a real economic basis for a wage increment.

In determining the size of the wage supplement the majority has taken into account that the country's good economic situation is due in large part to the favorable price and market situation confronting our export industries (especially paper and shipping) which results from the tense international situation and rearmament. The country's economic position is, therefore, unstable and may be vulnerable in case of an economic reversal and less favorable terms of trade. . . .

Further we have had in mind that economic conditions differ in individual sectors of the economy and that some of the firms in the domestic industries have marketing difficulties.

A part of the rise in the cost-of-living index is connected with the financing of our defense expenditures. The majority believes that the wage increase awarded will provide wage earners in reality with full compensation for the rise in the cost of living up to September 15, reasonable account being given to the increased burdens on the nation imposed by the tense international situation.[32]

Interestingly enough, the arithmetic of the decision (not adduced by the board majority in its written decision) was reminiscent of the 1940 and 1945 cost-of-living awards. The 21 øre award was some three øre more than the amount required for compensation if the effects of the increased sales tax were eliminated from the 10.8 increase in the cost-of-living index (some 18 øre more if the "wage drift" according to the NAF's calculations was also eliminated). However, the fact that 21 øre did amount to "three-quarters compensation" for the total cost-of-living demand by the LO makes it a warranted assumption that the figure was decided upon as an acceptable compromise in line with the three-quarters principle first incorporated in the agreements of 1940.

With this award of 21 øre, there was some expectation that a new stabilization line could eventually be established. The Economic Coördination Council in December 1951 noted that if the main trends in the prices of raw materials continued, movement of prices might soon become more dependent on internal conditions. Consequently, it recommended that "the government authorities take the question [of stabilization] up for consideration with the large economic organizations in order to reach, if possible, a basis upon which to build further." [33] There were also indications from the union side that a new stabilization level should be the objective.[34]

The issue confronting the authorities, however, was considerably broader than whether or not to establish a new "stabilization line." The fundamental question was the extent to which it would be the policy of the government to maintain detailed regulation of the economy. Government economic strategy had been successful in restoring the production base of the economy and bringing it record levels of output. Per capita net national product was some 20–30 per cent above the prewar level. Inventories had been restocked; supplies of basic consumer goods had become ample enough to permit abandonment of rationing on most items. Furthermore, monetary and fiscal policy had reduced bank reserves to about one-quarter their level in 1945, while the upward price movement of 1950–51 had let quite a bit of the steam out of the inflationary engine. In short, a reasonably stable equilibrium maintained with less reliance on direct controls appeared within striking distance.

Progress toward the goal of internal financial stability depended in large part upon the avoidance of a wage-price spiral. The danger of such a spiral was acute, first, because during 1952 virtually all the collective agreements were scheduled to expire making inevitable a new round of wage negotiations almost immediately, and secondly, because of the index clause in the 1950 agreements providing extension of the semi-automatic cost of living increase. Under this latter provision the new "red line" was 130.8 (1949 = 100), five points above the September 1951 level, which, if exceeded on March 15, 1952, would lead to new negotiations. It was estimated that the effects of the December award would in itself result in a rise of the cost-of-living index extremely close to the "red line." [35]

A great deal hung on the outcome of the 1952 wage negotiations. In retrospect, they may be viewed as the opening skirmish in a struggle that is still going on — the struggle to maintain wage-price stability in a full-employment economy.

CHAPTER 5

The Struggle for Wage-Price Stability, 1952–1958

From the beginning it was apparent that the 1952 wage settlements would introduce a new phase in the evolution of wage policy in postwar Norway. The problem of the 1952 contract negotiations had already come before the LO Representative Council meeting at the end of October, 1951. Concerned over the far-reaching, pattern-setting effects of the general wage settlements with the Employers' Association throughout the economy, the council decided to eliminate centralized negotiations, leaving the various national unions to work out individual contract renewals on their own. The chairman of the LO also urged as justification for this decision the desirability — after six years of centralized settlements — of making contract revisions "on the basis of conditions within the individual branches of industry" which would permit, among other things, a widening of skill differentials so as "to stimulate and increase the supply of skilled manpower." [1]

The LO decision to seek further wage increases in 1952 — notwithstanding the reversal in strategy — produced considerable strain within the government. The fading of the Korean boom in world prices removed the rationale for increased subsidization as a stabilization measure designed to control the impact of external price changes. On the other hand, despite cost of living adjustments, large groups of wage earners had undoubtedly suffered real wage declines during the inflation of 1950–51. Consequently, rank-and-file sentiment — and the ever-present threat of Communist exploitation of worker disaffection — apparently precluded the possibility of stabilizing on the current contractual wage level. After a cabinet shift including the resignation of Prime Minister Einar Gerhardsen, the new prime minister, Oscar Torp, announced the government's decision in a speech to the Storting.

Taking everything into account, the Government has concluded that at present it does not appear as though increased pressure on prices from abroad will, in the near future, affect our price level through imports . . . the Government for the present will not introduce new extraordinary measures to influence directly the price level. . . . The individual groups and their organizations will now have themselves decisive influence on the future development of prices. . . . [2]

With this announcement it appeared that the stage was set for a wide-spread revision of individual wage agreements without, for the first time since the war, either compulsory arbitration or overt governmental influence on the terms of the general settlement. But in the event, while the 1952 negotiations undoubtedly represented a considerable loosening in the collective bargaining process, governmental influence and central control by the LO over the negotiations played much the same role as in earlier settlements.

The National Budget for 1952 provided for a 4 per cent increase in consumption in order to make up for the decline in consumption which was thought to have occurred during the inflationary movement of 1950–51. In spite of the fact that the Representative Council had adopted the resolution calling for individual settlements, the LO Secretariat decided to provide the various unions with an "orientation" setting out the framework within which any wage settlement should be worked out. The general import of the orientation was that on the basis of the National Budget estimates, an average wage increase of about 5 per cent was economically justifiable, although some unions probably should get more and others less.[3]

An additional objective of the LO in attempting to decentralize the 1952 negotiations was the technical revision of the contracts, specifically the incorporation of the cost-of-living bonuses into the basic contract rates with the consequent readjustment of incentive rates.

The actual course of the 1952 settlements exhibited both increased flexibility and variability in the collective agreements and general adherence to the more or less centralized wage policy. The key settlement which set the tone of succeeding negotiations occurred in the iron and metal industry. The two parties to the dispute found it impossible to make any fruitful progress on their own in their negotiations or in subsequent mediations. The principal reason appears to have been the insistence on the part of the employers' organization in the industry (Mekaniske Verksteders Landsforening) that the LO indicate at the very beginning of negotiations whether the Metalworkers' demands were approved by the secretariat in their entirety. Unless the LO's position was made clear from the beginning, the employers felt that real bargaining could not take place since the LO could, under the terms of the existing Labor Disputes Law, always refuse to approve the Metalworkers' position and, thereby, force arbitration by a government wage board. This was seen as an evasion of responsibility on the part of the LO and an indication of bad faith in carrying out the announced intention of permitting decentralized negotiations; the unions, without facing up to the prospect of a strike, always had the option of seeking to obtain through an arbitration decision more than it seemed possible to get via the bargaining process.[4]

The result was that, with the breakdown in negotiations and the failure of mediation, the Metalworkers' Union indicated to the LO in unmistakable terms that it did not want to strike and that the dispute should be settled by compulsory arbitration. The LO, therefore, accommodatingly refused to approve the union's demands, thus forcing arbitration.[5]

The award of the Wage Board on April 4, 1952,[6] broke new ground in several directions. It provided a substantial wage increase but, for the first time since the war, it differentiated among skills. The basic rates of skilled workers were raised 20 øre per hour while semi- and unskilled workers received 15 øre and 13 øre respectively. Incentive rates were raised 5 per cent, which represented a 16–17 øre increase for skilled workers. Secondly, it called upon the two parties to negotiate the incorporation of the cost-of-living supplements into the basic structure of both hourly and incentive wage rates — such incorporation to be worked out so that no increase in earnings resulted from it. Finally, the board majority, because of "the uncertain economic situation," eliminated the cost-of-living index regulation and limited the duration of the contract to one year.

The general outline of this decision was incorporated into the collective agreements during 1952. There was a clear tendency for differentiation in the wage settlements between the skilled and unskilled groups. Moreover, the cost-of-living provisions generally disappeared and efforts were made to incorporate the existing supplements into the rate structure. The problem of the adjustment called for under the 1950 settlement when the cost-of-living index crossed the "red line" in May 1952, was solved by providing a 10 øre supplement for those working under contracts which had not been revised before June 15, 1952. This 10 øre was viewed as an advance on the wage increases to be made when the contracts came up for revision and was to be incorporated into the rate structure, even though no agreement was reached in the coming negotiations on the incorporation of other cost-of-living supplements.

The quantitative effect on the wage level of the 1952 wage rate increases is estimated to have been on the order of 4 or 5 per cent.[7] However, the incorporation of the cost-of-living supplements into the basic rate structure undoubtedly resulted in additional increases during 1952 and 1953. By 1952 the sum total of cost-of-living supplements awarded since 1939 and paid to most workers as a separate absolute addition to earnings irrespective of wage classification, amounted to around 30 per cent of average hourly earnings in mining and manufacturing. In theory, incorporation of these separate supplements into the rate structure was to be accomplished via adjustments in the basic hourly and piece rates distributing the total amount paid out as cost-of-living bonuses without, however, producing any change in average rates.

Needless to say, it could not be expected that a revision of the rate structure of the magnitude and complexity this process involved could be carried out without any impact on the average level of wages. The inevitable tendency would be an additional upward movement in wages. In fact, it is generally acknowledged that significant increases did occur, although it is impossible to specify their quantitative importance.[8]

On the whole, even though the LO found it necessary to exercise a certain amount of central authority over the negotiations and the key settlement could only be reached via compulsory arbitration, the 1952 revisions of collective agreements must be judged of unique importance. In the first place, they represented a partially successful attempt at decentralization of collective bargaining, with the deliberate purpose of introducing greater flexibility into the bargaining processes and permitting particular conditions within the various industries to be reflected in the collective agreements. In the second place, the elimination of the cost-of-living clauses in the agreements permitted the government somewhat greater freedom in its choice of economic policies, and, in particular, opened the way for increased reliance on the indirect and aggregative instruments of monetary and fiscal policy.

The effect of loosening the formal ties between wages and prices was, however, limited by the fact that the agreements in general were to expire within one year (contract terms of greater length without cost-of-living provisions would undoubtedly have been rejected by the workers). Consequently, there was still considerable pressure on the government to achieve price stability if it was not to be faced with increased wage demands in 1953.

The 1953 Extension of Wage Contracts

The apparent slackening in 1953 of economic growth in Norway and throughout Western Europe, the continuing drop in raw material prices, and a drastic deterioration in Norway's terms of trade confronted the policy of greater flexibility and freedom in the labor market with a severe test. Although import and export prices dropped sharply throughout 1952, wholesale prices continued to rise until late in the year when a moderate decline set in. With the removal of rationing and subsidization of certain food products, the cost-of-living index rose until September and appeared to reach a plateau. The decline in export and import prices emphasized the dependence of future price developments on domestic factors and raised the question whether the tendency for the domestic price level to continue upward could be overcome. The future course of agricultural prices seemed to be crucial. The Central Bureau of Statistics calculated that of the 7 per cent rise in the cost-of-living index from the fourth quarter of 1951 to the third quarter of 1952, somewhat less than half could be attributed to the increase in wage and other nonagricultural incomes, about half to increased money incomes in agriculture and fishing, and the rest to the net effect of lower import prices and changes in subsidies.[9]

The rise in food prices led to increasing restlessness among trade union members who made growing demands on the LO leadership to take the question up with the government.[10] In October and November, after discussing the possibilities with the various economic organizations, the government prevailed upon the cooperatives to introduce a series of price reductions on food items which eventually spread throughout private trade channels. The government also undertook to increase the subsidy on milk and to eliminate the tariff on sugar and coffee, the effect of which measures alone was expected to bring the cost of living index down 1 per cent. By the turn of the year it appeared that prices had been more or less stabilized.

The prospect of continuing deterioration in the external situation made it increasingly important to avoid any wage increase during 1953. The National Budget for 1953 assumed a deficit on foreign account of 600 million kroner, arising almost entirely from the adverse shift in terms of trade. Private consumption was estimated to increase by 1.5 per cent on the basis of increased disposable income resulting from higher levels of production, scheduled reductions in taxes, and the effects of wage increases granted late in 1952. No provision was made for increased wages, the stated objective being "to increase the standard of living without raising the rates of money income and wages." [11]

In January, the Finance Minister urged on the Representative Council of the LO a general policy of renewing contracts without wage increases.[12] He emphasized the likelihood that any wage increases would be dissipated in subsequent price increases and that only by maintaining control over the cost level so that Norwegian exports remained competitive in other countries would it be possible to avoid a serious problem of unemployment. On the other hand, he stressed that the reduction of taxes the government planned to introduce would provide a basis for an increase in real incomes without an upward movement in the cost level.

The council, after debate, passed a resolution recommending that all contracts expiring in 1953 be renewed. A significant qualification was appended to this resolution:

> During recent years the wage increases which the Landsorganisasjon has obtained for its members, have been appealed to both by wage earners not organized in association with the Landsorganisasjon and by other groups in society as a basis for demanding corresponding or larger wage and income increases. When the Representative Council recommends prolongation of collective agreements in 1953, it is assumed that all other groups in the society will also in this case follow the Landsorganisasjon's example and show the same moderation and social feeling.

For the trade unions' wage policy it will be of decisive importance that there occur no violation of this assumption.[13]

In undertaking this policy it seems clear that the principal concern was the threat of unemployment stemming from external influences. This fear of unemployment was reflected in the LO Congress in May, 1953. The report of the secretariat on the economic situation expressed concern over a possible increasing trend toward deflationary policies in Western European countries and concluded:

Should developments continue in this direction, it will have to be a major objective of the trade unions to cooperate with the authorities in using every means permissible within a democratic framework in a modern society to prevent the effect of an international deflation from introducing unemployment via our external economy.[14]

To a substantial degree the effort to avoid wage increases by voluntary action and without benefit of the Wage Board was successful. With minor exceptions, agreements were renewed for another year without major wage adjustments. The absence of wage rate increases and a continuation of the stagnating tendencies which developed throughout Europe in the latter part of 1952, contributed to a high degree of internal stability during 1953. Prices were stable, the cost of living in January 1954 standing only seven-tenths of 1 per cent above the peak reached in September 1952. Employment remained high, and production again began to increase in the last half of the year. The foreign trade situation, however, continued to be serious in spite of some improvement in commodity terms of trade, principally because of a continuing low level of freight rates. The balance-of-payments deficit for the year amounted to over one billion kroner, compared to the 600 million kroner deficit assumed in the 1953 National Budget.

The 1954 Negotiations

The balance-of-payments situation once again brought the Finance Minister to the fall meeting of the LO Representative Council to urge upon the trade unions a policy of no wage demands in the negotiations of 1954 contract renewals. Again the major emphasis was on the problem of maintaining high levels of employment and the futility of a wage-price spiral.[15]

The council's recommendations to the unions were based on a compromise position which stressed the difficulty of the situation, but left the question of whether to extend the contracts up to the individual unions. It was acknowledged, however, that the unions might desire to press for such fringe benefits as payments for sick leave and variable holidays falling on week days, shortening of the work week where it was now over 48 hours, diminution in the wage differential between men and women, and perhaps, some wage increases for those receiving considerably below the average wage.[16]

There was a feeling that the 1954 negotiations might well present the most serious problems confronted by the unions since the war. The chairman of the LO warned that there was some desire among the employers to re-open the agreements for purposes of obtaining wage decreases. And he concluded:

I believe that this will be the most difficult contract settlement since the end of the war. Many things serve to indicate that the external period of prosperity we have had is now finished, and that we are beginning on the journey down the trough of the wave, and there it is not easy to make any progress.[17]

The actual course of negotiations as they took place during the spring of 1954 was not smooth. It soon became apparent that the employers were unwilling to participate in peacemeal negotiations with individual unions on fringe benefits and individual wage adjustments. To avoid a widespread outbreak of strikes as the bulk of the contracts expired during March, April, and May, the LO secretariat, on April 5, proposed to the NAF that joint negotiations take place between the two central organizations on all the demands for welfare benefits raised by the unions in the spring contract negotiations. The NAF agreed to such negotiations on the condition (accepted by the LO) that they also include a general wage settlement.

After rather complicated and tense negotiations, agreement was finally reached providing compensation for variable holidays (not falling on Sundays) of 25 kroner per day for men, 20 kroner for women, 10 kroner for apprentices, and compensation of 5 to 10 kroner per day for days lost due to accidents occurring while at work. No general wage increase was granted, but increases of 10 øre per hour for male workers on time rates and 8 kroner per week for those with weekly rates (7 øre per hour and 6 kroner per week for women) were fairly widespread; actual rates, however, varied somewhat from industry to industry, depending on the wage level. Piece rates remained unchanged, except in the textile industry and for women in the canning industry. The pattern for these increases, which were designed to raise the wages of the lower paid workers, was set by an April 30 decision of a wage board convened in March by the Storting to settle the dispute arising from the demands of the land transport and dock workers.

The term of contract renewals was set at two years and there was reintroduced a semi-automatic cost of living clause permitting reopening of negotiations if on March 15 or September 15, 1955, the cost of living index had moved seven points from its level on March 15, 1954. In spite of the fact that the negotiations were concluded without any general increase in wage rates, the settlement represented a significant improvement in the workers' terms of employment. In total, it was estimated that the contract revision gave benefits equivalent to an average wage increase of roughly 3 per cent.[18]

Nevertheless, the negotiations and settlement provoked a significant amount of disagreement within the ranks of the unions. The decision of the LO secretariat to undertake centralized negotiations including the subject of wages was not universally accepted as appropriate.[19] The Communists were able to make enough of an issue out of a call for a fight to win the unions' demands completely to bring forth strong rebuttal in a leading editorial of the LO journal.[20] And the vote by the union membership to accept the terms of the final settlement showed a substantial minority opposition (over one third of those voting); five of the 25 unions involved polled majorities for rejecting the settlement.[21]

The latent dissatisfaction among the workers began to take on a more serious aspect when the cost-of-living index began to rise shortly after the agreement had been concluded. The cost-of-living clauses included in the settlement were based upon the level of the index in mid-March of 139 ($1949 = 100$); by July 15 the index had climbed to 145, within one point of the "red line," while under the agreements it was only if the "red line" had been crossed on March 15, 1955 that the question of compensation could be reopened. To have the price assumptions, upon which the wage settlements had been predicated, eroded to such an extent and so soon after the collective contracts had been signed — particularly when the terms of settlements had not been overly popular in the first place — placed the central leadership of the LO in a difficult position.

Events during the fall months of 1954 bore a striking resemblance to those following the 1952 settlements. In early October the LO secretariat made a formal representation to the government expressing profound concern over the price developments and requesting that the government take action to bring about a reduction in the cost of living.[22] Toward the end of the month the situation was felt to be sufficiently serious to warrant formal statements by the Prime Minister and the Minister of Finance to the Storting explaining the government price policy, and the subject was brought up for debate in the Storting at the end of November.

To a considerable extent the price developments during the summer and fall of 1954 raised issues of fundamental importance to the future course of general economic policy in Norway. A major issue in the election of 1952 had been the proposed enactment of a permanent price control law providing the government with broad powers to regulate prices and competitive practices when it was judged necessary for the economic well being of the country. In presenting the proposed law to the Storting, however, the Finance Ministry emphasized that direct price regulation was to be considered as only one of a variety of instruments available to carry out economic policy and that price controls were to be instituted only when a specific situation made them necessary.[23] And, in fact, with the coming into effect of the permanent price law[24] on January 1, 1954, a general removal of specific price controls took place and elimination of direct regulation continued throughout the year.[25] Against this background of relaxation of economic controls, the unfavorable price movements during 1954 can be seen as providing the first severe test for the policy of increasing the role of private and individual decisions in the economic life of the country.

Although the movement of the cost-of-living index under the impact, primarily, of increases in food and agricultural prices was the focal point of the unions' concern, it was only one symptom of more general inflationary tendencies which by the end of 1954 were recognized as presenting extremely serious threats to the stability of the economy. Despite efforts to reduce the rate of capital formation, the level of net investment had continued to rise. The deficit on the balance of payments in 1954 amounted to over one billion kroner, although export industries were running at full capacity, the physical volume of exports had increased some 15 per cent over 1953, and commodity terms of trade (excluding ships) during the year were more favorable than at any time since the liberation, with the single exception of the boom year of 1951.

Early in 1955 the government introduced a whole series of measures designed to reduce the rate of investment expenditures in order to relieve the pressure on the internal price level and the balance of payments. Actions to limit bank credit included enforcement of bank reserve requirements under the new bank reserve law, floating of government loans amounting to 500 million kroner, imposition of ceilings on the lending operations of the state banks, a reduction of 20 per cent in the licensing quota of the state housing bank, and direct regulation by the Norges Bank over private bond flotation. More direct attacks on investment demand were made by imposition of a 10 per cent tax on expenditures for new investment, a 20 per cent levy on contractual payments for ships on order, special taxes on cars and tractors, as well as certain tax remissions for investment funds set aside by businesses for a period of three years.

In addition, the central bank rate was raised to 3.5 per cent from the 2½ per cent level which had been maintained since the war. The latter step gained in significance, perhaps out of proportion to the actual impact on investment demand, because of the political importance that had become attached to a policy of low interest rates since the war. The conservative opposition, by emphasizing the necessity of higher interest rates to control inflation, had made the interest rate policy a focal point of controversy between differing economic philosophies, so that the decision to raise the bank rates had the appearance of a major shift in economic policy. The more immediate significance of the higher interest rate was in connection with the government's efforts to restrict the availability of credit to the private sector. The higher interest rates eased the process begun in 1954 of placing government loans with the private banks and insurance companies, the proceeds of which were used to finance the lending operations (principally for housing) of the state banks. Previously the state banks had received support via direct transfers from a special government account in the Norges Bank or by appropriations over the fiscal budget.

The introduction of these stringent measures coincided with the resignation of Prime Minister Oscar Torp and the formation of a new cabinet under the leadership of Einar Gerhardsen. The reasons underlying these shifts are complex and somewhat obscure. Both the new premier and the new finance minister emphasized their general agreement with the anti-inflationary policies which the Torp government had set forth in the 1955 National Budget shortly before the cabinet changes took place, and stated their intention to introduce additional measures felt to be necessary to control the situation. While the cabinet changes certainly are not to be interpreted as resulting primarily from differences within the Labor Party over the general line of policy to be followed in counteracting the inflationary pressures, there is reason to believe that the frictions and tensions which the issue of price stability had aroused were important underlying factors in the decision to form a new government.

It is worthy of note that the reaction of the government to the threat to stability posed by the price increases of 1954 took the form, in the first instance, of policy measures directed at the underlying inflationary pressures. But these actions could not be expected to solve the immediate short-run problems of cost-of-living increases that might make necessary a new round of wage negotiations in the spring of 1955. Through a series of price decreases negotiated with certain producer and distributor associations, and a combination of increased subsidies, imposition of price ceilings and tariff reductions on certain food products, the task of keeping the cost of living below the March 15 "red line" in the wage contracts was successfully accomplished. With no new wage negotiations of any import (only 40–50,000 workers were covered by contracts expiring during the year) and with only a modest rise in import prices concentrated on items not directly important in the cost of living, the cost-of-living index showed virtually no variation during the year, standing in January 1956 at the same level as the previous winter.

The Wage-Price Settlements of 1956

The apparent stability in price developments was to some degree deceptive. Pressures were still present or even increasing which would pose the same issues of maintaining wage-price stability in connection with the renegotiation of collective agreements expiring in 1956. Not the least important of these pressures stemmed from the demands of the agricultural producers. A severe drought during the summer of 1955 had led the government to undertake certain emergency measures to provide relief to the farmers. Negotiation in the fall with the agricultural organizations on drought relief measures resulted in no agreement. The government, nevertheless, undertook to increase subsidies on milk and milk products, feedstuffs and freight, and provide special credit facilities to the stricken areas. It agreed, however, to open new negotiations for an agricultural price settlement in January 1956 (even though the old agreement was not due to expire until July), at which time the government would not oppose some increase in the price of milk, which had been a focal point of the demands presented by the agricultural organization. This meant that, contrary to the usual practice, negotiations for an agricultural price settlement would precede rather than follow the opening of spring wage negotiations.

In an attempt to coordinate the wage and price negotiations and to carry out a revision in subsidy policy which had been under study for some time, the government appointed a special committee consisting of the Minister of Finance and representatives of the LO, the NAF, the farmers' organizations and the federation of commercial associations. In early March the government made public the terms of what it considered a reasonable settlement. Essentially these consisted of an increase in the price of milk of 8 øre per liter and an average wage increase of 20 øre per hour, which together were calculated to result in an increase in the cost-of-living index of 3.5 points. The government would limit the reduction of subsidies in order to have a further increase of only 2 points in the index. Altogether, these actions were calculated to bring the cost-of-living index up to 150 (1949 — 100), or an increase of some 5 per cent from the end of 1954. However, since the organizations involved were unwilling to commit themselves to the government's proposals, the attempt to produce a "master" wage-price settlement was abandoned and the special committee disbanded.

The government itself took the first move in the separate actions that followed. On March 19 it announced a series of subsidy reductions totaling some 135 million kroner and calculated to increase the cost-of-living index by just under 2 points. It appeared that in spite of the failure to achieve a favorably coordinated settlement, the hope was that the separate negotiations would produce results more or less in conformity with the government's proposal.

The agricultural negotiations, which had been underway since the middle of January were concluded a few weeks after the government's revision of subsidies. The agreement signed by the agricultural organizations and the Ministry of Wages and Prices on April 19 was somewhat in excess of the limits previously indicated by the government, providing an increase in the price of milk of 9.5 øre per liter, with equivalent increases for other dairy products. The effect of these increases alone was calculated to raise the cost-of-living index by over 2 points. An innovation in the agreement, which was to run for a period of two years, was a series of four "escape" clauses linking the price agreement to the wage settlement and to movements in the level of agricultural costs.[26] First of all, provisions were made for a reopening of negotiations if the coming wage settlements resulted in an average increase above the 20 øre limit indicated previously by the government. Secondly, if the spring agreements between the LO and the NAF included, as a rule, cost-of-living index clauses, negotiations were to be opened for the addition of corresponding clauses into the agricultural settlement. A third provision called for reopening of negotiations in March and April 1957, if the rise in the level of agricultural costs as calculated meant an increase in costs of more than 50 million kroner (roughly 5 per cent) from 1956/57 to 1957/58. Finally, the two-year duration of the agreement was to be effective only if the spring wage contracts were also generally for a two-year period. All these provisions were a direct result of the fact that the agricultural settlement was concluded before the completion of the spring wage negotiations and were designed to hedge the farmers' position vis-à-vis the terms of the wage agreements. Thus, the advantage to the trade union from the prior determination of the subsidy and agricultural price policy, making it possible for wage negotiations to be carried out with more precise calculations of what the future course of prices would be, was substantially limited by the saving clauses of the agricultural price agreement. In a sense, the problem of a price-wage spiral had been substituted for that of a wage-price spiral, and the pressures to limit the wage revisions in order to avoid too great an upward movement in the price level were bound to be of the same character as in previous years.

Throughout the period of uncertainty concerning subsidy and price policy which came to an end with the subsidy revisions and agricultural agreement described above, attempts to reach a wage settlement had been going on. Not a little anxiety about the difficulties of accomplishing reasonable wage revisions without serious work stoppages had developed during the last months of 1955. A strike of the transport and dock workers in November 1954 emphasized the nature of these difficulties. The workers in the union involved were among the lower paid groups and had not benefited from increases in wages above the contract rates — the "wage drift" — to the same extent as in other industries. Moreover, wage settlements in recent years had been reached only via compulsory arbitration by a wage board. The dissatisfaction of the workers with the imposition of contract revision through arbitration was reflected in a series of resolutions passed in a number of the Transport Unions' local organizations in favor of a strike against any attempt to utilize compulsory arbitration procedures. The temper of the workers was judged by the government to be such that the strike was permitted to take place without placing the issue of instituting compulsory arbitration before the Storting, even though the hardships imposed by even a short stoppage (especially because of the cessation of fuel deliveries) were bound to be substantial. The existence of a significant amount of Communist strength among the transport and dock workers undoubtedly was of importance to the decision of both the LO and the government regarding the strike. After a twelve-day work stoppage the dispute was settled through mediation procedures with a wage increase of around 8 per cent for transport workers and somewhat less for the dock workers. But the experience did not bode well for negotiations in the spring when the bulk of the collective agreements expired. The general strikes in Finland and Denmark during the early part of 1956 also contributed to the sense of uneasiness with which the spring contract revisions were anticipated.

In mid-January the Representative Council of the LO set forth for the national unions the general lines recommended for the coming negotiations. No general position was taken on the size of wage increases that might be demanded, but it was emphasized that first consideration must be given to workers in the lower wage brackets and those not benefiting from the "wage drift."

"The unions which wish to renegotiate existing contracts must postpone final formulation of eventual wage demands until there is a better view of the price situation, but the Representative Council would underline that in the contract revisions primary consideration must be given to the groups whose real wages are relatively low and who have not had a share in any wage drift." [27]

An unsuccessful attempt was started in February to reach a general settlement between the LO and the NAF on wage revisions and certain other general issues regarding compensation for absences because of illness and payment for variable holidays. Exploration of the possibility of achieving a general settlement with the aid of a state mediator also ended in failure. Consequently, the emergence of a more or less definite price policy on the part of the government as represented in the March subsidy revision and the agricultural agreement of mid-April, found the unions confronted with the task of negotiating separate settlements for each industry or contractual unit. The absence of any explicit framework for wage revisions set by the central leadership of the LO did not mean that central coordination of wage settlements was in fact absent. In effect, the government with its announcement of its willingness to stabilize the cost-of-living index at 150 if the average wage increase did not exceed 20 øre, and its conclusion of an agricultural price agreement on the same assumption, may be said to have performed the function (previously exercised by the central leadership of the LO) of laying down the general guide lines for the wage revisions. Without too much exaggeration, it may be said that the only difference was that the government proposed a settlement publicly and on its own responsibility instead of doing so privately to the LO and leaving it to the LO leadership to formulate and coordinate wage demands in a manner consistent with general economic policy. The task of central coordination remained, but the position of the LO authorities vis-à-vis the national unions could be somewhat more flexible since the LO itself had not formally committed itself in advance of the wage negotiations.

Considering the anxiety with which the 1956 contract revisions were approached, the actual course of negotiations and settlements was surprisingly smooth, although marked by the first series of major strikes since the end of the war. Within two weeks after the signing of the agricultural price agreement, settlements were reached (with the aid of mediation) in the textile and iron and metal industries, covering in all some 50,500 workers. By the end of June agreements covering almost 60 per cent of the workers under contracts expiring prior to May 1 had been signed and ratified; proposed settlements for the remainder were in the process of ratification.

The size of the wage increases varied considerably and, not surprisingly, tended to press against the limit of an average increase of 20 øre indicated by the government. The character of the actual rate revisions was so complex as to make estimates of the average magnitude of the increases difficult to arrive at and of uncertain reliability. Calculations by the LO and the NAF the latter part of June indicated that the average increase resulting from revisions of contracts expiring prior to May 1 was between 19–23 øre, or roughly 4 per cent. The contracts generally were for a two-year period and included a cost of living clause (which had been centrally negotiated between the LO and NAF) permitting reopening of wage negotiations if the cost-of-living index had risen 6 points or more above the "stabilization" level of 150 by March 15 or September 15, 1957.

In July, the relative quiet surrounding the contract revisions was severely broken by the outbreak of two major strikes — one in the pulp and paper industry, the other in building and construction. In both cases strikes followed the workers' rejection of terms of settlement proposed by the state mediator and recommended for adoption by both the Employers' Association and the unions' leadership. The economic impact of the strikes was softened by the fact that the first three weeks in July is the usual vacation period. In any event, the government did not impose emergency arbitration procedures. The settlement in the paper industry came after two weeks and provided for increases of 3.5 per cent (minimum of 20 øre) in incentive earnings and a 25 øre increase in time rates. The building strike lasted somewhat longer — six weeks in all — and resulted in a general increase of 36 øre per hour for time rates but the central demand of the union for a general increase in piece rates was not fulfilled. Since a substantial part of hours worked in building and construction is on a piecework basis, the impact of the settlement on the level of average earnings was considerably less than 36 øre.

In general, the 1956 contracts revisions may be said to have been a less than completely successful approximation to the framework set down by the government in its March proposal. A special arbitration court ruled early in 1957 that Norwegian milk producers were entited to a price adjustment, roughly estimated at 10 million kroner, as compensation under the terms of the 1956 price agreements, for the wage increases actually negotiated. The fact, however, that the wage settlements were reached after the subsidy revisions and agricultural agreement meant that the unions looked upon the government's indication that a position of stability could be achieved with the cost-of-living index at the level of 150 as a firm commitment to keep prices from increasing above that level. By the middle of June the cost of living had already increased to 151 and the trade union began once more to demand government action in the pattern familiar from the aftermath of the 1952 and 1954 negotiations. Apparently in response to this pressure the government, in a partial reversal of its previous position, announced in mid-August that it would begin September 1 to subsidize the consumption of milk by 7 øre per liter — which would reduce the price of milk 10 per cent and the cost-of-living index by slightly under 1 point. At the same time the removal of all quantitative restrictions on imports of shoes and clothes from members of the OEEC, free import of machines and raw materials, and the possibility of larger imports of fruits and vegetables were announced. These actions were sufficient to bring down the cost-of-living index to 149 and maintain it at that level during the remainder of the year.

Upward pressures on the price level continued to mount, however, aggravated by the effects of the Suez crisis in the fall of 1956. By the end of the year the cost-of-living index was once again turning up, reaching 153 in March. The government's response was to direct its efforts toward preventing any significant additional increases, despite the reversal in subsidy policy which such efforts would entail. As a result, subsidy payments which had been reduced to under 300 million kroner during the second half of 1956 amounted to over 425 million kroner in the latter half of 1957. This increase in price subsidies — the effect of which on the price index was calculated at about 3.75 points — kept the cost of living stable for the rest of the year. It was an atmosphere of considerable uncertainty which surrounded the LO and NAF as they confronted the task of negotiating new agreements in early 1958.

On the one hand, internal pressures pointed to the likelihood of another turn of the inflationary spiral with probable downward revision in government subsidy policy. Average hourly earnings in manufacturing in the third quarter of 1957 had increased some 12 per cent above the level prevailing immediately prior to the 1956 wage agreements; less than half of this increase could be accounted for by contract rate revisions, the remainder being due to wage "drifting." On the other hand, the United States recession was casting a long shadow, leading to heightened concern over the course of the external economy and its impact upon domestic levels of production and employment.

A further complication was added by the prospect that legislation reducing the maximum work week would be passed during the spring session of the Storting. A government-appointed commission to study the problem had recommended in April 1957 that the legal work week be reduced from 48 hours to 46½ hours by January 1, 1959, and subsequently to 45 hours by January 1, 1960. (Representatives of the Employers' Association on the commission had dissented from this recommendation; the trade union representatives indicated in a separate statement their view that such legislation could be considered only as a step toward the attainment of a 40-hour week.)

The leaders of the LO and the NAF entered into preliminary discussions in December 1957. As a result of these talks the secretariat of the LO obtained in mid-January the approval of the federation's representative council for centralized renegotiation of all contracts with members of the Employers' Association due to expire in 1958. Agreement was reached with unprecedented speed on January 31 — one week after the opening of formal negotiations.

The settlement provided for a three-year extension of expiring contracts without a general wage increase. Instead, the work week was to be reduced to 45 hours, effective March 1, 1959 (ten months before the date set in proposed legislation). Hourly wage rates were to be increased 6⅔ per cent to compensate for the reduction in hours (or by the appropriate percentage where the work week was already under 48 hours). Maximum compensatory increases in incentive and premium pay scales, however, were set at only 4½ per cent; weekly and monthly rates were to remain unchanged.

A special supplement of 18 øre per hour was provided for men earning under 4.50 kroner per hour and women earning under 3.20 kroner per hour (roughly 15 and 10 per cent respectively below average earnings levels). Less than one third of the covered workers were expected to be affected directly by these special supplements; the effect on the average level of earnings was calculated to be less than 1 per cent. Agreement was reached in principle on the establishment of pensions to supplement the state old-age security program, and a joint committee was formed to work out the details of the pension program. Finally, provision was made for reopening wage negotiations whenever the cost-of-living index showed a change of seven points form its level of 153 with the maximum wage change limited to the percentage change in the index. Subsequent negotiations for cost-of-living adjustments were provided for only if the index, after a minimum period of six months, showed a change of at least six points from the level prevailing at the time of the preceding index regulation.

The defensive character of the terms of the agreement from the point of view of the trade unions is apparent. The real net gains achieved were small, consisting only of a one-year advance in the reduction of hours and the wage increases for low paid workers. And these gains meant virtually nothing to those workers whose work week was already substantially below 48 hours and whose earnings did not qualify as substandard. As an editorial in *Fri Fagbevegelse* — the monthly journal of the LO — put it, the ratification of the central agreement by the unions was indeed a test of trade union "solidarity." However, the absence of any fixed date for the first cost-of-living adjustment and narrower limits for subsequent variations in the index represented significantly greater protection from price increases. With the submission of the fiscal budget shortly after the ratification of the agreements, the government announced its intention of limiting subsidies to 500 million kroner in 1958/59 — a reduction of 40 per cent. Such a reduction made it inevitable that the cost-of-living index would cross the "red line" of 160 by early summer. The struggle for wage-price stability continued.

This brings us to the end of our account of the course of general wage negotiations in Norway since 1945. Because our major concentration has been on the development of wage policy decisions by the trade unions and the government, whole areas impinging upon the wage bargain have been left out of account. Before we take up the task of attempting to place wage policy and wage movements in a more general context, however, certain patterns in the process of collective bargaining in Norway since the war may be noted in a preliminary fashion.

Of primary interest, of course, is the way in which the relationships between the various sources of organized economic power developed over the period. Norwegian experience lends some support to the often expressed opinion that trade unions will be forced to adopt additional functions, to a certain extent completely foreign to the ones previously exercised, when government undertakes the responsibility of maintaining full employment and controlling economic development. Certainly, it is clear that the labor government in Norway looked to the trade unions, and in particular to the central leadership, for what amounted to administration of a wage policy appropriate to the other economic policies and programs of the government. One consequence of this new role for the trade unions was to shift the center of the collective bargaining process away from the usual union-employer relationship. The most important decisions were bound to be a matter of union-government determination with the employers left somewhat to one side. The fact that our chronicle of wage settlements devotes only cursory attention to the position of the Employers' Association is a reflection of the secondary role played by the association in the decision-making process. The employers themselves were, of course, extremely sensitive to the shift in economic power relationhips resulting from the election of a Labor government. To them it appeared that the real bargaining between the parties tended to become impossible, since the coercive power of the government itself, a creature of the unions, always hovered in the background.

But the apparently secondary role of the employers in determining wage policy does not mean that that position was unimportant. Certainly the employers had not been stripped of all their power in the economy or, even, it may be argued, a major part of it. But as a group whose interests were to keep wages down, their power to withstand the wage demands of the unions was, in effect, rendered superfluous by the superior power of the government whose efforts also were directed at imposing restraint on wage rises. Under the circumstances of general excess demand that existed, employers' ability to pay was simply a question of ability to raise prices in domestic industries and the competitive status in foreign markets for export industries — or in other words, the problem of inflation and balance-of-payments deficits. It is not surprising, therefore, that the employers' usual contribution to wage policy decisions was to emphasize the impact of wage increases on the price level and the balance-of-payments deficit, to refuse on these grounds to grant any increases, and to force the trade unions to work out a settlement, formally or informally, with the government, which took these broader consequences into account. Thus the system operated to focus the responsibility for maintaining stability squarely upon the trade unions and the LO leadership in particular.

Perhaps equally as significant as the changed pattern of relationships existing between the parties directly involved in the wage settlements has been the increased awareness on the part of the trade unions of their relation to other organized economic groups. The tendency of centralized wage negotiations to set the pattern for the income demands of the agricultural and fishing organizations made the secondary impact of the unions' wage demands obvious not only to the leadership but also to the rank and file. The clear recognition of their direct interdependence among sources of economic power in the society was bound to have its repercussions on the development of union policy.

The way in which the trade unions have reacted to the demands placed upon them by their role in a planned economy, highly organized, interdependent internally and extremely dependent externally is one of the most striking features of postwar developments in Norway and will claim our attention in later chapters. Here only a few brief comments are in order.

First, it seems quite clear that the trade unions have found the burden of increased "responsibility" somewhat irksome. Instead of a trend toward more organic unity between the unions and the labor government, there has been continuing emphasis on union independence. Instead of working toward the establishment of increasingly comprehensive and centralized negotiations, the unions have sought to meliorate the high degree of centralization which already existed (though not with signal success).

On the other hand, in spite of these indications of restiveness, Norwegian trade unions appear to have exercised a remarkable degree of restraint in the use of their economic power. The why and how of this policy of forbearance will be returned to in later discussion. One key factor, however, stands out: the workers' willingness to make what appear to be relative sacrifices depends upon a belief that the distributive arrangements in the economy are so managed as to produce results more or less in conformity with the ideas of social justice prevalent in the labor movement. The central importance of the stabilization and equalization policy of the unions is one reflection of this fact. There is no question but that the system of profit and dividend limitations, price control, government direction of investment, low interest rates — in fact the whole fabric of the labor government's economic planning — was an integral element in union wage decisions since the war.

But, finally, it must be said that one of the apparent weaknesses of the system of wage control was, in certain respects, also one of its strengths. For undoubtedly of great importance to the ability of the LO leadership to exercise restraint in wage demands and contract revisions was the possibility for wage adjustments to take place outside the formal contractual procedures, with the resulting tendency for money wages to drift upwards during the contract period. So long as this "wage drift" did not exceed certain bonds it provided an advantageous avenue of wage change, more flexible and without the organizational and political impact of formal contract revisions. There were, of course, disadvantages flowing from this phenomena of "wage drift," and its significance, both in relieving and producing pressure for upward wage movements in a wage determination system such as existed in postwar Norway, can hardly be overemphasized.

CHAPTER 6

The Evolution of General Wage Changes

Under the highly organized and centralized system of wage bargaining in Norway, the central wage bargain undoubtedly has been the single most important proximate influence on the general level of wages, and, as we have seen in the preceding chapters, the general wage settlements were the prime focus of governmental efforts to control the wage level. That these efforts did not take the form of authoritative and essentially unilateral stipulation by the government concerning the terms of settlement has been sufficiently emphasized in the description of the course of these negotiations. The control the government exercised over the general wage level through influence on the central wage bargain was in this sense indirect in that it was effected through the collective bargaining institutions whose independence and autonomy were respected. The limitations which such a system imposes on the processes of national economic planning and control stem, of course, from the power of the parties to the negotiations (and particularly the trade unions) to force modifications in economic policy by a refusal to shape the wage settlements in accord with the national economic plan.

The first degree of indirectness in government control over wages through the bargaining process is compounded by the possibilities for actual wage movements to deviate from the changes stipulated in the wage agreements. The effectiveness of governmental wage policy depends not only on the extent to which wage settlements are in accord with that policy but also on the degree to which the contractual agreements in fact determine wage rates actually being paid. Even in Norway, with widespread and centralized union organization, there remains considerable room for the operation of influences on the general level of wages more multifarious and pervasive than can adequately be explained in terms of the central negotiations alone. The present chapter is devoted to an examination of actual wage movements and an attempt to determine more precisely the nature of their relationship to the wage decisions incorporated in the general contractual agreements.

Money Wage Changes, 1945–1955

As is not unusual in economics when the attempt is made to quantify a conceptual category, there is difficulty connected with the discovery of a satisfactory statistical measure of movements in the money or real wage level. In Table 2 are given a few of the available money wage indexes, no one of which can be said to represent the general level of money wages, but which, together, have sufficient coverage to warrant the assumption that all should be strongly influenced by those pervasive factors relevant to the concept of wage level.

Table 2. Money wage indexes, 1938–1957
(1946 = 100)

Year	Mining and manufacturing[a]		Agriculture[b]	All employees[c]
	Total	Employers Assoc. Men	Men	
1938	59	65	38	53
1944	78	78	80	—
1945	87	87	85	—
1946	100	100	100	100
1947	111	110	113	109
1948	120	117	123	118
1949	126	122	128	122
1950	133	129	137	130
1951	152	148	153	145
1952	172	165	167	162
1953	182	172	173	172
1954	191	181	183	180
1955	200	190	192	190
1956	—	205	207	—
1957	—	218	—	—

Source: Statistisk Sentralbyrå, *Produksjonsstatistikk, Statistiske Meldinger and Nasjonalregnskap*.
[a] Average hourly earnings. Colum 1 is calculated from earnings and man-hour data published annually in Norwegian production statistics. Column 3 is calculated from the Statistisk Sentralbyrå old wage series through 1952, extended to 1957 by applying the per cent change in the new wage series.
[b] Daily earnings of men without board during mowing operations.
[c] Average annual income, calculated from Norwegian national accounts data.

The pattern of money wage movements stands out clearly. The immediate upward wage adjustments of 1945 and 1946 were associated with a rise in average hourly earnings in the neighborhood of 45 per cent by 1947. The period of wage restraint during 1947 through 1949 brought a sharply reduced but still substantial rate of increase, amounting to almost 20 per cent by 1950. The revision of the stabilization policy following upon devaluation and the Korean war brought another wave of increases lifting money wages by some 25 per cent in the two years 1951 and 1952. Since the latter year there has been a fairly steady rate of increase of about 5 per cent a year.

Some indication of the unequal distribution of wage increases is evident, particularly in the stronger upward movement of agricultural wages during the earlier years of the period. The extent and significance of these differential movements will be the subject of a later chapter. In the present connection, however, it is the parallelism of the broad wage movements that deserves emphasis. Two facts are particularly noteworthy: the relatively slight deviation between all of the series and in particular the close correspondence (over the period where comparisons can be made) between the series for mining and manufacturing based upon earnings in member firms of employer associations and the earnings series which includes non-member firms as well. This parallelism among the series (which persists into the second differences) lends plausibility to the assumption of a strong link between wage levels within and without the unionized sectors. But of course it provides no clue to the nature of that link. Some progress toward an evaluation of the impact of the bargained wage settlement can be made by closer consideration of various "avenues" of wage change and their importance in postwar wage movements.

Avenues of Wage Change

If we adopt some measure of average earnings per unit time as an indicator of movements in the general level of wages, changes in that level may be viewed as arising from (1) changes in the rate structure, that is, in time and piece rates which govern the calculation of actual wage payments to workers and (2) nonrate changes in earnings associated with shifts in the proportion of man hours worked within a given rate structure and changes in the time rate of output of workers on piece rates. Applying this distinction to employees working under and outside of contractual agreements, and recognizing the possibility of rate changes within the unionized sector which are not the result of stipulated changes in the wage agreements, we have the following five-fold classification of "components" of wage change:

(1) Changes in contract wage rates for workers under union agreements
(2) Changes in wage rates for workers under union agreements which are not stipulated in the wage contracts
(3) Changes in wage rates for workers outside union agreements
(4) Changes in earnings of workers in the unionized sector not associated with rate changes
(5) Changes in earnings of workers in the nonunion sector not associated with rate changes.

Such a definitional scheme brings out clearly that union wage agreements can give only partial control over wage developments at best and that contractual wage changes, even in a highly unionized economy, must be viewed as only one part of the larger system of wage determination. To establish with any high degree of precision the relative importance of the five "components" of wage change would require a detailed and quantitative specification of the structure of the whole system of wage determination. We shall have to be satisfied in the present context with considerably less than this, for we can hope to obtain what are, at best, only crude approximations.[1]

The "Wage Drift"

The importance of noncontractual changes in the wage determination process in Norway received explicit recognition in the development of the concept of *lønnsglidning* or "wage drift" as a measure of the difference between the change in average hourly earnings which it is calculated would have taken place as a result of revisions in wage contracts and the change actually occurring in average hourly earnings. We have already had occasion in the preceding chapters to emphasize the role that the existence of the wage drift phenomenon played in the central wage negotiations; we need now to probe somewhat further in the attempt to assess its quantitative importance.

The concept itself has enjoyed considerable attention in postwar discussions of wage policy problems by Scandinavian and British economists.[2] In addition there have been continuing efforts to measure it statistically. Unfortunately, since the definition of wage drift is essentially a residual one, it tends to be surrounded by a haze of analytical imprecision. In terms of the components of wage change classified above, the concept emerges as a hybrid of sorts, but this is not so important as the fact that, in any case, the distinction between rate and nonrate changes as well as that between contractual and noncontractual changes often becomes difficult to apply in practice.

In Norway, statistical calculations of wage drift have generally been restricted to the manufacturing sector. Inasmuch as the great majority of workers in this sector are subject to union agreements, the estimates of the wage drift provide approximations to the noncontractual components of wage changes in that sector — that is, items (2) and (4) of the classifications outlined above. The actual procedure of estimation involves only those workers in manufacturing covered by collective agreements. Generalization of the results to all manufacturing workers in effect imputes a "contractual" component to workers in manufacturing not covered by union agreements. Such an imputation is not unreasonable since wages in nonunion manufacturing establishments very likely were adjusted on the basis of union agreements and, in fact, for a period following liberation, were legally bound to the negotiated settlements.

Table 3. Wage drift for adult males in manufacturing, 1944–1956

Year[a]	Increase in average hourly earnings	Calculated contractual increase	Wage drift (col. 1, less col. 2)	Drift as per cent of total increase
1944–1946	24.	24.4	0.5	2.0
1946–1947	10.8	7.9	2.9	26.9
1947–1948	7.1	3.0	4.1	57.7
1948–1949	5.2	2.4	2.8	53.8
1949–1950	5.0	2.3	2.7	54.0
1950–1951	9.8	6.3	3.5	35.7
1951–1952	15.1	11.0	4.1	27.1
1952–1953	6.9	4.2	2.7	39.1
1953–1954	3.7	—	3.7	100.0
1954–1955	6.2	2.7	3.5	56.5
1955–1956	5.2	—	5.2	100.0
1944–1950	61.1	44.5	16.6	27.2
1950–1956	55.9	26.4	29.5	52.8

Source: Statistisk Sentralbyrå *Lønnstatistikk 1951* for years 1944–1952; Lars Aarvig, *Lønnsutvikling og lønnspolitikk i Norge etter krigen* (Oslo, 1957) for years 1952–1956.

[a] Second half 1944 and first quarter for subsequent years.

A general idea of the magnitude of the wage drift in manufacturing since 1944 can be obtained from the figures in Table 3. These indicate that roughly one quarter to one half of the total increase in average hourly earnings was not directly connected with contract revisions. Over the whole period the wage drift provided an average annual increase in earnings of some 2 to 4 per cent. From year-to-year calculations of wage drift it appears that the relative magnitude of the drift itself has been fairly stable since the war, consistently adding between 2 to 5 per cent to average earnings each year. The result is that the percentage relationship of the wage drift to the total increase in earnings seems to vary inversely with the size of contractual wage changes.

The hybrid character of the wage drift concept makes it impossible to distinguish the extent to which the phenomenon is associated with wage rate changes above and beyond those stipulated in union agreements compared with influences generally producing a discrepancy between rates and earnings. With respect to the former category, while there is no reliable evidence concerning the extent to which contract wage provisions were avoided, it seems that so-called "black market" wages had a rather minor role for the period as a whole in producing the wage drift in manufacturing. On the other hand, merit increases, up-grading and other types of individual adjustments within the terms of the wage contracts undoubtedly were of significance, not only as a general response to the persistent labor shortage, but also because of the efforts on the part of both workers and management to adjust differentials in the face of flat cost of living supplements.

Increases (such as those granted in 1948 and 1949) restricted to lower-paid workers are likely to have similar and probably even more powerful effects. The only quantitative evidence of the significance of this phenomenon, however, are calculations of the Central Bureau of Statistics covering only selected manufacturing sectors and indicating that "the contractual wage increase has been largest for those groups which had the lowest average earnings at the end of the war, while the wage drift in large part has been strongest for the higher wage groups." [3] The ability to make adjustments in wages without disturbing basic rates varied, of course, according to the system of payments embodied in the contracts. In this respect those working under incentive and "minimum rate" systems had considerable advantage over those in firms where the "standard rate" prevailed. The discrepancies which this situation brought about were serious enough to cause the LO, as we have seen, to make a persistent effort to eliminate them. [4]

Of the factors contributing to the wage drift which tend to produce differences between changes in rates and earnings, the most obvious — variations in the amount of overtime — has not been important. Overtime has remained fairly stable and at a low enough level (around 3.5 per cent of total man hours) so that it cannot have had substantial influence on the rate of increase in average earnings.

A factor of substantially greater importance, however, has been the increasing use of incentive pay systems. In spite of the shortage of the statistics available on the extent of piecework and premium pay in manufacturing, they indicate a more or less continuous increase in the proportion of man hours worked under such systems — rising from 35 to 40 per cent in 1945 to about 60 per cent in 1952. [5] On the assumption that incentive systems tend to yield earnings some 25 to 30 per cent above time rates, a shift of this magnitude could account for an increase in average hourly earnings on the order of 1 per cent a year in the early postwar years. More recently the trend toward adoption of incentive wage systems has been halted or perhaps even reversed.

This crude estimate of direct impact of the structural shift in methods of wage payments should probably be considered a maximum. Nevertheless, it may understate the significance of this shift for the course of money wage developments. Incentive pay schemes (in addition to providing for a built-in wage drift resulting from the tendency toward increased earnings over time with the accumulation of small productivity increases), involve a wider range of possibilities for adjustments in rates within the contractual rate structure. The spread of these schemes represented, therefore, opportunity for broader participation among manufacturing employees in the wage drift.

The factors connected with wage drift that we have considered thus far have been those essentially dependent upon adjustments and decisions within a given firm. Another possible source for a continuing discrepancy between changes in rates and earnings is associated with shifts of workers between firms and industries. An increased proportion of man hours worked in higher-wage firms and industries under a given rate structure will have the same type of effect on average earnings as upgrading within firms. No data is available to make a satisfactory assessment of the influence of interfirm shifts in general. We can, however, obtain some evidence from calculations of the effect on average hourly earning caused by man hour shifts alone among the various industrial subsectors. Calculations based on the earnings and man hour data of the Norwegian production statistics reveal that between 1946 and 1951 the influence of this factor appears to have been negligible or absent so far as movements between industrial subgroups in manufacturing are concerned. The calculations were based on relative shifts in man hours worked among 23 subgroups in manufacturing. A change in the classification system used made adjustments for comparability necessary which in some cases could only be approximate and, hence, may affect the reliability of the final results. Because shifts within the subgroups are not taken into account, it cannot be said that the phenomenon was completely absent, although the presumption seems justified that it was small within the manufacturing area during this period.

The picture that emerges from extending the analysis to the whole economy is somewhat different. Relative employments shifts among the major economic sectors appear to have been of some importance in raising average annual earnings. Calculations using the income and man-year data in the Norwegian national accounts indicate that shifts among the major economic sectors which took place from 1938 to 1953 would have raised average earnings by about 10 per cent, even if the earnings structure of the economy had remained unchanged. The significance of the positive correlation which this result reveals between the expansion in employment within a given economic sector and the initial position of that sector within the wage structure will be further considered in Chapter 9. In the current context we need only note the fact that the general level of earnings for the economy as a whole was subject to a small but nevertheless significant upward influence from intersectoral shifts in employment.

With the aid of some rough calculations, we can now attempt a quantitative assessment of the direct impact of contractual wage changes on changes in the general level of employee earnings. We may, thereby, gain more insight into the limitations on the leverage which can be exercised in a system of wage policy implemented through the terms of centralized wage negotiations. The single most important limitation, of course, stems from the fact that union membership averaged somewhat less than 50 per cent of total wage and salary earners during the postwar years. Since wage increases in the nonunion sectors fall by definition in our noncontractual category, the contractual component of postwar wage changes could not have amounted to much more than half of the total. There is an implied assumption here that neither the wage levels nor the size of wage increases differed greatly between the union and nonunion sectors during the period. Such an assumption is probably valid, although there is no direct evidence to confirm it; in any case, such variation as might have existed almost certainly would not significantly affect the extremely gross estimates involved here.

Within the union sector, our analysis of wage drift indicates that in mining and manufacturing from one quarter to one half of the increase in average hourly earnings appears to have occurred outside the contractual settlements. There is no information on how large the noncontractual wage changes were in other unionized sectors, which account for roughly half of the LO membership. The magnitude of the wage drift for workers affected by collective agreements will, of course, vary from sector to sector, according to the nature of the work performed and the opportunities provided to increase earnings within the framework of contracted rates. It is unlikely, however, that the drift in the nonmanufacturing sectors exceeded that in manufacturing.

On these assumptions, we may summarize as follows: in the period under consideration, contractual changes in the wage provisions of collective agreements probably accounted directly for a maximum of 35–40 per cent of the total increase in employee earnings or a minimum of about 25 per cent, if wage drift in all unionized sectors approximated that observed in manufacturing. It is necessary to emphasize the weakness of the quantitative data used. The magnitudes obtained represent only an *ex post* assignment of the "components" of wage change, making any direct inference about the intrinsic functional importance of the contractual element in the process of wage determination in postwar Norway almost impossible. The assignment of percentage magnitudes in itself implies that the various factors considered are not only independent but additive in their effects, whereas in fact the relations between these factors undoubtedly are not independent and most probably are more complicated than simple linearity.

While it is conceivable that the sources of wage drift might perhaps act independently of the change in contract rates — for example through a nonmarket-induced trend toward greater use of incentive wage systems or the rising tendency of earnings with the accumulation of small productivity changes — the quantitative effect of these factors cannot be presumed to be simply additive. Their effects on changes in earnings must certainly be expected to be different at different levels of basic wage rates. In the absence of more detailed quantitative information (or indeed the detailed and comprehensive analytic framework necessary to handle such information if it were available) the analysis given will have to suffice.

Despite the shortcomings cited, there remains the basic fact that even under an extensive, highly organized and centralized process of collective bargaining, a substantial, if not major, part of the wage determination process took place outside the confines of collective agreements. This conclusion clearly implies that an explanation of the wage determination process, even in an economy with the degree of planning and control existent in Norway, cannot be framed simply in terms of policy decisions arrived at and implemented by the parties to central negotiations. Wage and income movements inevitably arise independently of, or follow only indirectly from, wage policy decisions executed through the institution of national bargaining. These movements are subject to the logic of impersonal economic processes, both directly and through their influence on the operation of the system of wage control itself.

"Drift" and "Decision" in the Determination of Money Wages

The evidence on what have been called the "components" of wage change appears to be sufficient to underline the oversimplification involved in assigning to centralized wage decisions an exclusive and autonomous role in the determination of money wages. The facts presented force recognition of the complexity of the relationships involved, but they do not provide much guidance for explaining the character of the mechanisms connecting wage decisions incorporated in the collective contracts and actual wage movements. To gain further insight into these processes it is necessary to marshal more direct evidence on the factors influencing the various wage components.

Unfortunately, such evidence as exists is scanty and far from conclusive. Indeed, with respect to the influence of the national wage settlements on wages outside the contractual area, it is not possible to do much more than engage in some more or less plausible speculations. The scope and importance of the centrally negotiated settlements quite obviously rules out any assumption that wages in the nonunionized sectors were determined independently of those settlements. Even in the absence of direct "nonmarket" influences, the terms of the collective contracts could not fail to have an effect in the nonunion labor markets. Under conditions of a general shortage of labor, the policy of relative "wage restraint" might lead to the expectation of relatively more rapid rates of increases in wages outside the unionized sectors. Such an argument — a reversal of the usual analysis of union-imposed wage rates — depends on the assumption that the increase in the relative demand for labor in the unionized sector actually tends to produce a shift of employment to that sector and thus reduces the supply of labor in the non-unionized markets. In effect, there is implied the view that the employment adjustment to contract wages is essentially "demand determined."

The course of actual developments is not inconsistent with this analysis. The results of the analysis of earnings increases and employment shifts among major economic sectors do in fact yield evidence that relative changes in employment were correlated with below average rate increases, as measured by a base year weighted index. It may be significant that this is true only as between all the major economic sectors, including both the unionized and nonunion labor markets, and not within the manufacturing sector alone. To the extent that unionization was connected with the relatively high wages and low rates of wage increase, the pattern of movement is consistent with *a priori* expectation as well as with the observed intersectoral compression of earnings differentials.

All this, however, will be more properly considered in connection with relative wage movements in a later chapter. The central issue connected with movements in the general level of wages is not the effect of collectively bargained settlements on the relative rate of increase in nonunion sectors, but on the absolute sizes of the increases. Here the emphasis is more appropriately placed on the wage-determining influences of the union settlements operating directly through the supply side in nonunion labor markets. From this point of view, it could be argued that the policy of "wage restraint" holding down the level of wages in the unionized sector tended to reduce the absolute size of the money wage increases in nonunion labor markets. In other words, "wage restraint," while it may have stimulated a more rapid relative rate of increase in noncontractual wages, at the same time may have made it possible for that relative shift to take place within the span of smaller absolute increases than otherwise would have been possible.

It should be noted that the power of the national wage agreements to limit movements in the level of wages in sectors outside the contract area is dependent upon the relative structure of wages and the demand for labor actually existing. It is unlikely that the system would have operated in the same way if the union wage settlements had not covered those industries with relatively high wages, on the one hand, and relatively high rates of expansion on the other. This is only to say that the power of the central negotiations to act as a kind of "super key bargain" for the economy was rooted in the economic environment and did not exist in a vacuum. Had the situation been reversed so that the problem in nonunion labor markets tended to be that of attracting rather than holding workers, the "key" character of the union settlements in limiting the absolute size of money wage changes might very well have been considerably diluted.

Evidence in support of this proposition regarding the relation between contractual and noncontractual influences can be found in an examination of the crucial role the "wage drift" played in the collectively bargained wage decisions within the contractual area. Here, a sharper distinction between organizational and market forces can be drawn, since theoretically the authority of collective contracts in setting wage rates was unquestioned. Nevertheless, as the mere existence of "wage drifting" testifies, this authority was far from complete. In so far as it is legitimate to identify "wage drifting" with the operation of "market forces," it is clear that the power of contractual authority over wages was limited by the modification which wage drifting introduced into the effect of contract decisions or, equally important, by the degree to which the "wage drift" affected the decision making process itself.

The data are not available to establish conclusively the association of wage drifting with economic forces of the market place. Nevertheless, such an interpretation is plausible in view of the individualistic character of the wage adjustments upon which the phenomenon depends.[6] Statistical evidence indicates that the incidence of the wage drift varied widely among industries between 1944 and 1951, amounting to only 10 per cent in canning compared with some 45 per cent for skilled bookbinding workers.[7] In general, these variations seem to have been of a character to soften the impact on the wage structure of the equalizing tendencies involved in the "solidaristic" policy of the unions. This conclusion is consistent with the relatively minor narrowing of interindustry differentials which (as set forth in some detail in Chapter 9) characterized the mining and manufacturing sector, particularly in the latter part of the postwar period when "wage drift" accounted for over half the total increase in average hourly earnings.

In addition, Swedish experience with the "wage drift" provides corroborating evidence with respect to its "market oriented" character. In a 1949 survey of local union leaders in Sweden, the cause of wage drift was ascribed first and foremost to the shortage of labor.[8] A later and more extensive statistical analysis tends to confirm the association of wage drifting with the excess demand for labor.[9]

However clear the general connection between the wage drift and labor market shortages, there remains an "institutional" element depending on the degree to which such things as various methods of payment afford differing opportunities to workers to take advantage of excess demand for their labor. Certainly a relative wage advantage accrued to those workers under incentive wage systems, minimum wage contracts, or generally in situations where, by contract or custom, individual wage adjustments were frequent. Very probably these institutional arrangements were themselves responsive to the market; the postwar increase in piece rate and premium pay systems can perhaps be attributed in part to the pressure of labor shortages, and it is only to be expected that the administration of contract wage provisions by employers tend to vary in rigor with the scarcity of labor. Nevertheless, differentials produced by such institutionally determined rates of participation in wage drifting bear no relation to the equitable principles governing wage policy, nor can they be rationalized in terms of market criteria. The resulting anomalies which therefore tend to accumulate in the wage structure place an effective limit on the exercise of a centrally negotiated policy of wage restraint. Such a policy depended in large measure on the "solidaristic" philosophy of the unions which emphasized the equitable character of equal rates of increase, modified by the presumption that any above-average increases should be limited to lower-paid workers. The erosion of the very foundations of union wage policy because of the pervasive and perverse impact of wage drift on the structure of wages is reflected in the responsiveness of union wage policy to the internal pressures generated among the union membership by the existence of wage drift and its diverse distribution.[10] In this respect the crucial role of wage drifting in the dynamics of money wage determination is bound to be understated by attempting calculations of the size of the drift component of money wage increases. Both the realized effects of previous wage drifting and the likelihood of similar movements in the future have directly influenced the size and timing of money wage decisions in collective agreements. A direct link was thus provided between the impersonal operations of the labor market under general conditions of labor shortage and the wage policy decisions arrived at in the centrally negotiated settlements. It would be obviously wrong to conclude that the course of money wages in postwar Norway, all appearances to the contrary notwithstanding, is simply to be explained in terms of the immutable and indefeasible law of supply and demand. It is equally clear, however, that "market influences" cannot be left out of the account.

What emerges from this analysis of the interrelation between "drift" and "decision" in money wage determination is the ambivalent role of noncontractual influences. The existence of a certain amount of "play" in the system revealed by wage drifting may have contributed to wage stability by allowing for adjustments to market forces without forcing general wage revisions upward. The importance of this aspect of the wage drift is underscored in the analysis of relative wage movements undertaken in Chapter 9 which indicates that what shifts there have been in interindustry differentials appear more closely related to "market" than to "policy" decisions. On the other hand, it is the corrosive influence of wage drifting on the policy of wage restraint which most deserves emphasis in the present connection. Such an emphasis brings clearly to the fore the "partial" character of wage control exercised through nationally bargained contracts. Control of money wage levels in the postwar Norwegian economy cannot be separated either in its execution or its effects from the other economic policies followed during the period. These broader perspectives — interaction between wages and the general structure of economic policy and control — are the central concern of the following chapters.

CHAPTER 7

Wages, Prices, and Labor Costs

The preceding chapter has concentrated on the general level of money wages. But the ends pursued in wage policy — by government, business, or trade unions — and the effects of money wage changes can be evaluated only in relation to price and income changes generally and ultimately to the structure and magnitude of the real flows of goods and services. The first step within this broader perspective, which we undertake in this chapter, is to probe into the relation between money wages and prices, with the object of throwing some light on the course of real wages on the one hand, and the level of labor costs on the other.

Real Wage Movements, 1938–1956

The definitional and statistical problems of obtaining an appropriate index of real wages as a measure of worker welfare are sufficiently well known to warrant no extended comment here. In Table 4 are presented three indexes of postwar movements in real wages based on three money wage series and two price series.

With regard to the two price indexes, one — the official cost-of-living index — is a fixed weight index based on sample surveys of consumer budgets, while the other — the consumption price index — is currently weighted, as well as more broadly based, since it is derived implicitly from the calculation of private consumption in constant prices in the national accounts.[1] The cost-of-living index is designed to approximate the living costs of an average industrial worker's family which differs in size and income from the average Norwegian household; this may suggest it as an appropriate deflater of average hourly earnings in mining and manufacturing, while the consumption price index may be more appropriately used in deflating average employee income for the economy as a whole.[2]

The greatest indicated rise in real wages is exhibited by the average hourly earnings series deflated by the cost-of-living index. Compared with the two annual income series, this is in part a reflection of a greater increase in money hourly earnings in mining and manufacturing than in annual money incomes. More important, however, is divergence between the two price series. As might be expected, this divergence in rate of increase was greatest prior to the 1950 abandonment of the stabilization line. We have noted earlier that government efforts were directed during this period toward immobilizing the cost-of-living index. The success of these efforts, of course, meant that money wage increases gave equal real wage increases insofar as the official index provided an accurate measure of living costs. That it did not do so completely is evident from the 13 per cent increase in

Table 4. Real wage indexes, 1938–1957

Year	Cost-of-living index	Consumption price index	Mining and manufacturing Real wage indexes[a]		Average annual real income, total employees[b]
			I	II	
1938	63	61	94	103	87
1945	97	—	90	90	—
1946	100	100	100	100	100
1947	101	107	110	109	103
1948	100	110	120	117	107
1949	100	113	126	122	108
1950	105	122	127	123	107
1951	122	138	124	121	105
1952	133	146	130	123	111
1953	136	149	134	127	115
1954	142	153	135	128	118
1955	143	154	140	134	123
1956	148	—	—	139	—
1957	152	—	—	144	—

Source: Statistisk Sentralbyrå, *Økonomisk utsyn over året 1953* and *Nasjonalregnakap*.
[a] Average hourly earnings from *Produksjonstatistikk* (I) and Statistikk Sentralbyrå Wage Series (II) deflated by the cost of living index.
[b] Average annual employee income (all industries) deflated by the consumption price index.

the consumption price index at the same time the cost of living showed virtually no change whatsoever. This does not mean that as a measure of living costs the movement of the official index is really irrelevant, except for the psychological influence it had on wage bargaining. During the stabilization period, in spite of its outmoded and restricted base and the well-known difficulties of cost-of-living measurement in a period of extensive rationing, immobilization of the index provided as close an approximation to keeping stable the actual cost of living for the average worker as could reasonably be expected. Until January 1950 the index had been weighted on the basis of a 1927/1928 budget study with some revisions undertaken in 1939. Since 1950, however, the index has been brought up to date by new consumer budget studies. For the entire postwar period the index can probably be accepted as a minimum measure of the increase in living costs of industrial wage earners. On the other hand, the consumption price index may be taken as a reasonable maximum measure of cost-of-living increases covering, as it does, all consumer goods in the proportions currently consumed by the entire economy.

Under these assumptions, the data in Table 5 seem to indicate that by 1946 real wages had already exceeded their prewar level and during the following ten years increased between 35 and 45 per cent in mining and manufacturing and between 25 and 30 per cent in all industries. This is an average rate of increase of about 2.5 to 3.5 per cent, which compares with an approximate 2.5 per cent rate of increase in real private consumption per capita and a rate of increase something over 3.5 per cent in per capita net national product over the same period.

Movements within the period are also of considerable interest and significance. It appears that the upward movement in real wages ceased as early as 1949 and did not again begin until 1952. During 1950 and 1951 real wages actually seem to have dropped.

In general terms this pattern of movement is readily explicable. After the cost-of-living award in September 1946 — actually an "advance productivity increment" of 15 øre to be paid in three five-øre installments over the following twelve months — no general changes in contract wages of substantial magnitude took place until the fall of 1950. The wage drift and the 1948–1949 supplements to low wage groups did result in a continuing, though slower, increase in average money wage levels. But in spite of the freezing of the cost-of-living index up to the abandonment of the stabilization line in the spring of 1950, the rise in prices of commodities outside the index continued strongly enough so that the advance in real wages can reasonably be said to have halted by 1949. After the reduction of subsidies in the spring of 1950 and the general price rises associated with devaluation and the Korean war boom, money wages seem to have had a tendency to lag until a new level of relative price stability was reached in 1952.

That no real wage gains were made during the period of fairly rapid price rise in spite of substantial money wage increases has important implications for the structure of wage and price determining factors in Norway, and, consequently, for the attitudes of trade union leaders toward wage policy. In perhaps somewhat too simple terms, the situation can be described as one in which, so long as there existed considerable inflationary pressure, an upward movement in money wages, even though in response to a previous or expected price rise, provided the occasion (if not the cause) for a further proliferation of price increases throughout the system with an aggregate inflationary effect of uncertain magnitude.

All this, of course, could be interpreted as simply another instance of the process of the wage-price spiral familiar in other Western countries. Certainly, the object lesson in the mechanics of inflation (if any were needed) which 1950–1951 provided the Norwegian trade unions was not lost upon the union leadership.

If we could not manage more than to maintain the same living standard we had before, that was because in this period [1950 and 1951] we have been witnesses to a large price rise. But it must also be added that we have had a large wage increase. Here we have then a typical demonstration of how closely we must view wage policy in relation to price policy, that it was not possible to maintain the same prices as before was the result of many factors which I shall not go into. But I want to emphasize here that wage supplements alone do not better the people's standard of living if there is no mastery over prices.[3]

But while the Norwegian experience with inflation reveals mechanisms similar to those characteristic of countries with a lesser degree of direct and quantitative control over the economy, there remains the fact that these mechanisms were called into play by deliberate policy decisions. The bases for these decisions were among the factors which the chairman of the LO did not feel it necessary to emphasize. The significant point is the trade union leadership's acceptance of the validity and appropriateness of those decisions and the recognition of their relevance to the formulation of money wage demands.

In the inflationary movement of 1950–1951, it was, of course, the devaluation and the world-wide price rise associated with the Korean war that appeared to be the dominating factor affecting the "mastery over prices" and forcing abandonment of the government's efforts to hold the stabilization line. The prominence of these "external" influences could not entirely obscure the internal pressures on the government price policy which had accumulated in considerable measure from the wage revisions and wage drift that had taken place. In the contract negotiations after 1952 these internal problems came to the fore and were reflected in the fact that the government's price policy came to be, directly or indirectly, a prime issue in the central negotiations between the LO and the Employers' Association.

The willingness of the trade unions to take explicit account of wage-price relationships in their wage bargaining can, in a sense, be interpreted as a measure of union "responsibility." But it seems clear that this "responsibility" had its roots in the traditional trade union objective of increasing the *real* wages of the workers. The centralization and extent of the collective bargaining system in Norway added, in effect, a new dimension to the wage bargain in that the effects on the price level of the general wage settlement were, to a certain extent, calculable. That the unions did, in fact, take account of these effects testifies, in the first instance, to their "rationality" rather than their "responsibility." The latter attitude, if it has meaning at all, can be evaluated only in terms of the way the calculated impact on prices of union wage demands entered into the actual wage decisions and the extent to which coordination between union wage policy and government price policy was achieved. Such an evaluation must wait upon an examination of the course which costs, prices, and incomes took during the postwar period.

The Cost Impact of Postwar Wage Movements

The attempt to analyze the effects of wage increases on the cost level and to evaluate the success of the Norwegians in controlling the level of costs is beset with theoretical and statistical difficulties. The relevant factors in such an analysis can be set down without difficulty; the problem arises in seeking to establish mutual interrelations and their respective quantitative importance. Unfortunately, in spite of a mass of statistical data, only generally qualitative conclusions can be derived, with occasionally some indications of relative orders of magnitude.

It is important to note at the outset the limitations involved in the abstract and ill-defined concept labeled the general cost level. As with other such aggregative concepts, this is a construction created for the purpose of squeezing an almost infinite multiplicity of complex relationships into a manageable whole. From one point of view, however, the necessity of having to deal in grossly aggregative terms has some positive justification. The wage and price policies of the Norwegian government were themselves conceived and executed in those terms. While the stabilization program had as a primary objective the maintenance of a competitive cost level both in the export and import-competing industries, there was no general attempt in that program to accord differential treatment to those industries exposed to competition from the rest of the world. A major exception was the subsidization of agriculture. It is fair to say that the weight of government stabilization policy was to limit or prevent increases in the general level of costs, in spite of the fact that detailed price controls and the extensive system of indirect taxes and subsidies might well have been employed on a large scale for differential purposes.

During the stabilization period, 1946–1949, the pivotal role was played by the cost-of-living index. By manipulating subsidies and indirect taxes on commodities heavily weighted in the index, variations in the cost of living were kept within a range of 3 per cent with no sustained upward movement until the spring of 1950. Wholesale prices, however, rose by 9 per cent and in spite of the immobilization of the cost of living, average annual employee income increased by 22 per cent. As perhaps might be expected, the largest cost increases appeared in the agricultural sector where incomes increased by 65 per cent. This was where the main weight of the subsidy program was directed because of the importance of food prices in the cost of living. Moreover, the Labor Party was committed to the establishment in agriculture of income levels comparable to those in other sectors.[4]

While a major objective of the stabilization period was to insulate Norway as much as possible from the inflationary impact of increases in world prices, the movement of costs and prices would seem to indicate that a considerable, if not major, part of the stabilization effort had to be directed toward containing pressures on costs stemming from internal rather than external sources (if such a distinction can be made). Even if the general level of prices had tended to rise in proportion to the 22 per cent increase in employee incomes over the period, the magnitude of the improved efficiency of the economy (roughly indicated by a 16 per cent increase in real gross national product per employed) would probably have been sufficient to counteract most of the external pressures on prices. Given a subsidy program to eliminate disproportionate effects on commodities entering the cost-of-living index and special export duties to limit profit inflation in the export industries, the problem of "external" pressures on the price level could presumably be reduced to negligible proportions. That, in fact, upward pressures on the cost-price structure continued strong, with wages and prices not weighted in the cost of living rising steadily throughout this period can, therefore, reasonably be ascribed to "internal" pressures which the system of controls was not able wholly to contain.

With the devaluation and later the Korean war boom, the objective changed from that of immobilizing the internal level of costs to that of controlling cost increases so as to avoid seriously cumulative inflationary processes. Such a policy implied the cessation of efforts to neutralize completely the effects of rising import prices on the wage levels through the cost of living. Prices and wages were to be permitted to increase generally in consonance with the rise in import prices. Such a development actually took place. The cost-of-living index moved upward by 33 per cent, with employee and farm incomes rising some 34–35 per cent between 1949 and 1952, while import prices were increasing by 36 per cent.

The release of inflationary pressure in the form of price increases did not mean, of course, that efforts to hold down internal costs lessened. There is no reason to expect that limitation of income increases within bounds set by productivity and external price changes poses any less difficult problems than limitations gauged by productivity criteria alone. And in some respects, since the former operation involves sharper and greater upward movements, there is perhaps a greater chance of powerful cumulative processes developing. In addition to the cost-inflationary pressure of maintaining living standards in the face of rising world prices, there was during this period the demand-inflationary pressure of high production and price levels in the export sectors and the resultant reduction and elimination in 1951 of the import surplus. To offset the inflationary effects of this export boom required that the increased flow of incomes generated in these sectors be prevented from entering the wage income stream so as to permit them to be immobilized in the form of increased private or public savings. The manner in which this was accomplished is a subject of the next chapter.

The upward pressure of internal cost increases became increasingly prominent with the slackening of the Korean war boom. In spite of a 9 per cent fall in import prices from 1952 to 1955, wages continued to rise —average annual employee incomes increasing by about 17 per cent. As we have already noted, noncontractual changes and wage drift accounted for the greatest portion of the upward movement during this period. Even in mining and manufacturing, where the union wage settlement had their most direct impact, contract changes accounted for less than half of the 23 per cent increase in average hourly earnings from the first quarter 1952 to first quarter 1956. While no final judgment of causal relationships can be made, the character of wage-price movements during this latter period does seem consistent with an interpretation emphasizing the level of aggregate demand rather than union wage policy as a basic source of inflationary pressure.

Calculated Components of Price Change

The rough picture of postwar cost-price variations can be supplemented to a certain extent with the aid of calculations made from national accounts data by the Central Bureau of Statistics[5] of the changes in aggregate cost components of total available goods and services, i.e. gross national product plus imports. The method employed consisted essentially of deriving an index of the price level by dividing gross national product plus imports in current prices by its value figured in constant prices, and then viewing changes in this total price index as a weighted arithmetic average of price changes in six major aggregate cost components — wages, property incomes, depreciation, indirect taxes, subsidies and imports. To obtain these component price changes (with the exception of the import component), the assumption was made that their "volume" changes were proportional to the volume change in gross national product. Within the somewhat severe limitations which this assumption imposed (it suppresses, for example, the role of productivity changes and shifts in profit margins), estimates were made of the relative importance of these components in the total price change as well as the effect on the price level of the calculated changes in the individual components if they had "worked alone."

The results of this study are summarized in Table 5. It goes without saying that extreme caution must be exercised in drawing any conclusions, considering the restrictive assumption upon which they are based. More-

over, the figures provide only an *ex post* description of price-cost movements; this makes any analytic implications inevitably dependent to a great
extent upon the assumptions made regarding the structural interrelations
involved in the price-determining mechanism.

Table 5. Aggregate cost-price relationships, 1946–1955

A. Component price changes as a per cent of total price change

	1946–1949	1949–1952	1952–1955
Wages	25	22	101
Property income	22	23	1
Depreciation	17	12	53
Indirect taxes	6	11	−3
Subsidies	−16	2	7
Imports	46	30	−59
Total	100	100	100

B. Calculated "separate" effect of component price changes

	1946–1949	1949–1952	1952–1955
Wages	4.3	7.9	2.8
Property incomes	3.7	8.2	0.0
Depreciation	2.9	4.3	1.5
Indirect taxes	1.0	3.9	−0.1
Subsidies	−2.7	0.7	0.2
Imports	7.9	10.8	−1.6
Total price change	17.1	35.8	2.8

Source: "Prisutviklingen i Norge etter Krigen," *Statistiske Meldinger*, No. 10 (1956), pp.
346–364.

Nevertheless, certain characteristics which distinguish the three different
periods in postwar price development stand out clearly and tend to confirm
the general impressions outlined in the preceding section. In both the
stabilization period from 1946 to 1949 and the inflationary movement of
1949 to 1952, the wage, property income, and import components of the
total price change appear to have assumed roughly the same relative importance, while the relative importance of import price changes was somewhat
greater in the first period. On the surface the major difference between the
two periods would seem to be the shift in government subsidy and indirect
tax policy from damping down the price impact of cost changes to reinforcing it. The aggregative character of the figures, however, obscures an equally
important difference in the composition of the property income component.
In the earlier period this component was mainly influenced by increases in
farmer incomes, whereas in the succeeding period a major factor was the

boom profits of the export industries. Moreover, the export boom influenced the level of indirect taxation through the imposition of special export duties. External price developments can reasonably be accorded the dominant role in both periods with the difference that during the stabilization period government policy worked to prevent changes in external prices from triggering internal price reactions. Abandonment of the stabilization line permitted greater room for "secondary" reactions to the impact of past as well as current changes in external prices (although, as we have noted previously, such reactions cannot be said to have been entirely uncontrolled).

With the drop in import and export prices from the peaks of 1951–52 and their relative stability thereafter, the picture changed markedly. The absolute magnitudes of price changes were, of course, considerably smaller, but the calculated change in the wage component alone was sufficiently large to account for the change in the price level. Significantly enough, the government subsidy policy also worked to increase prices. The statistical evidence would seem to indicate that the forces tending to initiate upward movements in the price level have become, in the last years, more closely connected with "internal" than with "external" forces. Actually, the figures are somewhat deceptive, in this regard, since the 1952 contract wage revisions may justifiably be connected with the upward price movements of the preceding years. The 1956 wage revisions and subsidy policy changes cannot, however, be similarly connected with previous price changes. Consequently, the general conclusion concerning the "internal" character of cost-price movements is a reasonable one in the light of all the evidence, although strictly it cannot rest on the calculated changes in price components from 1952 to 1955.

The apparent relative importance of the wage cost component in the upward movement of the price level during the more recent years does not, by itself, provide a basis for ascribing prime "causal" significance to contractual wage changes during the period. The upward pressure on prices which increased wage costs appear to have been exercising must be viewed in the light of the wage drift and noncontractual wage increases which were taking place, together with the impact on the cost-of-living index of the government's subsidy and agricultural price policy.

With respect to the first consideration, the noncontractual upward drift of wages of some 3 or 4 per cent a year left little or no room for noninflationary contract revisions; the increase in real wages that occurred during the period was roughly equivalent to the margin of money wage increase achieved through wage drifting. For the unions to forego any wage increases in the face of such wage drifting would amount to abandoning any control over the incidence of wage changes, leaving them to the vagaries of those forces determining the rate of the wage drift. Since such a course of action would be contrary to the fundamental *raison d'être* of unionism, it is not surprising that it was not adopted.

The link between wage changes and the cost of living raises more complex issues. Contract revisions undertaken under the pressures of wage drifting presumably will work to reduce such drifting; wage changes in response to increases in the cost of living, on the other hand, will tend to produce further price increases in the traditional pattern of the wage-price spiral. It is difficult to get a precise and reliable quantitative estimate of what price reaction might be expected from a given wage change. The *ex post* magnitudes we have been considering, which show a variation between 25 to 100 per cent in the price-raising impact of wage increases, emphasize the fact that the reaction will be dependent upon the general situation prevailing at any given time. Using the results of an input-output study carried out at the University of Oslo, one Norwegian labor economist has estimated that a 10 per cent increase in wages could be expected to increase prices of consumer goods, as well as the general price level by about 3 per cent.[6] By taking into account certain assumed repercussions on the farmer's price demands and the impact of tax rates, however, he concludes that "roughly 70 per cent of the nominal increase in wages is lost in increased prices and taxes."

This brings us back to the proposition advanced earlier — that union leadership, in attempting to serve the economic interests of union members through a centralized wage policy is forced to take into account the probable repercussions of its decisions. These are intimately bound up with the actions of other groups in the economy and, particularly, with the price policy of the government. The conclusion seems justified, therefore, that a central element in whatever "responsibility" the trade unions exhibited with their policy of "wage restraint" was the "bargain" struck with the government on price policy. This is, of course, obvious for the stabilization period when the government undertook to immobilize the cost-of-living index. But it also applies to the later years and stands out very clearly in the 1956 negotiations where the government explicitly employed its control over consumer prices in the attempt to influence the size of the money wage settlement.

Labor Costs and Gross Margins in Industry

In order to supplement the extremely aggregative data upon which the preceding analysis has been based and, also because the structure of collective bargaining institutions was such as to make the industrial sector most crucial to the formulation and execution of wage policy, cost developments within mining and manufacturing deserve somewhat closer scrutiny. Even here, it is impossible to delineate in any great detail the intricate cost interrelationship within the sector, but sufficient data are available to form a general picture of the cost movements within the sector.

Quite striking in the figures of Table 6 is the rapid recovery of industrial production from the low levels reached at the end of the occupation. Increases in production were large enough to restore or exceed prewar levels by 1948. The movement in output per man hour was somewhat slower, but followed generally the pattern of total output. Such a development in production and productivity is generally consistent with what one would expect, given the situation that existed in Norway at the time of liberation. The gradual improvement in the supply of raw materials, the repair of war damage and restitution of productive equipment was bound to influence favorably both total output and efficiency and to bring large increases in both as the economy approached capacity in the sense of fully utilizing its capital equipment. This process was naturally extended by the high rate of new investment being undertaken, at the same time, to expand capacity beyond prewar levels. The direction of capital and labor into the industrial sector, together with the high level of internal and external demand combined to produce annual increments in the volume of industrial production of 10 to 15 per cent until the slackening of demand in 1952 brought a temporary halt.

Table 6. Production, productivity and labor cost indexes for
mining and manufacturing, 1938–1954
(1949 = 100)

Year	Production	Output per manhour[a]	Average hourly earnings	Wage costs[b]
1938	74	(90)	47	(52)
1946	70	(87)	80	(92)
1947	81	(90)	89	(99)
1948	91	(94)	96	(101)
1949	100	100	100	100
1950	113	110	106	97
1951	121	114	121	106
1952	122	116	137	118
1953	129	122	144	118
1954	141	131	151	115

Source: *Produksjonsstatistikk*.
[a] For years prior to 1949 both the coverage and the method of calculating the productivity index limit its reliability for use in estimating wage costs variations.
[b] Output per manhour divided by average hourly earnings.

The substantial increases in productivity that accompanied the rehabilitation and expansion of industrial capacity provided the margin to enable virtual immobilization of labor costs in industry during the period of reconstruction, despite continuing upward movements of money wages during the latter part of the stabilization period. After the immediate postwar wage adjustments of 1945–46, wage costs appear to have remained stable until 1951 in the face of money wage increases of about 20 per cent. Even during the inflationary movement of 1951–1952, increases in productivity appear to have been large enough to offset one-third of the cost impact of money wage increases and these two years account for the whole increase in wage costs since 1947. From this evidence, the Norwegians have been remarkably effective in their objective of holding down wage costs in industry. It should be remarked, however, that the rise in labor incomes outside of the industrial sector (particularly in agriculture) which took place in conformity with, if not because of, the government's "equalization" policy, would imply *falling* wage costs, rather than stability, if wage increases were to be "noninflationary."

The evident success in holding down labor costs naturally raised the corollary question of the course of profit margins. Under the extensive system of controls prevailing in Norway after the war, it might be expected that, with prices but not wages subject to direct regulation, there might be a tendency for upward wage pressure to squeeze profit margins. What statistical evidence there is (Table 7) however, indicates that profit margins, while declining in per cent of gross value of production since the war, have done so more under the impact of increased raw materials prices than from increases in wage costs. Both wages and salaries and gross margins appear to have declined since the end of the war, while the cost of raw materials as a per cent of gross value of industrial production moved upwards until 1953, when both seem to have turned slightly upward once more. In the light of our previous examination of the role of import prices, this pattern may be interpreted as supporting evidence of the increasing importance of internal factors in the cost-price structure.

Table 7. Costs and gross margins in mining and manufacturing, 1946–1954

Per cent of gross value of production	1946	1947	1948	1949	1950	1951	1952	1953	1954
Wages and salaries	23	22	21	21	20	18	19	21	20
Raw materials, fuel, etc.	47	49	51	51	54	55	55	54	55
Gross margin[a]	30	29	28	28	26	27	26	25	25
Adjusted gross margin[b]	—	—	21.9	22.7	21.0	20.3	19.4	20	20
Gross value of production	100	100	100	100	100	100	100	100	100

Source: *Produksjonsstatistikk.*

[a] Gross value of production at market prices *minus* wages and salaries, raw material, fuel, and so on.

[b] Gross margin *minus* indirect taxes and *plus* subsidies.

The maintenance of gross margins in manufacturing gives some basis for the tentative conclusion that profits maintained at a high and probably increasing level. The modest decline in gross margins could easily have been offset by the substantial increases in the volume of production. In the absence of more direct evidence, however (some of which will be considered in the next chapter), it is difficult to come to any firm conclusion. Overhead costs were undoubtedly increasing substantially with the volume of investment activity that was taking place, although the low levels of interest and rent that prevailed would serve to keep down the level of overhead expenditures.

More important in this connection, and a factor which qualifies all the conclusions reached thus far in the discussion of wage-price relationships, is the fact that a substantial and almost certainly increasing portion of total labor cost took the form of nonwage supplements. It is difficult to quantify this aspect of labor costs because of the definitional problems involved. National accounts data show wage and salary supplements rising from 3.6 per cent of total wage and salary income in 1946 to 4.6 per cent in 1955. A survey made by the Employers' Association (concentrated on the larger employers and therefore perhaps giving an upward bias) estimates the level of payments for the benefit of workers, but not included in the measure of average earnings we have used here, to be around 10 per cent of workers' earnings and closer to 15 per cent of the income of salaried employees.[7]

On the evidence considered thus far, it would appear that in spite of the subjection of both the trade unions and the government to strong pressures for increased money wages, there was no discernible tendency for the government to adopt price policies which would permit wages to increase at the expense of profits. On the contrary, there is some indication that the combination of wage and price policies which actually followed, permitted, if it did not encourage, a relatively high profit level.

One distinction needs to be kept in mind. High profits in the sense used above should not be identified with high personal incomes for profit receivers. Under the Norwegian system of economic planning and control, profit incomes were not left completely at the disposal of profit recipients. Hence, they played a role somewhat different from that usually assigned to them in less "controlled" economies. This will stand out more clearly after the discussion in the following chapter of the structure of income flows and their relation to the saving-investment process.

CHAPTER 8

Wages, Incomes, and the Financing of Investment

One of our central themes is that wage determination in the controlled economy necessarily is intimately associated with over-all planning decisions and, in particular, with the fiscal and monetary policy decisions derived from the real resource programs of the planning authorities.

Economic planning within the framework of national budgets has meant that Norwegian policy formation in these areas is very much a joint process. The planning process in Norway is far too much a matter of mutual adjustment and compromise between competing considerations to make it possible to single out "wage policy" for separate and independent analysis. The fundamental decisions around which all else appears to revolve deal with the magnitude and composition of the investment program, especially because of its direct bearing on rapid postwar reconstruction, a continuing high rate of economic growth, and full employment.

The 1946 reconstruction program — crude as it was compared to the detail and attempted precision of later planning — laid down the basic design of economic policy which stayed in effect until 1952. The Long-Term Program of 1948 covering the period 1949–1952, worked out in conjunction with Norway's participation in the Marshall Plan, was essentially a continuation and expansion of the 1946 plan.[1] This was followed in early 1953 by another long-term program for the years 1954 to 1957 which in turn has been superseded by the latest program for 1958–1961.[2] It would take us far afield to essay a detailed analysis of these programs and the degree to which they were successfully carried out.[3] It is nevertheless necessary to look briefly into the objectives embodied in these programs, particularly their allocation and use of real resources, in order to understand the interdependence between wages and general economic policy.

Aggregate Resource Allocation, 1946–1957

The original reconstruction program of 1946 contemplated a 20 per cent increase in national product by 1950.[4] It was thought that this would restore production to its prewar level. In fact, the prewar level of national product was reached in 1946, but the Norwegian authorities were not aware of the fact until a revision of national income statistics completed in 1951. It might be mentioned in passing that it was the extensive revision in the national accounting system concluded in late 1951 which makes difficult any previse evaluation of plans in light of actual events. The substantial changes made in estimates of some of the basic magnitudes upon which plans and policy decisions were being based in the years prior to 1952 also raise interesting issues about the effect of statistical errors on planning decisions. However, it is doubtful that any major differences in policy would have resulted had the revised figures been available as early as 1946 or 1947.

Achievement of the goal of a 20 per cent increase in national product was predicated on a net rate of domestic capital formation of over 20 per cent, compared with a prewar rate of between 10 and 12 per cent. By holding the ratio of consumption to national product down to its prewar value, it was felt that the program could be implemented with the aid of import surpluses financed by use of foreign exchange reserves and borrowing abroad.

The rise in world prices (and hence depreciation of real purchasing power of foreign exchange reserves), plus an underestimation of the import requirements and the difficulties of obtaining loans in postwar capital markets, rapidly made obsolete the estimates of necessary foreign financing. In July 1947 the government "had to put on all the brakes and curtail imports to such an extent that it would have meant an even lower consumption than in 1946 and a serious slowing down of economic recovery." [4] The Marshall Plan, however, provided the external resources necessary to continue the rapid rate of development. In the Long-Term Program of 1948 the plan was to continue with a net investment rate of over 20 per cent and to achieve by 1952 an increase in output over the 1948 level of 15–20 per cent while raising per capita consumption to the prewar level. In terms of the figures then available, this called for about a 10 per cent increase in per capita consumption from 1946 to 1952, while output per capita was to increase by around 40 per cent in the same period. Obviously such a program was bound to place priority on the limitation of personal incomes if any approach to balance in the consumer sector was to be looked for, even if there had been no backlog of consumer demand stemming from the privation of the occupation period.

While actual developments deviated from the expectations of these programs, the basic nature of the problems remained very much as foreshadowed in the original plans. A net investment rate of 20 and 25 per cent throughout the period — a higher rate than in any other country in Western Europe or North America[5] — was maintained by holding private consumption significantly below its prewar ratio to national product (although public and private consumption together approximated the prewar level) and by incurring substantial import surpluses.

The limitation of consumption, however, was not so strong as to prevent an increase considerably above that allowed for in the original programs. By 1949 real private consumption per capita had increased by 15 per cent over

1946 and by 1952 had gone up another 4 per cent. This meant by the latter year the per capita consumption level in real terms was about 16 per cent above 1939, compared to the programmed objective of merely reaching that level. That this improvement in consumption could take place without jeopardizing the investment program is primarily due to two factors. In the first place, the budget and national account figures of the first postwar years considerably underestimated the level of consumption relative to 1939. Although the basic programs were predicated on a belief that consumption in 1946 would be only 90 per cent of the 1939 level, the later estimates indicate that consumption in 1946 was already about 98 per cent of the former year. Consequently, from 1947 on, increases in consumption were improving consumption standards above those of prewar, rather than merely regaining them, as was thought. However, the unavailability of certain consumer goods, especially prior to the lifting of rationing in 1951 and 1952, makes the comparison of consumption standards subject to considerable uncertainty; while it was apparently generally believed as late as 1950 that *average* consumption standards were below those of 1939, it was recognized that large groups in the economy, particularly those in low income brackets, were undoubtedly better off than before the war.[6] A second factor in the situation was the underestimation of the rate of increase in output up to 1951. The goal of a 20 per cent increase in net national product by 1950 had been exceeded by 1949. The relative stagnation in production from 1951 to 1952, due mainly to a slackening of demand rather than to lack of productive capacity, was accompanied by a correspondingly low increase in consumption.

After the inflationary movement of 1950–1951, greater emphasis was given to raising consumption. Nevertheless, the Long-Term Program for 1954–1957 planned on maintaining net investment at its absolute level in 1953. Under the assumption of a 12.5 per cent increase in national product from 1953 to 1957, this implied a gradual reduction in the ratio of investment to net national product from 20 per cent to roughly 17–18 per cent. By stabilizing investment at this high level and barring a major adverse movement in the terms of trade, it was assumed that both public and private consumption could be increased by around 15 per cent over the four-year period without necessitating an average annual import surplus of more than 250 million kroner.

The preliminary figures available indicate that the production and consumption goals have, in fact, been exceeded with increases in both national product and consumption of 16–17 per cent. On the other hand, investment also continued to rise although at a lesser rate. The result has been deficits on the current balance of payments of roughly twice the magnitude contemplated despite the fact that terms of trade were slightly more favorable than anticipated.

The greatest single factor in these developments was the extraordinarily high rate of growth in the merchant fleet. Investment in shipping, which accounted for over 25 per cent of gross investment during the period, exceeded the programmed amount by almost 28 per cent. But of more fundamental interest was the general shift in policy toward greater reliance on indirect measures of control. By 1957 the abandonment of quantitative import restrictions under the trade liberalization program of the OEEC had progressed to a point where well over 80 per cent of imports from Western Europe had been liberalized. This meant a substantial weakening of direct control over both investment and consumption. The latter, for all practical purposes, was completely uncontrolled, whereas the only major direct regulation of investment operative (outside of restrictions on the import of tankers) was the system of building and construction licenses. To a certain extent, therefore, these years had the character of a transitional period, with more and more stress being laid upon fiscal and monetary instruments as the means for implementing economic policy.

The general picture of the growth and allocation of aggregate resources during the postwar period may be seen in Tables 8 and 9. Over the whole

Table 8. Net national product and major components, 1938–1957
(Millions of Kroner)

Year	Net national product	Private consumption	Net domestic investment	Public Consumption		Export surplus	Exports	Imports
				civil	military			
1938	4994	3827	610	361	57	139	1682	1543
1946	9286	6816	1728	890	464	−612	2635	3247
1947	10963	8087	2803	982	331	−1240	3815	5055
1948	11756	8396	2763	1031	307	−741	4430	5171
1949	12402	9174	2980	1103	331	−1186	4625	5811
1950	13758	10275	2751	1179	353	−800	5694	6764
1951	17314	11581	3612	1289	574	258	9045	8787
1952	18722	12583	3942	1420	818	−41	8995	9036
1953	18716	13021	4078	1548	993	−924	8179	9103
1954	20232	14117	4594	1648	1051	−1178	8786	9964
1955	21510	14673	5005	1770	891	−829	10058	10887
1956	24085	15634	5422	2014	938	77	12139	12062
1957	25829	16738	5631	2251	994	215	13225	13010

Source: *Nasjonalregnskap*.

period, gross domestic investment in real terms increased somewhat faster than gross national product while private and public consumption grew at a substantially lower rate. With respect to the relative allocation of net national product, there appears to be a fairly definite break between 1950 and

Table 9. National account components as a per cent of net national product, 1938–1957

	1938	1946	1947	1948	1949	1950	1951	1952	1953	1954	1955	1956	1957
Net national product	100	100	100	100	100	100	100	100	100	100	100	100	100
Export surplus	2.8	−6.6	−11.3	−6.3	−9.6	−5.8	1.5	−0.3	−4.9	−5.8	−3.9	−0.3	0.8
Exports	33.7	28.4	34.8	37.7	37.3	41.4	52.2	48.0	43.7	43.4	46.8	50.4	51.2
Imports	30.9	35.0	46.1	44.0	46.9	49.2	50.8	48.3	48.6	49.2	50.6	50.1	50.4
Private consumption	76.7	73.4	73.7	71.4	74.0	74.7	66.9	67.2	69.6	69.8	68.2	64.9	64.8
Public consumption	7.2	9.6	9.0	8.8	8.9	8.6	7.4	7.6	8.3	8.1	8.2	8.4	8.7
Civil military	1.1	5.0	3.0	2.6	2.7	2.5	3.3	4.4	5.3	5.2	4.1	3.9	3.8
Net domestic investment	12.2	18.6	25.6	23.5	24.0	20.0	20.9	21.1	21.7	22.7	23.4	22.5	21.9

Source: *Nasjonalregnskap.*

1951 in that the ratio of private consumption to net national product tended to fluctuate between 65 and 70 per cent since 1951 rather than between 70 and 75 per cent, as in the preceding years. This, together with a slight downward tendency in the net domestic investment rate, permitted substantial relative improvement in the foreign balance, in spite of increased government absorption of goods and services (see Table 10).

Table 10. Indexes of gross national product and major components in constant prices[a] 1938–1957

Year	Gross national product	Private consumption	Public consumption[b]	Gross domestic investment	Exports	Imports
1938	93	91	54	84	176	115
1946	100	100	100	100	100	100
1947	113	110	96	127	135	129
1948	118	112	90	126	154	120
1949	122	119	95	129	168	137
1950	127	123	98	123	199	144
1951	132	123	105	139	215	156
1952	138	129	112	140	217	156
1953	140	131	118	143	229	165
1954	148	137	122	155	255	185
1955	152	141	116	166	268	197
1956	158	145	119	178	291	211
1957	163	149	123	180	300	216

Source: *Nasjonalregnskap.*
[a] Calculated from national accounts figures in 1938 prices for years 1938–1951 and in 1954 prices for years 1952–1956.
[b] Including military expenditures.

The task before us now is to explore the role of wage policy in conjunction with fiscal and monetary policy in determining the general pattern of resource allocation. The general line of attack will be first to investigate the manner in which the investment program was actually financed in order to seek out the influence of changes in disposable income and private saving. Then we will link these changes with changes in wage incomes. Finally, we will give attention to the efforts of the government to establish the conditions for and subsequent increased reliance on monetary instruments of control.

Public and Private Saving and Investment

In the Norwegian system of national accounting, total government use of goods and services is divided into public consumption and public investment expenditures. Corresponding to this distinction is the concept of public saving defined as public disposable income (public net income from capital plus taxes and other transfers from private sector and from abroad less public transfers to private sector and abroad), less public consumption. Total net capital formation (net domestic investment plus net foreign investment) is accordingly equal to or "financed" by the total of public and private savings.

A substantial proportion of total saving since the second World War was accomplished in the public sector. Public saving amounted to roughly 40 per cent of total capital formation over the whole period. After the beginning of the Marshall Plan, large amounts of foreign aid, as well as the substantial government surpluses on current account when the level of private saving was relatively low, led to exceptionally high ratios of public saving to net capital formation — rising from 50 per cent in 1948 to almost 75 in 1950. In spite of the fact that public investment rose from about one-seventh to roughly one-quarter of total net investment, public saving has tended to decrease in relative importance since the early postwar years. Nevertheless, since 1947, public saving has consistently exceeded the level of public investment and thus, in effect, provided resources for use in the private investment sector.

The role of government fiscal operations in relation to private domestic investment and the balance of payments may be brought out more clearly by considering the excess of government internal net receipts (that is, net of transfers received from abroad) over total government expenditures on consumption and investment. Net private domestic investment may then be viewed as being financed by the government "surplus" plus private "domestic" saving (also net of foreign transfers) and the import surplus of goods and services.[7]

The movement in these components are presented in Table 11. From 1947 through 1952 the government managed to maintain a sizeable surplus and thus to offset significantly the inflationary impact of the excess of investment over saving in the private sector. During the stabilization period,

Table 11. Private investment, domestic saving and the import surplus, 1946–1957

Year	Private domestic saving	Government "surplus"	Import surplus of goods and services	Net private domestic investment
	(millions of kroner)			
1946	902	−84	647	1465
1947	867	234	1287	2388
1948	1110	337	804	2251
1949	884	246	1245	2375
1950	768	429	867	2064
1951	2356	688	−181	2863
1952	2261	630	105	2996
1953	1727	131	997	2855
1954	2076	113	1285	3474
1955	2533	292	963	3788
1956	3421	539	102	4062
1957	3487	636	−25	4098
	(percentage distribution)			
1946	62	−6	44	100
1947	36	10	54	100
1948	49	15	36	100
1949	37	10	53	100
1950	37	21	42	100
1951	82	24	−6	100
1952	76	21	3	100
1953	60	5	35	100
1954	60	3	37	100
1955	67	8	25	100
1956	85	13	2	100
1957	85	16	−1	100

Source: Calculated from figures in *Nasjonalregnskap*.

when the government was burdened with large and gradually increasing price subsidy payments, this offset amounted to only about one-sixth of the private capital "deficit." In the succeeding three-year period the government, because of the cut in subsidies and the export boom after the outbreak of the Korean War, was able to increase the surplus substantially and, hence, to accentuate the reduction in inflationary pressure associated with the rise in internal prices. The increased surplus was achieved in part because of the lag in defense expenditures behind the planned increases which had been the basis for an increase in indirect taxation and special excises on exports during the 1950–1951 boom. The combination of the inflationary movement and the anti-inflationary fiscal policy produced sufficient balance in the consumer sector of the economy to permit the elimination of rationing on virtually all consumer goods by the end of 1952. There was at the same time a substantial reduction in quantitative restrictions on imports.[8] The approach to equilibrium in the consumer sector cannot properly be ascribed solely to developments during 1950–1952, however, if only because of the importance of the reduction in the backlog of consumer demand left from the occupation and the accumulation of inventories which was taking place over the whole postwar period (to say nothing of the increases in the level of production).

The years 1953–1954 saw a sharp reduction in the government surplus as a result of increased public investment and defense expenditures and a lesser rate of increase in tax collections. These were connected in part with the decline in export demand and a slackening in the rate of economic growth. In succeeding years, the surplus again increased with improvement in the foreign balance.

The basic pattern that emerges shows government fiscal policy operating to raise the level of internal saving through consistent maintenance of a government surplus, with the level of the latter, however, tending to vary inversely with fluctuations in the import surplus. This pattern is a reflection of the fundamental policy objectives of maintaining a volume of investment substantially in excess of the level of private saving and of maintaining domestic investment and employment in the face of fluctuations in the external economy. Thus the long-run objectives with regard to domestic investment and employment have tended to be accorded priority over short-run balance-of-payments considerations, with the result that the rate of domestic saving increases in periods of favorable external demand and decreases when adverse movements occur.

The budgetary pattern that emerges from the figures used above is, it must be emphasized, based upon national accounts data in current prices and has, to a large extent, been shaped by policies affecting wage and price developments since the war. Of particular importance, of course, have been those decisions concerning indirect taxation and subsidies. From 1946 to 1949 indirect taxes less production and price subsidies dropped from 41 per cent to 22 per cent of total net transfers from the private to the public sector. This resulted from the combination of increasing indirect subsidies connected with the stabilization program and the imposition of certain extraordinary direct tax levies connected with war damage and wartime capital gains. Since devaluation and the abandonment of stabilization the ratio of net indirect taxation to net private transfers to government rose to over 50 per cent in 1956. The absolute size and relative importance of indirect taxation and subsidies inevitably tied budgetary decisions directly to wage and price policies. The interplay between these policies will become clearer in the examination of movements in private disposable income and private saving.

Private Disposable Income, Saving, and Distributive Shares

The reverse of the government's role in financing domestic investment is its control of the level and distribution of disposable income in order to limit the demands placed on the economy by consumers.

It is in connection with the attempt to control the level and distribution of money receipts from production that the strategic importance of wage policy becomes fully apparent. Under the circumstances existing in postwar Norway, it was generally felt that the marginal propensity to save out of wage incomes was probably very close to zero and, conversely, the marginal propensity to save out of profit incomes was very high. The problem of developing sufficiently large savings, therefore, resolved itself into maintaining a relatively high flow of income to the business and government sectors where the saving of the economy was actually being accomplished.

The dependence of private saving on profit incomes is the root of a fundamental conflict between the objectives of stabilization with a high rate of capital formation and the goal of income equalization. Without too much exaggeration it may be said that the history of postwar economic policy is generally a story of successive efforts to resolve this conflict. Unfortunately, Norwegian statistics do not include any measure of corporate saving or personal income so that it is difficult to obtain a detailed picture of this process in quantitative terms. The general outlines, however, can be observed in the available national-accounts breakdown of factor incomes.

Examination of movements in the components of private factor incomes shown in Table 12 reveals significant differences over the whole postwar period. The principal distributional shift between 1938 and 1946 was an increase in the relative income position of employees and independent income recipients at the expense of profit, interest, and rental incomes. Behind this shift were the tight control of rents and the decline in the rate of interest associated with the high level of liquidity left from the Occupation. During the stabilization period, total wages and profits both increased by almost the same amount as total private factor income, while independent incomes in agriculture, forestry, and fishing increased by considerably more, and independent service incomes by considerably less. During the same period, moreover, private factor incomes increased more rapidly than the value of net national product because of the increase in price and production subsidies (relative to indirect tax collections) connected with the effort to stabilize internal prices. The net benefit of the stabilization program, from the re-

Table 12. Percentage increases in private factor income components, 1938–1957

	1938–1946	1946–1949	1949–1952	1952–1955	1955–1957	1946–1957
Wages and salaries	105	37	44	22	22	184
Independent incomes in agriculture, forestry and fishing	100	53	32	14	11	153
Corporate profits and other incomes	78	34	48	—	24	146
Interest and rental incomes	−34	−3	11	109	30	185
Total private factor income	85	37	43	15	19	168
Private disposable income	79	30	48	16	17	161
Net national product	85	34	51	15	21	178

Source: Calculated from *Nasjonalregnskap.*

stricted point of view of relative income shares, seems to have flowed almost exclusively to the agricultural, forestry, and fishing sectors.

Turning now to the 1949–1952 period, we find a different situation. Moving to a higher price level during these years meant that the policy problem shifted from attempting to hold a "stabilization line" to that of avoiding serious cumulative movements which would jeopardize an approach to a more balanced situation. From the evidence it appears that the effort to control the increase in wage incomes was extremely effective during the period of price increases. In the three years after devaluation, wage incomes increased by only 45 per cent, compared to 37 per cent from 1946 to 1949, the period of a wage restraint policy. At the same time, profits after devaluation were increasing on the order of 55 per cent (compared to 36 per cent in the previous period) and total private money incomes by some 44 per cent. Incomes in agriculture, forestry, and fishing increased by only 32 per cent, while the value of net national product increased at a considerably faster rate than private factor incomes. The latter movements are explainable principally by the revision of agricultural subsidy policy and an increase in the general sales tax and certain export duties.

The years since 1952 again exhibited a distinctly different pattern. Employee earnings and incomes in agricultural, forestry, and fishing increased some 25–30 per cent more than the increase in total private incomes, while the increase in corporate profits and other incomes was only one quarter the increase in private money incomes. Interest and rental incomes advanced sharply with the rise in interest rates in 1954 and revisions in rent control regulations.

While no quantitative evidence can be adduced concerning the effect of these relative shifts in factor incomes on the propensity to save, it is possible to establish a connection with developments in private saving. The wage-price-subsidy policies of the stabilization period do not appear to have contributed to the easing of inflationary pressure in their effect on the distribution of income. Rather, in view of the equalizing consequences of that policy with respect to agricultural income, the contrary is more probably the case. If account is taken of other probable distributional shifts associated with direct taxation, the income effects of stabilizing prices of those goods which enter workers' budgets, and the growth of public consumption and welfare — the conclusion must be that up to 1949, changes in structure of income flows to individuals almost certainly represented a net addition to the latent inflation in the economy.

But this conclusion refers only to the effect of shifts in the functional and individual distribution of income. The increase in private disposable income was kept below that of private factor income through the imposition of heavier direct taxation making possible a substantial government surplus, despite the burden of price subsidies. Combined with the increased availability of goods and services, the production increases and import surpluses, and the consequent reduction of the backlog of consumer demand, this was sufficient to produce a net reduction in inflationary pressure by 1949 but not to eliminate it.

The ratio of private saving to private disposable income remained relatively low and showed a tendency to decline during the stabilization period until it reached a postwar low of 7 per cent in 1950. This tendency was sharply reversed in 1951–52, when private saving rose to 16–17 per cent of private disposable income. From the pattern of developments after devaluation and during the Korean war boom the conclusion might be drawn that wage policy was sufficiently stringent (and price-profit policy sufficiently liberal) not only to prevent an excessive increase in wage incomes and consumption demand, but actually to reduce it via a shift in flow of incomes to the business and government sectors. The result, as we have already had occasion to note, was a drastic increase in the level of public and private domestic saving and the elimination of any inflationary pressure in the consumer sector. The increased volume of profits and indirect tax collections, in large measure, however, was directly connected with boom conditions in certain export markets. Consequently, the approach to a more balanced situation is more properly assignable to the bounty brought by improvement in the terms of trade. The significant point, however, is that the shift in the distribution of income toward profits, the decline in real wages and consumption, which were direct results of modest wage increments relative to prices, prevented the real income increase from being immediately incorporated into the basic consumption standard. By making possible the diversion of the increase in real income to the financing of real investment and the accumu-

lation of foreign exchange reserves, the policy of relative wage restraint
provided an effective "hedge" against future deterioration in the terms of
trade. The development of seriously cumulative processes in the movement
to a higher internal price level was avoided and the upward price movement had the desired effect of relieving inflationary pressure in the system.
From its 1951 peak the private saving ratio declined again to slightly under
12 per cent in 1953, rising thereafter to 17 per cent in 1957. In view of the
increases taking place in the relative share of employee and agricultural incomes since 1952, the movement in private saving in these years too appears
to have been dominated by external developments. In general, the fluctuations in private saving over the whole postwar period in Norway have
apparently been more closely connected with fluctuations in export markets
and terms of trade than with internal wage-price policies.

This conclusion is confirmed by an analysis of wage shares in the Norwegian economy made by Odd Aukrust of the Central Bureau of Statistics.[9]
Aukrust's results (Table 13) show that the greater part of the fluctuation in

Table 13. Wage shares of factor income and the private saving ratio, 1946–1957

	Wages and salaries as a percentage of factor income				Private savings as a percentage of disposable income
Year	Total	Ordinary business[a]	Home market sector	Export sector[b]	
1946	54.1	50.4	50.9	47.8	12.1
1947	52.6	49.3	51.0	41.2	9.8
1948	52.9	49.6	50.7	44.0	11.9
1949	54.0	50.9	51.5	47.5	9.0
1950	53.6	50.7	52.6	42.8	7.1
1951	49.6	46.4	52.1	30.0	17.0
1952	54.1	49.6	53.4	36.6	16.0
1953	57.8	52.9	54.3	46.6	11.8
1954	56.6	52.0	52.7	48.5	13.1
1955	57.5	52.6	54.9	42.8	15.0
1956	56.1	—	—	—	18.2
1957	56.5	—	—	—	17.4

Source: *Nasjonalregnskap* and Odd Aukrust, "Trends and Cycles in Norwegian Income Shares"
in International Association for Research in Income and Wealth, *Income and Wealth, Series VI,*
pp. 283–305.
    [a] Excludes government (except government enterprises), ownership of dwellings, domestic
services, hunting, construction and repair work on own dwellings, etc.
    [b] Whaling, metal mining, metal extracting, chemicals, pulp and paper, shipping.

the wage share during the postwar years (and prewar as well) is accounted
for by the variation in the wage-profit distribution in the six major export
industries — whaling, metal mining, basic metal processing, pulp and paper,
chemicals and shipping. Of the six, shipping is by far the most important,

accounting for over 40 per cent of factor income generated in the export sector in 1950.

The tendency for the rate of private saving out of disposable income to vary inversely with the wage share is the result of fluctuations in the export industries. The wage share in home market industries alone has shown little year-to-year variation. Of importance also are the opposite trends in the two sectors. What upward movement has occurred in the over-all wage-income ratio results from the upward tendency in domestic industries; the trend in the export industries, if anything, being downward. Moreover, one might speculate that the rising trend in the private saving ratio is not unrelated to both the relative faster growth of the export industries since the war and the relative favorable terms of trade Norway has enjoyed in recent years.

Monetary Aspects of the Savings and Investment Process

It will be recalled from earlier discussions that an essential part of the economic strategy underlying the Norwegian version of the "disequilibrium system" was to approach monetary equilibrium by mopping up excess liquidity over a period of time rather than through any drastic monetary reform. The task of monetary policy in this effort was to conserve the liquidity-reducing impact of the current government surpluses and the balance-of-payments deficit. From 1946 to 1950, government fiscal operations and the net sale of foreign exchange worked to reduce liquidity by about 5.6 billion kroner, but was offset to a large extent by the payment of over two billion kroner to the shipowners in settlement of wartime losses. "Liquidity" is here used, in accordance with Norwegian terminology and accounting practice, to refer to the net liquid financial claims on the central government and Norges Bank in the hands of banks and private individuals and organizations. Concretely, it consists of Norges Bank deposits, short term Treasury bills and currency held by banks and the public and is roughly equivalent to bank reserves plus currency in circulation in U. S. terminology. The resultant net reduction in liquidity, plus an increase in the cash holdings of the public, brought about a reduction in the reserves of commercial and savings banks of almost four billion kroner — a decline of about 80 per cent over the five years. During the same period, the banking system was expanding its loan by over 3.8 billion kroner.

The financial pattern of the reconstruction period from 1946 to 1950 has been described by the Ministry of Finance in the following terms:

The Restoration and development of capital equipment . . . has been accomplished via high domestic saving and substantial import surpluses. Because of the high liquidity of the banking system it has not been necessary to take any special measures to insure internal financing. In fact, the high liquidity has provided the most important internal financial basis for the development.

A considerable part of investment has been financed by loans from banks, which have increased their lending primarily at the expense of their liquid holdings. In the course of the five-year period 1946–1950, bank reserves fell by around 4 billion kroner.

The private nonbank sector has in turn given up liquid assets to the government sector. In the first place, deficits on the balance of payments have in the main been met by foreign exchange sold by the government to the private nonbank public. . . . In the second place, the government has withdrawn considerable sums by surpluses on the public accounts. . . . By sale of foreign exchange and budget surpluses, liquidity was reduced by a total of around 5 billion kroner.

The liquid position of the private sector, however, has not declined. The non-bank public has been supplied with new assets by the banks and, through the state's settlement with the shipowners, by the government.

There has thus passed a flow of funds from the banks to the nonbank public and, further, from the nonbank public to the government. This had led to a reduction in bank liquidity while the nonbank public has reduced its net financial capital [that is, increased its debt — principally to banks] in order to increase its real capital.[10]

The reduction in bank reserves came to a halt after 1950. Improvement in the balance of payments removed a major source of reserve contraction. The upward movement of prices in 1950–1951 in combination with past reserve contraction and expansion of loans reduced the "effective" liquidity of the system sufficiently to cause concern, for the first time since liberation, that the difficulties of internal financing might interfere with the accomplishment of real economic objectives. In particular, the market for State Bank loans, the proceeds of which were a major source of financing for housing and agricultural investments, had dried up at an interest rate of $2\frac{1}{2}$ per cent.

In this situation the government decided against a revision of the low interest rate policy and undertook to provide the State Banks with funds out of certain special accounts in the Norges Bank, at least until other ways of reopening the bond market as a source of funds could be explored.[11] These loans to State Banks, together with the elimination of the import surplus and a release of blocked deposits in the Norges Bank, more than offset the contractive effect of other government fiscal operations during 1951; bank reserves increased by some 350 million kroner.

Government budgetary and lending operations continued to augment the supply of liquid resources in private banks during 1952 and 1953, despite the development of a substantial balance of payments deficit in the latter year. It seemed that having come within striking distance of a situation where indirect monetary controls were once again in "contact" with the credit market, the government was unwilling to rely upon monetary policy to control the level and structure of investment.

The implications of these developments were elements which one government official referred to as a "structural crisis" which began to develop after 1951. The decay of the "disequilibrium system" confronted the government with the question of what to substitute in its place — or whether, indeed, the government could afford to permit its complete demise. The elimination of inflationary pressure was gradually making obsolete or eroding the effectiveness of direct and quantitative controls; in certain sectors sufficiency of demand began to appear as equal to supply limitations in determining the course of developments. Furthermore, the fact that the principal net effect of financial flows during the postwar period and substitution by the banks of claims on the government for claims on the real capital accumulated in the private sector meant that government fiscal and monetary policy had been used in such a way as to increase the potential economic power of both private business and private banks. The Labor Government found itself in the position of having deliberately followed an economic policy designed to make possible the accumulation of real capital in private hands and to reëstablish a condition where the availability and terms of financing from the banks had regained its importance as a determinant of investment. It was not to be expected that a Labor Government of socialist antecedents, whose power derived from the working classes in general, and organized labor in particular, would entertain any intentions of relinquishing authority over the use of existing capital equipment or the course of future development, even if there were no problem of employment. Instead the government moved to consolidate and put on a long-term basis its authority over private enterprise. This took the form of legislation introduced to make permanent the economic powers the government had exercised previously by virtue of emergency legislation dating back to the war. Of greatest importance was legislation empowering the government to institute direct regulation of the interest rate,[12] and a law providing permanent price control authority and strengthened antimonopoly regulatory measures, which granted sweeping powers over private business operations.[13] In securing passage for these measures, however, the stated intention of the government was not to revert to a system of extensive direct regulation. Rather were the measures considered necessary to the government's arsenal of economic instruments in order to supplement the more traditional fiscal and monetary measures and to reduce the risks involved in increased reliance upon them.

Continued large balance-of-payments deficits, despite favorable terms of trade and an upward drift of prices in 1953–54, provided the first test and brought about, after a reshuffling of the cabinet, the increase in the interest rate and the whole series of measures[14] designed to reduce the level of investment. The emphasis placed upon monetary instruments in these efforts to halt the upward movement of prices and reduce the payments deficit was sufficiently great to represent a fundamental shift in policy. It is difficult to evaluate how effective the new policy line has been; it has apparently contributed to reduce some of the strain on the economy without interfering with output increases and high levels of employment. But the tendency for prices to increase has not been completely forestalled. In the words of the governor of the Norges Bank: "the point of departure for framing the monetary and financial policy for 1957 [remained] the prevailing danger of rising prices stemming from internal factors and the lack of real resources which can be activated by a credit expansion." [15]

Whether these internal inflationary factors can be successfully controlled without interfering with employment and output objectives is, of course, the central question raised by the shift in economic policy to increased reliance on fiscal and monetary measures.

Against this background, the wage policy of the trade unions since the war may be said to have provided the necessary basis for achieving and maintaining short-run stability. The true significance of the relative wage restraint on the part of the unions lies in the willingness for the sake of longer-run economic interests to refrain from exploiting to the full their ability to obtain money wage increases in the short run. During the period of reconstruction and stabilization such a wage policy made possible the effective operation of the direct control system. In the inflationary movement following the abandonment of stabilization, it prevented the development of seriously destabilizing cumulative movements, conserved Norway's economic position vis-à-vis the rest of the world, and aided in an approach to a more balanced situation without the necessity for as an extensive direct control system as before. In the years after 1952, however, when the economic situation has not been dominated to such an extent by the problems imposed by the second World War and the Korean war, when the economy has been less subject to direct government regulation, the fundamental problems of wage-price stability and monetary equilibrium in the long run have come to the fore. Success in this latest stage of economic policy will depend, as it has in the preceding periods of stabilization and controlled inflation, in large measure on stability in the labor market. In this sense, it may be said that effective economic control continues to rest upon the responsibility and restraint of the trade unions. But the evidence of postwar economic developments which we have outlined clearly points to the grounding of union restraint and responsibility upon the whole structure of government policy and economic developments. Union wage policy has never operated as a wholly independent element but, as we have seen, has been adjusted to the shifts in economic circumstances.

The challenge implicit in the shift in emphasis toward more indirect and aggregative policy instruments is whether those instruments will be sufficiently powerful in shifting the economic environment and union policy sufficiently sensitive to the constraints imposed by that environment to make possible a stable economic development. In its broadest terms, the problem of future economic stability is simply one aspect of the fundamental problem of choice among the partially conflicting goals of full employment, economic growth, and the equable distribution of income. The past record, by revealing how the resolution of these conflicts has shaped economic events in Norway, can form the basis for some insight into possible future developments but can never eliminate the element inherent in the relative weight placed upon these goals by the various decision-making units in the economy. But further discussion of these issues is best deferred until we have supplemented the aggregative picture presented thus far by an analysis of relative wage movements and policy.

CHAPTER 9

Wage Structure and Employment

Heretofore the analysis of wage policy has been conducted with principal emphasis on comprehensive concepts such as the general level of wages and wage income. The differential aspects of wage developments in Norway since the war are equally important and suggestive. Furthermore, wage and income differentials was crucial to government and trade union policy.

Unfortunately, it will not be possible to carry out as complete an investigation into this area as might be desirable. The statistical basis for such research is deficient in important respects for the period prior to 1950. Because of the magnitude of the statistical effort which would be required to overcome these deficiencies and to adduce, in any case, comprehensive and reliable conclusions concerning movements in the relative wage structure, it will not be possible here to present the full-scale analysis which the subject deserves. The most that can be done is to rough out broad contours of development in the wage structure insofar as they can be more or less readily discerned.

Wage Policy and Relative Wages

From the more strictly economic point of view, wage differentials are important, in the first instance, as a means of directing the recruitment, allocation, and use of man power. Shifts in the wage structure take on full significance only in the context of associated changes in employment. Considerable space in this chapter, therefore, will be devoted to the relation between the patterns of relative wage and man power movements. Exploration of this relation, even if it could be satisfactorily carried out, leaves important considerations out of account. (That concentration on the wage-employment relationship gives too narrow a focus to permit a satisfactory analysis of either the wage structure or man power movements is perhaps now such a well-worn proposition that it does not need extensive justification.) Not the least of these is the fact that policy with respect to the wage structure in Norway ostensibly paid little heed to possible employment effects. Similarly, manpower policy tended to be determined and administered independently of the relative wage situation, or at least so it would seem on the surface. This independent treatment of wage structure and employment reflects, of course, an implicit judgment on the part of the government and the trade unions as to the weakness of the structural relation between wages and employment, particularly on the supply side — certainly not an unexpected attitude considering the skepticism with which uncontrolled price allocating mechanisms generally were viewed by both parties. To some extent, the analysis that follows should provide a basis for determining how reliable this judgment has proved to be.

It will be recalled that two basic objectives of postwar economic policy described in chapters 1 and 2 were to eliminate recurrence of the unemployment that had blighted the economy in the late thirties and, at the same time, to bring about a more equitable distribution of income among the various economic sectors of the economy.

With regard to the employment problem, the excess demand in the system associated with the high level of investment maintained throughout the postwar period effectively submerged any structural unemployment problem. Three aspects of an employment problem of a "structural" character may be distinguished. First was the combination of population and technological factors tending to generate a surplus of labor in agriculture and fishing, if it were not offset by absorption into other sectors. Secondly, there was the related problem of seasonal unemployment. Aside from the obvious climatic factors, this problem was associated with the economic dependence of many areas on a single seasonally affected industry. In particular, many of the Norwegian farms were incapable of providing a year-round living; capital movements in forestry and fishing tended to remove the basis for the combination of small farming in the summer and fishing or forestry in the winter. This was an important source of difficulty in the northern provinces and in some of the west coast districts.[1] Finally, attainment of "viability" (that is, approximate equilibrium on the foreign balance without deflationary pressures) required emphasis on expansion of those export industries where the comparative advantages of Norway's natural resources could best be exploited. Similarly, expansion of certain import-competing industries in the manufacturing sector appeared desirable; in others it was necessary to achieve and maintain a level of labor costs competitive with other countries if adherence to international obligations for trade liberalization and nondiscrimination was not to cause unemployment.

In sum, the structural problems associated with continued maintenance of full employment implied shifts in the industrial and geographical distribution of the labor force of a magnitude that could not be viewed with complacency and might have appeared to require rather extensive direct controls over the allocation of labor. Such direct controls, however, have not been invoked (with one exception) since the liberation. The exception was a prohibition without official permission of any building or construction in the Oslo area involving more than three workers. Certain reserve powers over manpower allocation do exist; under the Law of June 27, 1947, concerning measures to promote employment (which codified emergency provisions in effect since 1945), the government is given the authority to require (1) that no employer lay off 10 or more workers without permission of the Labor Directorate; (2) that no employees be hired except through the employment service; and (3) that all unemployed workers register at the employment offices. But these provisions have not been put into effect. What direct official influence there has been over employment shifts has been exercised only through the ordinary procedures involved in placing voluntary applicants at the labor exchanges, supplemented, in certain instances, by offers of financial assistance to job seekers willing to move into areas or industries particularly short of labor.[2] Such measures, although of some importance in such areas as forestry and building and construction, cannot be said to have been a major factor in the movement of labor during the postwar period.

In the absence of comprehensive man power controls, the allocation of labor was left subject to the influence of relative wage differences and employment opportunities. While it theoretically might have been possible for the government in collaboration with the trade unions to have carried out a wage policy that was designed to accomplish a distribution of the labor force appropriate to the programs for economic development, actually no general attempt was made. In part, failure to do so can be explained by the simple fact that there was no serious problem of obtaining flows of workers into the desired industrial sectors. But, equally, if not more important, the historical attitudes of the Norwegian labor movement toward wage differences militated against any extensive use of differential wage policy as a major instrument of economic control.

In view of the fact that "the prevailing philosophy of Norwegian labor has been Marxian, and that class consciousness has been an important force in shaping both the organization and activities of the Norwegian labor movement," [3] it is not surprising that the relative-wage objectives of Norwegian trade unions have had an equalitarian bias which has tended to exclude justification of wage differentials on economic grounds alone. In contrast to the unions' attitude toward wage level problems, where economic considerations loomed as the largest single factor, the labor movement explicitly and consistently appeared ideologically bound to what was called a "solidaristic wage policy" (solidariske lønnspolitikk). The policy of wage solidarity, while it undoubtedly had earlier origins, had, by the end of the thirties, become a major doctrinal element in the labor movement, with two chief objectives: 1) equalization of wages between industrial groups, 2) equalization of wages between industrial workers and wage earners in agriculture, forestry, and fishing.[4]

Wage solidarity, defined in terms of narrowing or eliminating intersectoral and interindustry wage differentials, however, constituted only one, albeit a primary, facet of the equalitarian policy of the Norwegian unions. In particular, the raising of "substandard" wages irrespective of trade or occupation, and the elimination of sex and geographic differentials were of continuing importance in the formation of wage policy. With regard to the questions of sex and geographic differentials, however, the objectives apparently were not absolute equality but "equal pay for equal work, i.e. for the same or equally *worthwhile* labor [which] springs from the simple and socialistic view that there shall be no differences among the people. . . ." [5]

In spite of the Marxist tradition in the labor movement, neither the "solidaristic" wage policy nor the principle of "equal pay for equal work" seems to have involved a tendency to gear wages exclusively to "needs" rather than to the work performed. Evidence on this score, aside from the indication in the above quotation, is provided by the unions' attitude toward incentive wage systems, skill differentials, and dependency supplements. The latter question arose at the time of the cost-of-living adjustments in 1950 and 1951, in connection with a proposal from the Economic Coördination Council for possible substitution of state-financed family allowances for wage increases. The Employers' Association also had suggested that, instead of cost-of-living compensation in the form of a wage increase, an amount be paid into a "family fund" out of which cash grants could be made according to size of family. The trade unions, however, refused to accept any substitution of family allowances for wages on the basis that it would "create many difficulties in the workshops." [6] Gøthe, in his exposition of postwar wage policy, explicitly rejects separation of wage payments from work performed:

Fundamentally, the view of organized labor is that wage contracts shall not differentiate according to dependency burdens. Such a differentiation can be an important source of discontent in the individual places of work if wages for the individual workers are adjusted according to conditions which have no connection with the worker's performance or his particular skill qualification. *The starting point for wage payments must be the work which is accomplished, and not the unit which is called the family.* [7]

The gradually increasing concern to maintain adequate skill differentials is also indicative of the trade unions' recognition of the difficulties associated with continued rigid adherence to "wage solidarity."

There has been general agreement in the responsible organs of the union movement that this [solidaristic] wage policy has been correct from the purely social point of view. But it has been clearly recognized that it also had its limitations. As a result of the equalization which has taken place, the difference between wages for skilled and unskilled manpower within many groups became so small that there no longer was the necessary stimulus to seek lengthy training in skills and more extensive education.

This problem had to be taken up for solution as soon as a point had been reached where *all* wage earners, irrespective of occupational training, had been assured a defensible living standard.[8]

At the 1949 trade union congress, the chairman of the LO noted that the problem of skill differentials "was a matter that had become currently relevant, especially because there has been a tendency for unskilled manpower to earn more than skilled." For adequate incentive toward apprenticeships and vocational training there must, he said, be a difference in wages between skilled and unskilled manpower.[9] But it was not until the negotiations of 1952 that any significant effort was made to widen skill differentials; for these negotiations the policy guidelines of the LO secretariat to the individual unions specified that "a greater differentation in wage levels must be sought with distinct distance between skilled and unskilled manpower." [10]

The 1952 negotiations also exhibited greater concern with the incentive effects of wage payments. The policy instructions of the secretariat to the national unions included the recommendation that "attempts should be made to obtain, to a greater extent than previously, agreements linked to production results through incentive and production bonus arrangements so that wage earners could as far as possible get their wages in accordance with production." [11] To a certain extent, the apparent deviation from wage "solidarity" (which emphasis on incentive wage systems appears to represent), can be explained by the fact that, as has been noted earlier, such systems provided an important source of wage advantage through the operation of the "wage drift" in the period when the policy of restraint placed severe limitations on rate increases. In addition, there was growing concern with the rate of productivity increase as the basis for wage increases, which undoubtedly is associated with the centralized system of wage bargaining and the relationship between the trade unions and the Labor government. Whatever the reason for it, acceptance and encouragement of systems of payment-by-results on the part of the Norwegian unions is additional evidence of their explicit recognition of the economic effects of relative wage differences and of the limitations economic considerations placed on the execution of a relative wage policy which was based solely on the ideological grounds of "solidarity."

To summarize, while the "solidarity" principle effectively prevented manipulation of wage differentials to influence the allocation of labor between sectors or industries, it appears to have taken into consideration the influence of wage differentials on the supply of labor between skill categories and on individual worker effort. That trade union wage policy during the postwar period generally was directed at a narrowing of differentials throughout the economy does not mean that the wage structure was an unimportant factor in directing the flow of manpower to those areas and industries where the greatest expansion was needed. For fortunately, as will appear from the discussion of shifts in employment which actually took place, and to which we now turn, the existing wage structure apparently was such as to assist in inducing the desired manpower movements as the flow of investment created additional employment opportunities. In fact, it might be said that control over the allocation of labor has primarily been exercised through the general controls over access to economic resources other than labor, administered by means of import regulations, construction licenses, price control, rationing, and so on.[12]

Sources and Uses of Manpower in Postwar Norway

In any discussion of the manpower situation in Norway since the war, the most important fact to be kept in mind is the extremely high level of employment. The general shortage of labor was not only influential in eliminating any transitional unemployment problem immediately following the liberation and in effectively submerging the continuing problem of seasonal unemployment, but it was also a major conditioning factor in the pattern of employment shifts. The annual averages of the number of applicants for work at the state employment offices varied between a low 7700 in 1949 to a high of somewhat over 14,000 in 1953 — that is, between 1 and 2 per cent of the total workers covered under the compulsory unemployment insurance system, or between a half of 1 per cent and 1 per cent of the total labor force. Monthly unemployment figures, because of seasonal influences, showed considerably greater fluctuations, dropping as low as 2000–3000 during the summer of 1949 and 1950 and rising as high as 25–30,000 in the winter of 1952–53. While these figures probably understate the amount of unemployment, the figures on the percentage of unemployed members of certain trade unions (which may overestimate employment because of overrepresentation of seasonally affected building trades) show unemployment rates of between 2.5 to 3.5 per cent since 1946. From the available data it is probably safe to say that average annual unemployment has been between 2 and 3 per cent of the labor force, and would have been lower except for the importance of seasonal influences in Norway.

One effect of the extremely high level of demand has been to encourage, particularly during the reconstruction period, an increase in the ratio of labor force to population. Of an estimated increase in the labor force of something over 110,000 workers between the end of 1945 and the end of 1952, less than half is ascribable to increases in the population of working age. Another 15 to 17 per cent of the increase is accounted for by the return to work of some 18,000 collaborators while the remaining 33 to 35 per cent is presumably the result of increased labor force participation rates.[13] This increased attraction of manpower into the labor force, together with the reduction in the level of unemployment compared to prewar accounted for 30 to 40 per cent of the total increase in employment between 1939 and 1952 and is one reason for the rapidity with which Norway regained and exceeded prewar production levels.

The general shortage of labor has also undoubtedly been a fundamental factor behind the substantial shift of manpower out of agriculture and domestic service. Between 1946 and 1955 the decline in own-account workers, principally members of farm families, amounted to about 30 per cent of the total increase in employment of wage and salary earners (Table 14). The only

Table 14. Shifts in employment of wage and salary earners by sector, 1938–1955 (thousands of man-years)

	1938–1946	1946–1949	1949–1952	1952–1955	1946–1955
Total employment	64	84	44	12	140
Own account workers	−1	−23	−11	−24	−58
Wage and salary earners	65	107	55	36	198
Agriculture	−18	−7	−9	−9	−25
Forestry and fishing	−7	5	6	−5	6
Mining and manufacturing	35	63	16	18	97
Building and construction	35	12	6	10	28
Utilities and distribution	1	12	6	10	28
Ocean transport and whaling	−19	16	6	2	24
Other transport and communication	13	8	6	1	15
Government, financial and business services	59	1	18	12	31
Personal services	−35	−3	−3	−6	−12

Source: *Nasjonalregnskap*. (Items may not add to totals because of rounding.)

other sector showing a substantial loss of self-employed persons during the period was building and construction, where there was a drop of 13,000, almost all of it occurring between 1947 and 1949. The flow of manpower out of agriculture has been augmented by the steady and apparently accelerating decline in agricultural wage earners. Personal services has been the only other sector consistently releasing labor to other industries since the war and here the outward flow has been largely made up of workers in domestic service.

The structural shift of employment out of these low productivity sectors has also contributed significantly to the growth of the economy since the war. Preliminary estimates of the Central Bureau of Statistics indicate that some 40 per cent of the total increase in real national product is connected with the shift of employment between sectors, the greatest component of which is the relative decline in agriculture and domestic service.

In general, the pattern of movement in the employment of wage and salary earners is readily understandable in terms of the structure and level of effective demand and the resultant impact on the labor market in the various sectors. A word of caution needs to be entered here. The employment statistics are among the least reliable of any of the national accounts figures. The Central Bureau of Statistics remarks in a footnote that the "statistical basis for the estimates of employment is rather poor for many industries, particularly for 1938" and warns that "care should be taken in drawing conclusions from the movement in the figures." For this reason, only a nine-sector breakdown has been used, instead of the 40-odd sector classification which the Bureau itself employs, in the belief that such aggregation will reduce the importance of errors in the more detailed figures.

The two cases where in spite of this procedure there is still serious question as to reliability are building and construction and personal services. The various items in its national accounts estimates indicates that the figures of employment in these sectors, insofar as their year to year movement is concerned, is based on weak basic data and may have little independent value. In view of these statistical defects in the basic employment data, therefore, an effort has been made to restrict any conclusions reached to those where the movements are sufficiently well marked to reduce the probability that they arise merely out of the statistical characteristics of the series involved.

From the indexes of Table 15 it is apparent that employment in the

Table 15. Employment indexes of wage and salary workers by sector, 1938–1955
(1946 = 100)

	1938	1946	1947	1948	1949	1950	1951	1952	1953	1954	1955
Agriculture	136	100	98	90	88	78	72	68	62	54	50
Forestry and fishing	129	100	113	121	121	125	133	146	125	121	125
Mining and manufacturing	85	100	113	121	126	129	134	133	134	137	140
Building and construction	60	100	106	105	114	117	111	121	134	139	132
Utilities and distribution	99	100	106	111	111	115	118	121	125	130	134
Ocean transport and whaling	150	100	116	129	140	150	158	158	155	155	163
Other transport and communication	78	100	107	113	113	118	121	123	125	125	125
Government, financial and business services	62	100	98	99	101	101	106	112	115	121	119
Personal services	138	100	99	99	97	97	95	93	91	89	87
Total	92	100	105	110	113	115	117	119	120	123	123

Source: *Nasjonalregnskap.*

mining and manufacturing, building and construction, and shipping sectors
has grown substantially faster than the average for the period; almost two
thirds of the total "supply" of workers as measured by net additions to the
labor force and the man power released from agriculture and domestic
service have been absorbed into these three sectors. This is only to be expected in view of the fact that some 40 per cent of postwar investment has
been in the form of building and construction, while a similar percentage
of total investment has occurred in the two sectors, mining and manufacturing, and shipping. The slower rate of increase in employment in industrial
occupations after 1949 is unquestionably connected with the relative stagnation in effective consumer demand in 1950–51 and the slackening of external
demand in 1952–53. On the other hand, the increased demand for building
and construction associated with the acceleration in the housing program and
the increases in defense construction after 1951 stimulated the flow of workers
into that sector up to 1954. Technological change, capital improvements, and
the generally high level of demand continued to release labor from agricultural employment. Insofar as the manufacturing sector could not absorb
the continued flow of man power out of agriculture, there was a tendency
for relatively unskilled labor to accumulate in the construction sector which
by 1951 began to show up in the form of increased seasonal unemployment.
Part of the effort to combat this unemployment took the form of increased
governmental expenditures on occupations like road construction (particularly in the northern areas where the problem was the greatest) which,
of course, to a certain extent, was bound to have a reinforcing influence on
the movement out of agriculture.

The difficulties associated with *flukten fra jordbruket* (the flight from
agriculture) present one of the most serious structural problems confronting
Norway at present. Not the least of the difficulties is the political influence
of the agricultural groups who view with alarm the depopulation of Norway's rural areas and the relative decline in the importance of the agricultural sector. While the government explicitly renounced in its long-term
programs any intention of completely halting the decline in agricultural
employment, its plans for investment and agricultural subsidies seemed
clearly intended to lay the foundation for an improvement in the level of
rural incomes while controlling more carefully the movement out of the
rural areas.

Through continued rationalization and especially by increasing the size of farms
it will undoubtedly be possible for the agricultural sector to manage significantly
higher production with less manpower than now. So long as this is reasonable the
State ought, moreover, to encourage such a development. But there must also
be taken up for solution the problems which are posed for the rural districts by a
decrease in the agricultural population.[14]

Intersectoral Income Differentials and the Industrial Wage Structure

Indices of average annual earnings based upon employee incomes and man-years worked in the major economic sectors (in spite of the statistical short-comings of the employment data) provide an imperfect picture of the differential movements in incomes that have accompanied the structural shifts in employment. Most marked in the figures presented in Table 16 is the large

Table 16. Indexes of annual employee income per man-year by sector, 1938–1955 (1946 = 100)

	1938	1946	1947	1948	1949	1950	1951	1952	1953	1954	1955
Agriculture	36	100	111	123	126	133	145	158	167	179	180
Forestry and fishing	43	100	115	129	140	129	134	177	211	218	218
Mining and manufacturing	61	100	113	122	123	133	153	170	178	187	197
Building and construction	51	100	113	115	115	122	136	150	155	165	175
Utilities and distribution	62	100	112	118	126	135	155	172	175	180	192
Ocean transport and whaling	41	100	95	96	96	101	109	122	120	126	125
Other transport and communication	60	100	108	123	131	134	143	166	173	185	192
Government (excluding military), financial and business services	67	100	108	115	120	128	138	152	162	164	169
Personal services	47	100	108	115	127	138	155	163	175	188	195
All employees	53	100	110	118	122	130	145	162	172	180	190

Source: Calculated from data on wages and salaries and full-time equivalent employment in *Nasjonalregnskap*.

increase in earnings in agriculture, forestry, and fishing, both absolutely and relative to all other sectors. By 1955, annual employee earnings in these sectors had increased five times from the prewar year of 1938, while the general average increased a little more than 3.5 times. The other sector showing the greatest rise is personal services with an average income in 1955 quadruple the prewar level. In both cases, however, it is to be noted that the greatest part of the increases took place during the occupation period, with agricultural wages falling behind and increases in earnings in personal services, only slightly above the average increase since 1946. In view of the fact that these two sectors were the low income sectors both before and after the war and that, as we have seen, they were the two sectors which experienced absolute declines in employment, the strong increase in average earnings is not surprising. It must be assumed that the prewar level of unemployment had its greatest depressive effect on wages in these two sectors where union organization and other factors tending to support the wage level were the weakest. Similarly, there is a clear presumption that these two sectors harbored a good portion of the disguised unemployment or underemployment of the prewar period. The inflationary pressure and general labor shortage of the occupation and postwar periods, therefore, reversed the situation, in the sense of producing the greatest relative wage-increasing and underemployment-reducing impact in these two areas.

The impact of these differential movements on percentage income differentials among the major economic sectors is represented in Table 17. The

Table 17. Average annual employee income differentials by sector, 1938–1955 (percentage difference from average annual employee income)

	1938	1946	1949	1952	1955
Agriculture	−58	−48	−36	−39	−41
Forestry and fishing	−9	12	29	22	28
Mining and manufacturing	11	−2	−2	2	1
Building and construction	12	18	11	8	8
Utilities and distribution	14	−4	−1	1	2
Ocean transport and whaling	40	87	47	40	23
Other transportation and communication	15	1	9	4	3
Government (excluding military), financial and business services	54	22	19	14	8
Personal services	−57	−52	−50	−52	−51

Source: Calculated from data on wages and salaries and full-time equivalent employment in *Nasjonalregnskap*.

major changes in the wage structure between 1938 and 1946 is clearly indicated; indeed, the changes in differentials after 1949 are generally of an order of magnitude small enough to make the basing of any more specific conclusions on them foolhardy in the face of the limitations of the data from which they have been calculated. But note should be made in passing that the severest loss in position in the relative wage structure seems to have been suffered by employees in government and the professions.

The broad movement in the wage structure indicated by the changes in annual employee incomes in the major economic sectors provide a background for a more intensive analysis of relative wage movements through the use of wage data which, though less comprehensive, may, on that account, perhaps be more precise. In any case, such an analysis will permit investigation of internal developments within the broader categories and between narrower industrial classifications, skills, and so on. The limitations imposed by the available data, however, will restrict our view to the mining and manufacturing sector.

From the man-hours and total earnings figures in mining and manufacturing published annually by the Central Bureau of Statistics in its *Produksjonstatistikk,* there have been computed average hourly earnings for 23 subgroups in mining and manufacturing since 1938 and 28 subgroups since 1948 (Tables 18, 19). From simple measures of dispersion which have

Table 18. Average hourly earnings in mining and manufacturing, men, 1938–1957[a]
(ore per hour)

	1938	1946	1947	1948	1949	1950	1951	1952	1953	1954
Average	148	249	272	298	312	332	375	426	447	469
Printing, bookbinding, etc.	188	297	319	336	355	371	409	456	494	507
Electro-chemicals	187	290	318	330	344	380	398	474	500	526
Rubber	153	264	300	327	344	354	382	435	452	483
Other basic metal	—	—	—	327	340	374	417	479	501	532
Other paper products	153	254	292	325	332	351	395	455	473	501
Gas	197	297	312	320	334	352	397	444	470	485
Electro-metallurgical	171	268	296	318	339	361	407	461	497	504
Metal products	—	—	—	313	322	342	393	440	455	479
Miscellaneous	—	—	—	310	318	340	381	433	461	474
Leather	143	248	283	306	316	331	374	404	433	443
Nonmetallic mineral products	144	256	276	305	327	348	389	445	460	476
Metal, metal products and machinery[b]	151	254	281	303	315	333	372	426	448	474
Petroleum, coal, and other chemicals	168	252	275	302	316	337	381	433	462	497
Transport equipment	—	—	—	301	312	328	362	415	439	467
Electronics	149	254	279	300	316	327	379	435	462	482
Metal mining	144	249	280	297	310	340	400	463	484	507
Nonelectrical machinery	—	—	—	290	308	324	367	417	441	462
Pulp, paper and cardboard	145	239	269	286	301	325	388	426	446	469
Beverages	177	256	280	286	299	321	352	413	426	446
Shoes	140	229	261	285	305	322	362	395	409	428
Fats and oils	147	226	259	285	295	316	360	395	411	444
Tobacco	162	245	289	282	305	322	368	436	455	483
Food (except fish and meat canning)	155	238	265	281	294	315	356	403	430	450
Textiles	143	238	256	281	292	316	353	395	406	428
Furniture and fixtures	117	228	258	280	293	307	349	398	426	448
Wood and cork	119	221	251	279	291	309	346	395	412	430
Clothing (except shoes)	150	238	258	277	295	314	359	394	416	436
Fish and meat canning	111	196	229	255	258	275	305	345	356	375

Source: Calculated from earnings and man-hours data in *Produksjonsstatistikk* adjusted for comparability.

[a] Arranged according to rank in 1948.

[b] Includes electro-metallurgical, other basic metal, metal products, and transport equipment.

Table 19. Average hourly earnings in mining and manufacturing,
total, 1938–1954 [a]

(ore per hour)

	1938	1946	1947	1948	1949	1950	1951	1952	1953	1954
Average	135	230	256	276	289	307	349	397	416	437
Electro-chemical	187	290	317	329	344	378	397	470	497	523
Other basic metal	—	—	—	327	340	374	417	478	500	531
Gas	197	297	312	320	333	352	395	443	469	484
Electro-metallurgical	170	267	296	318	337	360	405	459	495	502
Transport equipment	—	—	—	301	311	327	362	415	439	466
Metal, metal products, and machinery[b]	149	251	278	300	311	329	368	422	443	468
Nonmetallic mineral products	139	251	276	297	317	338	377	433	445	461
Metal mining	144	249	280	296	308	339	399	461	482	504
Metal products	—	—	—	296	304	325	375	422	437	460
Printing, bookbinding, etc.	164	254	279	294	315	333	369	413	447	459
Nonelectrical machinery	—	—	—	289	308	323	366	416	440	461
Leather	131	231	262	289	300	314	356	383	407	415
Electronics	142	242	264	286	301	315	364	419	447	464
Miscellaneous manufacture	—	—	—	285	290	308	350	400	426	436
Rubber	124	223	259	285	298	310	338	389	400	433
Fats and oils	146	225	258	284	293	315	358	393	409	441
Pulp, paper and cardboard	142	232	262	279	294	318	381	418	437	459
Furniture and fixtures	116	227	256	278	292	306	348	396	424	445
Wood and cork	119	220	251	277	289	307	345	394	410	429
Beverages	169	242	265	273	284	306	339	398	410	428
Petroleum, coal, and other chemicals	162	219	244	270	284	305	351	407	435	467
Other paper products	117	194	233	269	280	306	350	398	419	440
Food (except fish and meat canning)	138	215	240	253	266	282	333	366	388	404
Shoes	102	197	224	245	262	277	315	343	349	361
Tobacco	136	194	231	231	254	269	307	360	377	401
Textiles	131	186	203	222	233	249	288	322	335	356
Clothing (except shoes)	120	171	189	208	220	239	277	308	326	340
Fish and meat canning	85	158	183	205	211	223	253	287	292	307

Source: Calculated from earnings and man-hours data in *Produksjonsstatistikk* and adjusted for comparability.

[a] Arranged according to rank in 1948.

[b] Includes electro-metallurgical, other basic metal, metal products, and transport equipment.

been calculated (Table 20), the pattern previously observed seems to have been repeated within the mining and manufacturing sector. The range between the highest and the lowest wage industries in per cent of the average of all mining and manufacturing decreased by over 40 per cent

Table 20. Range and deviation in the industrial wage structure,[a] 1938–1954

	Range		Average deviation	
	(øre)	(per cent)	(øre)	(per cent)
Men				
1938	86	58.1	16	10.7
1946	101	40.5	17	6.9
1949	97	31.1	17	5.5
1952	134	31.4	25	5.8
1954	157	33.4	27	5.8
All workers				
1938	112	82.9	20	15.0
1946	139	60.4	25	10.7
1949	124	46.0	25	8.7
1952	191	48.1	34	8.6
1954	224	51.2	40	9.2

Source: Calculated from earnings and man-hours data in *Produksjonsstatistikk* and adjusted for comparability.

[a] Range equals difference between average hourly earnings in highest and lowest industrial sub-groups. Average deviation equals difference between average hourly earnings of the sub-groups and the average for all mining and manufacturing.

from 1938 to 1952 and by almost 25 per cent from 1946 to 1949. Similar declines took place in the average deviation of earnings in the individual categories from the mean for all groups. Since 1949, however, this movement seems to have been halted and even slightly reversed. Nevertheless, our conclusion that the tendency toward less dispersion in the wage structure was in the main associated with the inflationary pressure of the war and immediate postwar years appears to find confirmation.

Insofar as this conclusion is well founded, it tends to support the general judgment that the wage structure has responded in very much the way that might have been expected under the circumstances. Variations in the general economic situation — from the severe inflationary movement of the occupation period through suppressed inflation to a position approaching equilibrium — were reflected in the wage structure in a manner similar to that experienced in other countries where the power of organized labor over wages is considerably less and more decentralized.[15] This is at least indirect evidence of the continued primary importance of general economic influences relative to explicit union policy as determinants of relative wages.

Not only does the general pattern of movement appear "explainable" in terms of basic economic factors, but individual shifts within the wage structure also seem to make considerable "economic sense." (Here we must tread on less sure ground in the absence of extensive statistical analysis which cannot be undertaken within the confines of this study; simple observation of the movement of average hourly earnings in certain industries, however, is suggestive, if not conclusive.) Within the context of a general tendency toward narrower differentials, those industries which give the appearance of faring the best either in improving or maintaining their position in the wage structure during the postwar period tend to be the investment and export industries, where the pressure of demand has been the highest and expansion activities the greatest. Perhaps the clearest example in the case of nonmetallic mineral products which has moved from a below average wage position to one considerably above, presumably under the impact of the demand for cement, stone, and other building materials, arising out of the enlarged volume of housing and construction. Metal mining shows a similar movement, probably because of efforts to increase exports of ore. The marked increase in the position of the electronics industry in the wage structure is partly a reflection of the high internal demand for electrical appliances, which import restrictions have made difficult to obtain and which have contributed to the rapid development of the industry. The housing program and the continuing heavy investment of hydro-electric power development have also been factors in the relative high level of demand for electrical supplies and apparatus. The comparatively slight improvement in the relative wage position of the food, textile, clothing, and shoe industries, on the other hand, is probably associated with the more rapid approach to equilibrium in consumer markets and to a certain extent, the closer supervision of product prices in these markets. In the background, also, particularly in the case of textiles and clothing, has been the imminence, and gradual realization, as the trade liberalization program progressed, of competition from abroad.

Foreign competition has of course been a factor in wage developments in the export industries. As noted earlier, the objective of maintaining control over internal costs in order to preserve the competitive position of Norwegian exports in world markets was a primary consideration in the formulation and execution of the general policy of wage restraint. Still, the state of demand for Norwegian exports has been high and the effort to expand the capacity of the export industries has been vigorous throughout the postwar period. It is not surprising, therefore, to find that the increase in average hourly earnings since 1946 has been about 5 per cent greater in the export sector than in industries oriented to the domestic market. But this more rapid increase of earnings in the export industries was confined to the years 1949 to 1952, and should be connected with the impact of high profits following devaluation and the increase in international demand following the outbreak of the Korean war. In this case, too, there seems to be evidence of the responsiveness of the postwar Norwegian wage structure to general economic influences.

Two basic conditions appear to be primarily responsible for the continued responsiveness of relative wages to economic factors. First, of course, is the widespread use of piece rate and premium pay arrangements throughout industry and all other factors underlying the wage drift. The latter phenomena provided a major avenue by which the traditional market influences could make themselves felt within the wage structure. The role of such internal shift mechanisms within the Norwegian industrial wage structure provides another illustration of the importance of structural wage adjustments under high employment conditions and within the context of macroeconomic controls designed to limit aggregative movements.[16]

Emphasis on the way in which it was possible for wage variations to take place in spite of or in apparent disregard of the explicit wage policy objectives of the trade unions should not, however, obscure the fact that another basic reason for the conformance of relative wage variations to the patterns of economic change is to be found in the actions and attitudes of the unions themselves. In spite of the fact that the ideological objective of "wage solidarity" was the foundation upon which the labor movement's policy toward relative wage changes rested, in actual practice it was recognized that this social goal was only to be realized within the limitations imposed by the economic situation. Hence, part of the reason for the increased use of incentive wage systems can be found in the generally favorable attitude toward such systems by the trade union leadership. The major reservation concerning their use has not been based on ideological grounds of "worker solidarity" and equilitarianism, but on the possibility of cuts in piece rates as earnings increased.[17] During the postwar period, too, there were occasions when wage settlements above the pattern were obtained (specifically in forestry and underground mining) for the purpose of attracting labor rather than to promote wage equality.

Occupational and Skill Differentials

While the industrial wage structure has remained relatively free from serious anomalies introduced by the combination of inflationary pressure and "wage solidarity," the same cannot be said for the structure of skill differentials. The narrowing margin between skilled and unskilled rates has been pointed out previously as a problem that began to be a matter of some concern to the trade union leadership soon after liberation and eventually led to the decision to seek a widening of skill differentials in the 1952 negotiations. Difficulties of obtaining comparable wage data for various occupational and skill classifications over the postwar period prevent any definitive staking out of the precise dimensions and location of distortion in the occupational wage structure. Sufficient information does exist, however, to give some support to the general conclusion that the rewards for skill and training have become in some cases so small as to endanger the future supply of skilled manpower.

The situation seems to have become most serious in the metal trades. Figures of the Employers' Association on skilled and unskilled rates and earnings indicate a drop in the average per cent differential from 24 per cent in 1938 to about 11 per cent in 1951 with an increase to 13 per cent in 1952. The increase in earnings in the skilled occupations, based on the sample shown in Table 21 seem to have been generally below the average

Table 21. Skilled and unskilled earnings in the metal trades, 1938–1955
(1946 = 100)

(Third quarter)	1938	1946	1949	1952	1955
Toolmakers	61	100	113	149	172
Hand molders	60	100	124	165	189
Ship-plate workers	61	100	112	156	177
Core makers	61	100	122	166	187
Tin and copper smiths	64	100	116	153	179
Lathe operators	67	100	117	154	179
Machinists	64	100	118	158	176
Pattern makers	61	100	118	156	177
Skilled workers	62	100	117	158	180
Unskilled workers	58	100	119	160	181

Source: Norsk Arbeidsgiver Forening and Statistisk Sentralbyrå.

for the industry as a whole. How serious this differential squeeze has been in terms of restricting the flow of apprentices and younger workers into the metal trades is impossible to say. The extremely small magnitudes of the skill differentials give a presumption that the problem could become serious over the long run. And the percentage of workers in the metal industry below the age of 19 decreased from about 15 to 18 per cent immediately prior to the war to around 6.5 per cent in 1948. Since that time there has been both an absolute and relative increase in the number of "boy helpers and apprentices." [18] Notwithstanding the paucity of quantitative information, the net impression given by the information that exists on skill differentials is that the decreased dispersion within the occupational wage structure has been more serious than has been the case in the industrial wage structure. To what extent this development is to be ascribed to implementation of the principle of "solidarity" in wage settlements, however, is questionable. With-

out doubt the principal immediate cause for the narrowing of skill differentials was the granting of cost-of-living supplements throughout the postwar period in equal absolute amounts. Though the "solidarity" principle was
certainly a basic consideration in the decisions to make these supplements in
this form, experience in other countries without national wage bargaining or
any commitment to "wage solidarity" within the labor movement has shown
a general bias toward absolute money increments in cost-of-living wage
settlements. In this respect, Norwegian experience is not unique. The growing concern on the part of the union leadership with the problem of
differentials, together with its continuing effort to eliminate the deleterious
effects of flat increases on the occupational rate structure and the operation
of incentive systems may be taken as additional evidence of the increased
feeling of union responsibility for optimum economic performance. This
concern, however, cannot be separated from the traditional pressures of
skilled groups within the union to protect their relative position.

From one point of view, this survey or relative wage and manpower
movements during the postwar period leads to the conclusion that there has
been considerable success in achieving both the employment and relative
wage objectives. The shifts in employment have conformed roughly to the
desired pattern of industrialization. Similarly, the relative improvement in
the wage levels of the lower-paid groups in industry and the reduction in
industrial and occupational differentials generally would appear to be in line
with announced goals of "wage solidarity." This apparent coincidence of
policy and actual results, however, has a certain degree of speciousness. For,
the actual movements in the structure of wages and employment probably
should be ascribed in the main to the differential impact of the high level of
internal demand and not to any specific policy measures.

From this point of view, progress toward these objectives was made
possible through the exploitation of an existing situation and relied upon
more or less unregulated employment to the level and distribution of demand under conditions of full or overfull employment.

This is not to say, however, that the relative wage objectives of the trade
unions summed up in the principle of "wage solidarity" were unimportant
in shaping the actual course of events. On the contrary, "wage solidarity" has
been crucially important to the whole structure of postwar economic policy.
But, its importance has had a more negative than positive character; it was
the foundation upon which the policy of general wage restraint rested, and,
as such, was a basis for establishing short run wage stability. By providing
the rationale for restraining individual groups from fully exploiting the
possibilities for money wage increases in the general inflationary situation,

the "solidarity" principle was an essential element in making possible control over the general wage level.

The limitations and, to a certain extent, gradual erosion of "wage solidarity" as a foundation for a policy of wage restraint have been observable in our survey of relative wage developments — specifically in the existence of the "wage drift" as an avenue of wage adjustment, relieving some of the upward pressure on negotiated wage rates and mitigating the dissatisfaction of skilled groups over the narrowing of differentials which had to be taken into account in formulating wage demands. But an even more important limitation is the fact that "wage solidarity" to the trade unions does not include countenancing any substantial reduction in wages in some sectors in order that other wages may rise. The improvement in relative income standards since 1938, particularly in agriculture, has been bound up with the general inflation of the period and has increased some of the difficulties of eliminating inflationary pressure and upward wage movements while still maintaining a high, full-employment rate of growth. Changes in the wage structure can no longer take place in the context of general increases in the level of wages. As a consequence, with the difficulties of obtaining wage decreases under conditions of generally high employment, any development tending to bring about relative wage changes will almost inevitably involve a general upward movement in the wage level.

CHAPTER 10

Trade Unions and Wages
in a Controlled Economy

No amount of statistical and other empirical information concerning the structure, operation, and results of wage determination processes in postwar Norway can in itself lead to definitive judgments as to the long-run effectiveness and stability of the Norwegian system of collective bargaining within the context of economic planning and full employment. Certainly no claim can be made that the description and analysis presented in the preceding chapters cover all the relevant aspects of postwar Norwegian experience in the field of wages, employment, and industrial relations. Nevertheless certain features of wage developments in Norway stand out strongly enough to provide insight into the wage problems of any economy where the government undertakes to exercise some degree of control over the course of economic events.

Whatever lessons are to be derived from the broad survey of Norwegian wage experience, as described in the preceding chapters cannot take the form of supposed "solutions" to economic policy problems. The value of that experience lies in the nature of the alternatives that have been faced in order to carry out a systematic policy of economic control rather than in the specific course Norwegian economic policy has followed in choosing among these alternatives.

Goals and Achievements of Postwar Wage Policy

In the opening chapters and throughout the body of this study, the interrelation between wage policy and general economic policy in the Norwegian system of economic control has been constantly emphasized. From the basic economic objectives of full employment, rapid economic growth, and greater equalization of incomes were derived the principal goals of wage policy. These, it may be recalled were: (1) to prevent any inflation of the internal cost level which would jeopardize the competitive position of Norwegian exports; (2) to restrict increases in wage incomes sufficiently to keep increases in consumption demand within the limits set by increases in production, and thus to permit an extremely high rate of investment without over-increasing pressure on the internal price level and the balance of payments; (3) to accomplish a considerable reduction in wage inequalities within industry and between the major economic sectors, while at the same time not interfering with substantial shifts of manpower into those areas where expansion was most desired; and (4) to keep industrial unrest and work stoppages to negligible proportions. Moreover, it was generally accepted that the achievement of these goals was to be sought in an institutional framework which permitted considerable economic power to remain in the hands of private individuals and organizations who were not subject to direct governmental regulation.

The broad contours of policy development since the war reflect the shifting emphasis placed upon these goals which, like any set of objectives in this imperfect world, are, in general, not susceptible of being fully realized at one and the same time. While labor costs have been maintained at a level which conserves Norway's international position and the increases in wage incomes have generally been restricted sufficiently to generate a high level of domestic saving and bring consumer markets close to equilibrium, inflationary pressures have not been either wholly contained or eliminated. There have been significant improvements in the relative income positions of workers in the low-wage sectors of the economy, and the pattern of employment shifts has been more or less in conformity with planned export, investment, and production goals. Nevertheless wide dispersion in the relative wage structure persists, and distributive goals, to a certain extent, have had to give way before the need for an adequate supply of skilled manpower.

The nature of the compromises among objectives has been, of course, largely dependent upon the extent to which the government was unable or unwilling to establish absolute control over economic developments. The precise boundary of effective control must inevitably remain undefined, but it is nevertheless clear that, on the one hand, the impossibility of establishing complete control over external economic developments and, on the other hand, the unwillingness to establish direct control over the wage determination process contributed two of the most important constraints shaping policy decisions in the postwar period. It is the latter aspect of Norwegian economic policy which is of particular interest. One of the most significant features of the post war Norwegian economy — the deliberate demobilization of direct government regulations — has been closely connected with the desire to maintain autonomous collective bargaining institutions.

The Autonomy of Norwegian Trade Unions

The more than ten years of collective bargaining experience in postwar Norway not only provides evidence of trade union autonomy throughout the period, but in addition indicates a trend away from and not toward direct governmental authority over the collective bargaining process. In the early years after liberation, the task of reconstruction and the dangers of economic and financial chaos appeared sufficiently overwhelming to encourage, if not require, efforts to subordinate individual interest to the general economic welfare. The emergency character of the period led, as we have seen, to the institution of compulsory arbitration and a trade union wage policy centered on the task of helping the government to maintain the stabilization line. It was in this atmosphere, too, that the LO and NAF agreed to set up joint production committees within individual firms as a vehicle for union-management cooperation in increasing output and efficiency. Writing of these early years, Professor Galenson was understandably struck by the subordination of immediate trade union objectives to over-all governmental policy and the incipient tendencies for Norwegian unions to be "governmentalized" in the manner of Soviet unions. But even at that time he found it was "decidedly premature to conclude that the Norwegian trade unions will ever go the way of their Soviet counterparts, to become in effect administrative divisions of the state with little real autonomy."[1]

In the succeeding years, the trade unions have not only succeeded in maintaining their autonomy but, if anything, have strengthened their position of independence. Trade union primacy in the area of wage determination was preserved in 1949 by limitation of compulsory arbitration to cases where wage demands had not been approved by the central organizations. It was eventually completely eliminated in 1952. In spite of internal political pressures to bind the LO unqualifiedly to the political labor movement and to force explicit adoption of socialist or semisyndicalist doctrines, the LO has held uncompromisingly to the position that the trade unions should be independent organizations pursuing their economic objectives through the traditional avenues of collective bargaining and negotiated contracts.

At the 1949 Congress the LO constitution was amended to include maintenance of free and independent trade unions as one of the fundamental objectives of the federation. This position was reaffirmed at the 1953 Congress when a variety of amendments involving qualifications of trade union autonomy under socialism were voted down. In commenting on an amendment suggesting that the section calling for the LO "to work to see that the trade unions are always free and independent" be modified with the phrase "in connection with and with respect to the capitalistic social system," the chairman of the LO expressed himself as follows: "That is a sentence we cannot accept. It is clear that we will work for a free and independent trade union organization under any social system whatsoever. We must oppose any social system which seeks to break the trade union movement."[2]

An even stronger statement on the same issue is contained in a leading editorial in the official LO journal, *Fri Fagbevegelse,* published immediately prior to the congress.

This point in the Landsorganisasjon's statement of constitutional objectives [stipulating the freedom and independence of trade unions] was formulated and adopted four years after the end of the war and occupation. It contains no conditions whatsoever, and it means that trade unions shall be free and independent irrespective of what management the country has. Those who wrote it and those who adopted it had themselves lived through a period of five years when an occupying power and its Norwegian born pawns ruthlessly and with the most brutal means sought to place the trade unions under the mastery of the state authorities. These state authorities were Nazis and they opposed — professedly — capitalism. In another circumstance the state authorities could perhaps call themselves communists or the Latter Day Saints and proclaim war on capitalism. With respect also to such state authorities the trade unions shall be free and independent. — The Norwegian trade union movement shall never be any tool or pawn of the state, irrespective of which party or group has acceded to governmental power in the nation. This is a fundamental principle in the Norwegian trade union movement.

At the same Congress, the status and future operations of the joint production councils came up for discussion. In the face of proposals looking toward the endowment of the councils with managerial authority, the LO secretariat's recommendation for their continuation as "advisory and informational cooperative organs" was adopted. The secretariat's position was that "if the question of worker influence in the management of firms is to be taken up, it needs to be raised on a different basis from the right of co-determination through the production councils." [3]

The importance of the erosion of the formal structure of compulsory arbitration and these repeated union protestations of independence is made manifest in the increased willingness to strike in the face of government policy pronouncements on the appropriate basis for contract settlement. The unrest accompanying the 1956 negotiations which led to a loss through strikes of one million man days (ten times the previous postwar high) is both evidence for and a logical consequence of the increasingly independent exercise of trade union power as the emergency environment of the reconstruction period receded into the past.

Trade Unions and Economic Stability in a Controlled Economy

The absence of any trend toward increased governmentalization of wage determination in Norway runs somewhat counter to the speculations of those who see a basic incompatibility between collective bargaining between autonomous employee and employer organizations and a government policy of full employment.

The first stage in the argument of those who have given the most rigorous formulation of this paradox is that subordinating the objective of price stability to that of full employment as the basic criterion for governmental fiscal and monetary policy removes any upper limit on the price level.

Under conditions of guaranteed full employment, there is no economic mechanism to insure a finite upper limit to the wage (and price) level. Whatever wage level happens to be set, the government must alter the quantity of money and/or its rate of expenditure so as to provide full employment at that level . . . The removal of the upper bound upon the wage and price levels leaves the recipients of fixed money incomes at the mercy of whatever wage bargains and price policies happen to develop.[4]

This proposition is a simple deduction from familiar Keynesian assumptions. Thus, in its converse form, the proposition states that under a system of guaranteed price stability, the level of employment is indeterminate, that is, there is no upper limit to the level of unemployment — the actual level depending upon whatever money wage level is stipulated by the workers.

From the voluminous discussion that has centered on the character and validity of the Keynesian assumptions, it seems to have been fairly well established that wage determination is excluded from the explanatory system by assuming labor is supplied not with reference to real economic quantities but only with respect to the money wage rate.

The particular rationale for excluding wage determination from the system makes no difference to the argument. Whereas Keynes relied upon the so-called "money illusion" of the workers, others have found it more realistic to justify the noneconomic character of wage determination on the basis of the "political" elements which trade union power introduces into wage decisions. The greater the power of unions, the more "political" is presumed to be the process of wage policy.[5] In either case the system is left hanging, so to speak, on noneconomic or "political" wage setting processes.

The logical consequence of this trend of thought is the ascription to trade unions of primary power over and therefore primary responsibility for price stability. In effect, the monetary authority of the government is replaced by the wage-setting authority of the trade unions — a situation Professor Hicks has labeled "the labor standard." In his words:

So long as wages were being determined within a *given* monetary framework, there was some sense in saying that there was an "equilibrium" wage, a wage that was in line with monetary conditions that were laid down from the outside. But the world we now live in is one in which the monetary system has been relatively elastic, so that it can accommodate itself to changes in wages rather than the other way about. Instead of actual wages having to adjust themselves to an equilibrium level, monetary policy adjusts the equilibrium level of money wages so as to make it conform to the actual level. It is hardly an exaggeration to say that instead of being on a Gold Standard, we are on a Labour Standard.[6]

Whether wage decisions under trade unionism are essentially "political" is a question of definition and can be answered only with reference to the fruitfulness of analyses couched in such terms. Stress on the "political" aspects of wage determination processes involves the danger of directing attention away from rather than toward the constraints operating to produce decisions, which are the proper focus of any explanatory analysis.[7] In saying this we do not intend to minimize the importance of so-called "political" influences, but rather to express a judgment as to how they should be taken into account. The problem of the relative importance of "economic" and "political" elements in the determination of wages is the fundamental one (arising in any analysis of behavior as a decision-making process) of the structure of relationships which are presumed to connect decisions with the actual course of developments.

The character of this structure is, by definition, determined by "noneconomic" factors. The usefulness of the fundamental separation between the "economic" and "noneconomic" categories in any analysis depends on the relative invariance of the noneconomic or exogenous variables with respect to the economic or endogenous variables; in more formal language, on the degree of autonomy of the relationships postulated in the analysis. This degree of autonomy can never be established on *a priori* grounds so that where the line is drawn between economic and political or noneconomic elements will depend on the purposes for which the analysis is designed. As Professor Haavelmo expresses it, "The construction of systems of autonomous relations is . . . a matter of intuition and factual knowledge; it is an art." [8]

The relegation of the wage-setting process to the "political" sphere naturally removes any economic mechanism which will tend to ensure stable prices at a high level of economic activity. But this assertion of the possible incompatibility between the decisions of various economic units and the "instability" such incompatibility involves may be interpreted as simply the expression of ignorance of the determinants of those decisions. How the system will behave is left dependent on the levels actually stipulated by the decision-making units for those variables under their control, which levels are assumed to be given independently of the rest of the system. The usefulness of such a procedure, however, is limited to an examination of the possibilities in any given situation. Clearly, from the point of the decision-making unit, it is just such an analysis which is necessary in order to make a selection of instrument variables that best serves the objectives. But it is equally clear that from the point of view of the observer of decisions, the "power" of a given decision-making unit to select certain values for the instrumental variables under its control gives no insight whatsoever into what selection will actually be made. Such insight is only possible in terms of a broader analytic framework in which the "power" of a decision-making unit appears to be reduced insofar as the choices actually made are "explained" or "determined" by "outside forces," that is, by relationships to other variables in the system. The tendency, therefore, to argue that the inevitability of wage-price instability in a full employment economy results from the "power" of trade unions[9] involves a confusion of possibility and probability.

The conclusion to be drawn is that the characterization of wage determination as a political process in view of the "power" of trade unions does no more than set the stage. To arrive at the conclusions that chronic inflation (or abandonment of full employment) actually will result if trade unions remain free to exercise their power requires a second and separate step in the argument. Once the problem has been framed in "political" terms, however — specifying the absence of any mechanism whereby the political decisions will be coordinated — it seems but a short step to the assumption that, in fact, "powerful" unions will continually demand and obtain wage increases in excess of productivity increases — a proposition which Professor Morton has labeled Lewis' Law.[10] Given this assumption, the inevitable conclusion is that implementation of effective full-employment policies by the government is bound to force abandonment of "free" collective bargaining between unions and employers as a wage-setting mechanism if any kind of economic stability is to be maintained.

Several alternative possibilities have been suggested whereby trade unions as institutions might be preserved in spite of their apparent incompatibility with a full-employment economy. But all these suggestions involve a radical transformation of worker organizations and imply the destruction of trade unions as autonomous decision-making units.

One of the most common proposals is framed in terms of trade union "responsibility." As Beveridge succinctly puts it, "So long as freedom of collective bargaining is maintained, the primary responsibility of preventing a full employment policy from coming to grief in a vicious spiral of wages and prices will rest on those who conduct the bargaining on behalf of labour." [11] Thus, autonomous trade unions could continue to exist without threatening economic stability if there existed the central trade union leadership to develop a national wage policy on the one hand, and to enforce adherence by individual unions to such a centrally determined policy, on the other.

But the greater the emphasis upon "union responsibility" as a necessary condition for successful operation of collective bargaining in a full employment economy, the more insistent becomes the question of what precisely constitutes responsible trade union behavior. Merely to raise the question forces recognition that to invoke "responsibility" as a requirement for trade union behavior with respect to wage policy tends toward a circularity which robs the concept of any prescriptive value, however much heuristic value it may have. For, in the final analysis, the degree of responsibility exhibited by the trade unions can only be determined after the fact — that is, on the basis of an evaluation whether trade union behavior did, in fact, conform in some sense to the general public welfare. To attempt to imbue trade union "responsibility" with descriptive content *ex ante* necessarily involves the assumption of some larger interest or authority which the unions must serve if they are to act "responsibly." The greater the degree of union responsibility, therefore, the less the degree of trade unionism in the sense of autonomous organizations serving the economic interests of their members, and the less appropriate it is to speak of free collective bargaining. From this point of view, specifying a responsible national wage policy by trade unions as a condition for combining free collective bargaining and economic stability in a full-employment economy amounts almost to saying that the two are incompatible.

Other proposed solutions explicitly accept this basic incompatibility arguing that full employment requires abandonment of the private enterprise system and the transformation of trade unions from militant representatives of the economic interests of their members into organizations providing central regulation of wages and working conditions in accordance with general economic policy. The usual socialist view of the function of trade unions, which has been an important element in the thought of leaders of the Norwegian labor movement, is summed up in a statement by the "grand old man" of the political labor movement in Norway, as follows: "Trade unions representing social groups will continue to be necessary under socialism . . . They will then be administrative divisions of society rather than, as now, defensive and combative organizations." [12]

To avoid such a subjection of trade union action to governmental authority, an alternative sometimes proposed to the socialist "solution" is a kind of "industrial democracy." The central idea is syndicalist in its implications in that the workers in an enterprise or industry are to be accorded, through their unions, joint (or perhaps exclusive) authority over the management of the process of production. This solution, too, has had some vogue in Norwegian labor circles and has recently given rise to considerable discussion of such a form of industrial democracy as the "third alternative" to capitalism on the one hand and socialism on the other.[13] The "third alternative" as a solution to the problem of economic organization, however, is similar to the socialist one. It leaves no place for free collective bargaining and also entails a basic transformation in the character and functions of trade unions.

The analytic basis for these pessimistic conclusions about the compatibility of free collective bargaining may be summarized as follows: (1) the process of wage determination — under unionism or not — is primarily noneconomic in character so that in an economy placing heavy reliance on private enterprise there is "no inherent mechanism . . . which can with certainty prevent competitive sectional bargaining for wages from setting up a vicious spiral of rising prices under full employment";[14] (2) trade unions as political organizations are so constituted that it is virtually inevitable that they will, in fact, produce chronic inflation if the government pursues an active full employment policy; and (3) lacking any economic mechanism to provide stability, a government policy of full employment requires a political solution to the problem involving the explicit or implicit abandonment of free collective bargaining carried on by autonomous organizations. What light, if any, does Norwegian experience throw upon the validity of these propositions?

Wage Decisions and Economic Stability in Norway

Without denying the possible usefulness of an analysis which assumes that the determination of money wages is a result of factors relatively invariant with respect to the rest of the economic system, it is obvious that such has not been the case in postwar Norway. In spite of the fact that wage levels were to a substantial degree dependent upon the decisions resulting from centralized wage negotiations, there was by no means a one-to-one correspondence between those decisions and actual wage movements. It has been sufficiently emphasized in previous chapters that the less than universal scope of the central bargain and the amount of "play" between central wage decisions and actual wage rates and earnings (stemming in part from the very comprehensiveness of the central agreements) make invalid the assumption that wage developments were solely a function of "political" union decisions. Moreover, union wage policy, far from being formulated without reference to the economic consequences of wage decisions, appears to have been dominated by such considerations. The system of national wage bargaining under full employment did not result in any reduction of union interest in the real economic effects of wage decisions, but rather acted to shift that interest from the particular price-employment consequences appropriate to less centralized wage bargaining toward the general price-employment consequences of the "master wage bargain."

Primary among the economic restraints operating on union wage policy was the direct threat to employment, or, alternatively, to the standard of living, which internal wage-price increases involved through their impact on the competitive position of the export industries or of domestic industries exposed to the competition of imports. The weight which this consideration has had in influencing union attitudes in Norwegian wage settlements probably cannot be overemphasized. Of course, Norway is something of an extreme case in view of the substantial magnitude and directness of the effects via the external economy of wage-price increases. Yet, aside from this, there were purely internal factors operating to strengthen trade union interest in price stability. Open inflation even with automatic cost-of-living adjustments forced the bulk of union efforts to be devoted to preventing a fall in real wages with the consequent neglect of other objectives, both economic and noneconomic. Similarly, when the inflation was suppressed, the wage drift and the acute shortage of labor associated with the level of excess demand interfered with the achievement of organizational objectives by undermining union control over the labor market. To some extent, also, the hothouse atmosphere of suppressed inflation posed a threat to the maintenance of union wage standards by encouraging the growth of, if not nonunion firms, at least inefficient union firms.

In spite of all this there might still be objections that the "economic" rationale for trade union decisions in the process of wage determination has been overshadowed by the political responsibility the trade unions have had to bear as a consequence of their close relationship to the Labor government and the vulnerability to governmental pressure which that responsibility involved. Certainly, as a source for a great portion of the Labor Party's political strength, the trade unions have had political, as well as economic, reasons to take into account the effect of any action on the interests of other groups in the economy and the economic policies of the government. To do otherwise would subvert the achievement of the broad social-economic objectives which are the roots of trade union support of the Labor Party. The political position of the Norwegian labor movement, while it has been dominant since the liberation, nevertheless, is far from being unassailable, as is only to be expected in a political democracy. For the Labor Party to retain a parliamentary majority, the support of other groups in the economy is essential, particularly the rural population, whose interests are separate, and, in important respects, in conflict with those of organized industrial labor.

Even in the absence of this particular source of political vulnerability to governmental pressure, it might be argued that the centralization of the collective bargaining process and the corresponding concentration of wage-making authority in the trade union federation in itself is sufficient to produce the same subservience to governmental influence. In Professor Ross's words, "The master wage bargain, which alone could imply responsibility for the volume of employment or other economic objectives . . . [and] to which the government could not avoid becoming a party, is in many ways the antithesis of "free collective bargaining." [15]

To emphasize the burdens of political responsibility, however, is to present only one side of the picture. In Norway, trade union willingness to assume the restraints upon direct trade union action has rested to a large extent on the ability to secure governmental policies to serve the economic interests of the workers and, equally important, to prevent the benefits of trade union restraint from accruing to employers and the upper classes generally. Not the least important of these policies, of course, has been the full-employment policy itself, and perhaps equally important was the assurance of some degree of governmental supervision over prices and profits. The influence of the unions on the character and operations of government economic controls provided alternatives to increased money wages as a method of improving the workers' standard of living.

Without political power, trade unions are confined to the variable of money wages in seeking to increase real wages, although they may be fully aware of the implications of wage-price relationships. But when they can exercise control over prices through government, unions are able to pursue the goal of higher real wages through alternative means.[16]

The foundation of trade union "responsibility" has not been the sacrifice of trade union interests in the name of some larger overriding principle of the general economic welfare, but simply the willingness and ability to take account of the consequences of union action on the economic well-being of their members.

The course of general wage settlements since the liberation provides abundant evidence in support of this conclusion. Even in the first wage settlement after the liberation, when, presumably, the factors contributing to social unity were the strongest, the unions obtained wage increases in excess of what was considered desirable by the government because of dissatisfaction with the manner in which the burden of war losses was to be distributed. Similarly, the unions' insistence on cost-of-living clauses in collective contracts gives further testimony to the strength of the workers' desire to provide a form of direct protection of real wages instead of relying on government economic policy, in spite of the fact that such provisions imposed a considerable burden upon the implementation of government policy. Moreover, the emphasis on this protection from real wage declines implied, as we have noted before, that union policy would not contemplate a reduction in real incomes of nonagricultural workers for the benefit of the agricultural sector, irrespective of the level of farm incomes or any broad political principle of "worker solidarity." Finally, the influence of the "wage drift" on union wage policy is another indication of the continued primacy in that policy of the particular interests of the membership. For it is quite clear that the upward drift of wages from noncontractual influences was important in forcing the unions to seek wage increases irrespective of adverse economic conditions. "Wage drifting," consequently, so long as trade unions function as independent organizations, will continue to place a fundamental limitation on the extent to which broader economic considerations can enter into union wage policy.[17]

The fact that the determination of money wage level was subject to economic influences plus the fact that the trade unions exhibited a negative reaction to price increases lead to the conclusion that a unionized economy does not differ in any essential respect from the unorganized economy in terms of the theoretical tendency toward a full-employment equilibrium with wage-price stability. This does not, of course, exclude the likelihood that the supply of labor (or union policy) is not solely a function of the real wage rate. Money wages or the level of prices can still be taken as independent variables influencing the supply of labor. The theoretical significance of the existence of "money illusion" on the part of workers, unions, or other economic units is not to eliminate the possibility of a stable equilibrium but to make that equilibrium dependent upon the absolute level of prices.

The Norwegian system of wage determination is not inconsistent with a theoretical model of the economy incorporating a tendency, other things being equal, for the level of money wages to be set at a level compatible with full employment and stable prices. In other words, it simply establishes the claim of the unionized economy to as much "inherent" stability as the nonunionized economy. The essence of the problem of economic stability in a "market" or unionized economy is the coordination of the behavior of interdependent economic units including the government, whether that coordination of economic behavior takes place through the medium of the "market" or through collective negotiations. The question of whether a given system will be stable requires a specification of the nature of the interdependent relationships between the decision-making units and the character of the responses to the impact of autonomous changes imposed upon the system.

The apparent Norwegian success in avoiding economic instability and the destruction of independent collective bargaining institutions, therefore, is as much the result of government economic policies which took explicit account of this interdependence of economic behavior, both organized and unorganized, as it was to the "responsibility" of worker, employer, or farm organizations. The inexorability of the wage-price dilemma alleged to confront the full employment economy dissolves with the recognition of the interdependence between wages and monetary and fiscal policy; that, on the one hand, stable full employment cannot be achieved by monetary and fiscal measures alone, and on the other hand, other economic policies can contribute to producing the consistency between the actions of economic groups which is necessary for stability.[18]

But in blunting the force of the dilemma we have been able to push the problem back only one level by focusing attention on the interrelation between union wage policy and the policies of the government and other economic groups. It might with justice be said that notwithstanding the economic rationale of Norwegian union behavior which is emphasized in the argument above, the "political" problem remains the task of the government in formulating and carrying out an economic policy sufficiently well coordinated to achieve economic stability. There is a fundamental truth in the proposition that effective economic policy and, hence, economic stability rests fundamentally on a social and political "consensus." [19] But this is true in any economic system. Any conclusion about economic stability, therefore — whether in a purely competitive economy or a highly organized one such as Norway's — can only be stated relative to this "consensus."

In this sense, the stability exhibited by the Norwegian economy is closely connected with the stable social and political conditions in Norway since the war. Thus "responsibility" on the part of economic organizations is more appropriately described as a willingness to acquiesce in government policies, the very nature of which is to resolve conflicts of interest between economic groups, rather than a unilateral sacrifice of self-interest in the name of the public weal. While Norwegian trade unions have shown themselves to be unwilling to behave "responsibly" in the sense of formulating their wage policy in accordance with some criteria of the common welfare rather than in terms of the economic interest of their members, they have nevertheless clearly shown awareness that the corollary of "free" or "irresponsible" unionism is support of government policies which make such freedom consistent with stability.

The continuing emphasis of the Norwegian trade unions on the necessity of price stability as the foundation for real economic progress appears not as a deviation from traditional trade union principles but merely the application of those principles in a context of a full-employment economy which permits the emergence of price stability as an important consideration in union wage policy. No real paradox is consequently involved in the fact that with governmental responsibility firmly established for maintaining a high level of employment, Norwegian trade unions, far from appearing as a revolutionary force, are found to be a source of support for economic policies emphasizing financial stability and economic efficiency and which are designed to approach economic balance closely enough to permit free collective bargaining over the fruits of technological progress and economic development.

To interpret this behavior as evidence of trade union subservience to the government would be to distort its true significance. The trend of Norwegian unionism appears to conform to the pattern Sir Douglas Copeland discerned in noting that "an interesting reflection on the experience of recent years is that trade unions as a whole resist any wages policy that impairs their freedom, their prestige, and their traditional role as guardians of the rights of their members." [20]

The point of view advanced above is that whatever threat trade unionism poses to economic stability is best viewed as inherent not in union control over wages but in the burdens which the criteria for union wage decisions impose upon government economic policy; that the responsibility for economic stability or instability is rightfully placed upon any government which undertakes to resolve the conflicts of interest between various economic groups in the light of the "common welfare." Economic analysis cannot prescribe how government policy ought to resolve these conflicts of interest. It can only hope to indicate the probable consequences of any policy, given the specific structure of interests in the economy. Whether economic stability will obtain, therefore, is fundamentally a question of the balance the government economic policy strikes between the various economic interests in the community. The ability of the government to carry out a stabilizing economic policy depends in large degree on the political support given by the various economic groups to the measures adopted — support which cannot be rationalized solely in terms of the narrowly defined interests of the groups involved.

On a more abstract level, what this implies is that the problem of economic stability in a controlled economy is at base simply one aspect of the fundamental problem of social choice in a welfare state. A democratic government responsive to political pressures of private interest groups to conduct a stablizing economic policy requires criteria for its action which is generally acceptable to the participants in the economy. Such criteria, as Arrow has shown, cannot, in general, be derived in a manner which will avoid conflict with individual values.[21] If these conflicts between the collective choices embodied in government economic policy and private interests are to be kept within limits consistent with relative stability, the decision-making processes embodied in the structure of economic and political institutions must be accorded a value separate and independent from the results of those processes.[22] In other words, economic stability, like social stability, requires conformity to both the cultural goals and the institutionalized means of the society.[23]

The degree of conformity, and hence, long-run stability, however, must inevitably remain in doubt in a free society where the course of economic policy is sensitive to shifts in the economic environment and the structure of social and political interests. In such a society, economic policy cannot be reduced to rules of thumb and automatic mechanisms. As Professor Samuelson has shown in formulating what he calls the "neo-classical" view of policy, the ultimate basis for policy decisions is the democratically expressed desires of the people measured against the alternatives perceived at the time of decisions.[24] In a practical sense, however, this is just another way of saying that ultimate rationality is unattainable in a world where uncertainty surrounds both the "public interest" to be served and the nature of the alternatives available.

In the absence of this ultimate rationality of economic policy, economic stability, and therefore, economic control, will remain partial and incomplete — a principle illustrated profusely in the Norwegian experience we have surveyed. With respect to the specific problem of trade unionism, however, perhaps the more important significance of developments in postwar Norway lies in the illustration it provides of the link between organizational behavior and the uncertainty and conflicts of interest characteristic of a free society. It is in this "principle of bounded rationality" that Professor Simon has found the source of organizational behavior.

"It is only because individual human beings are limited in knowledge, foresight, skill and time that organizations are useful instruments for the achievement of human purpose; and it is only because organized groups of human beings are limited in ability to agree on goals, to communicate and to cooperate that organization becomes for them a 'problem.' " [25]

This principle makes it clear that unions are the result rather than the cause of instability and uncertainty and conflict; that theories emphasizing the incompatibility of unions and stability in the controlled economy are based on an invalid imputation of complete rationality and control to the economic policy-makers.

Rejection of the incompatibility argument does not prove compatibility. Rather it places us back in the perhaps less intellectually satisfying world of conflict and contingency. This is the only world in which labor organizations can perform their essential function of representing worker interests and offering some degree of protection from the uncertainties of modern economic life. The behavior of trade unions — the policies adopted and the organizational methods employed — in performing this function, therefore, cannot remain unaffected by changes in the institutional and economic environment. In particular, it is only to be expected that as the government becomes more and more directly concerned with economic welfare — that is, undertakes the deliberate measures to influence economic well-being and security which are the mark of the welfare state — both the unions' immediate objectives and the means of achieving them become more closely connected to government policy and action. The present study has in large part consisted of an analysis of this process of mutual adaptation in the area of wage determination. And the evidence we have examined reveals Norwegian trade union behavior in a "controlled" economy as an adaptive process in which the fundamental functional characteristics of autonomous labor organizations and collective bargaining institutions have been preserved.

Judgments as to the future based on this historical record must inevitably suffer from the usual shortcomings surrounding extrapolations of past trends. At the very least, however, it seems clear that the emphasis in Norwegian economic policy upon a high rate of investment and maintenance of full employment is likely to continue to make price stability loom large among the immediate economic problems. In Norway, as in most other Western economies, the balance of economic policy tends to accord relatively less weight to those interests which would be served by absolutely stable prices. In consequence, although government policy has a definite anti-inflationary flavor, it is not likely that it will ever take on a deliberately deflationary character, unless forced to do so by a deep and protracted world-wide depression. Under such circumstances, although the economic system may exhibit price stability in the sense that its response to change in the external or internal economy will tend to be in the direction of a stable equilibrium level of prices, there will be a long-run upward trend of prices. Such, at least, seems to be the characteristic behavior of the Norwegian economy in recent years and may, perhaps, be expected in any economy in which there is a tendency to give priority to goals of economic growth and full employment. Wage-price stability in the full employment economy seems likely to involve an unending struggle.

Notes

Notes

Chapter 1
Wages in a System of Economic Control

1. Walter Galenson, *Labor in Norway* (Harvard University Press, 1949), p. 77.

2. *St. meld. nr. 1 (1955): Nasjonalbudsjettet 1955,* p. 7.

3. *Norway's Economic and Financial Problems: Two Lectures by the Governor of the Bank of Norway, Erik Brofoss, at the University of Oslo Summer School for American Students* (August 1955), pp. 62–63. As a member of the cabinet (first as Minister of Finance and later as Minister of Commerce) for more than eight years following the end of the occupation, Mr. Brofoss exercised perhaps the most important single influence upon the development and execution of postwar Norwegian economic policy.

4. *Ibid.,* p. 68.

Chapter 2
The Institutional and Economic Framework of Wage Determination

1. These proportions are about one-half those in the United States where (in 1947) 25 per cent of total employment and 24 per cent of value added in manufacturing was contributed by firms of less than 100 employees.

2. These figures, however, exaggerate the concentration, since they are based on an annual survey of mining and manufacturing industries which excludes firms in which less than 12,000 (in some cases 6,000) man hours were worked. More complete figures based on industrial accident insurance statistics show about 20,000 firms in mining and manufacturing in 1951 compared to only 6,341 covered by the annual survey in that year. However, 90 per cent of the total man hours worked were in the surveyed establishments and the 13,000 excluded firms accounted for less than one-sixth of the gross value of production. Statistisk Sentralbyrå, *Norges Industri: Produksjonsstatistikk 1952,* N.O.S. XI 175 (Oslo 1954), pp. 8–10 and Table 9, p. 141. (This series under the title *Norges Industri* contains production statistics from an annual survey of mining and manufacturing establishments, as well as certain information on mining and manufacturing obtained from reports to the Industrial Accident Insurance System. Future reference to these statistics will be cited simply as *Produksjonsstatistikk.*)

3. For a general survey of the extent of trust and cartel arrangements in Norway and the history of control legislation, see the Ministry of Finance recommendations for a permanent price control law. *Ot. Prp. Nr. 60 (1952).*

4. For a general discussion of agricultural coöperatives, see O. B. Grimley, *Agricultural Coöperatives in Norway* (Oslo: The Coöperative Union and Wholesale Society, 1950).

5. Much of the following is based upon Professor Walter Galenson's study of the Norwegian labor movement, *Labor in Norway,* the definitive work in English on Norwegian trade unions. Although Professor Galenson was writing relatively soon after the liberation, the general character of wage policy had already taken definite shape so that his analysis of early developments under the postwar Labor government is, to a considerable extent, relevant for later years.

6. Galenson, *Labor in Norway*, p. 81.

7. Erling Petersen, *Norsk Arbeidsgiverforening 1900–1950* (Oslo, 1950), p. 5.

8. Petersen, pp. 66ff.

9. Petersen, p. 91.

10. Petersen, p. 64.

11. Petersen, p. 182.

12. Galenson, *Labor in Norway*, p. 43.

13. Galenson, pp. 44f. Galenson also points out that the moderation with which central authority was exercised by the LO and the small size of the Norwegian trade union movement generally were additional factors contributing to the maintenance of centralism in the federation.

14. Galenson, p. 31.

15. *Basic Agreement of the Norwegian Employers' Association and the Norwegian Federation of Labor,* paragraph 10, reproduced in English in Galenson, *Labor in Norway,* Appendix A, p. 344.

16. Quoted in Galenson, *Labor in Norway*, p. 13.

17. Galenson, *Labor in Norway*, p. 72.

18. Arbeidernes Faglige Landsorganisasjon, *Protokoll over Kongressen 1949*, p. 67.

19. *St. meld. nr. 1 1948, Nasjonalbudsjettet 1948*, pp. 95–96. (Emphasis in the original.)

20. It is perhaps gratuitous to point out that this distinction between macro- and micro-economic controls tends to break down if applied too rigidly; actually what is involved is a whole spectrum of economic administrative mechanisms rather than two mutually exclusive categories as implied by the above classification. Not only are macro-economic policies likely to have differential and direct effects, but also the direct and particular controls will typically affect both the composition and the magnitude of economic aggregates, directly and indirectly.

21. Odd Aukrust, "On the Theory of Social Accounting," *The Review of Economic Studies* 16 (3), no. 41:170–188 (1949–50). This article gives a concise and clear explanation of the system of national accounts developed in Norway. In addition to this article, the following references (in English) may be cited: O. Aukrust, P. J. Bjerve, R. Frisch, "A System of Concepts Describing the Economic Production and Circulation Process," University Institute of Economics (Oslo, 1948) (mimeographed); Ragnar Frisch, "Axiomatic Remarks on Some National Income Concepts," University Institute of Economics (Oslo, 1949) (mimeographed): OEEC, *National Accounts Studies: Norway* (Paris, 1953).

22. Aukrust, Bjerve, and Frisch, "A System of Concepts," p. 6. (Emphasis in original.)

23. Aukrust, Bjerve, and Frisch, *Ibid.,* p. 7.

24. Finansminister Erik Brofoss, *Norges Økonomiske og Finansielle Stilling* (Oslo, 1946). This is one of the early statements of the labor government's position on financial policy. There has been little or no change in basic attitude since, although, for reasons explained later on, considerable more emphasis has come to be placed on the use of monetary and fiscal measures for achievement of program objectives.

25. *St. meld. nr. 1 (1948): Nasjonalbudsjettet 1948*, p. 96.

Chapter 3
The Strategy and Structure of Postwar Economic Policy

1. The selection of these three basic problems confronting the Norwegians follows the presentation of Aukrust and Bjerve in their discussion of the transition to a peacetime economy (Odd Aukrust and Petter Jakob Bjerve, *Hva Krigen Kostet Norge* [Oslo, 1945], part II, pp. 103–164). A fourth problem, that of the government debt, is not considered separately since it is considered part of the general problem of inflation.

2. Norwegian Joint Committee on International Social Policy, *Housing in Norway* (Oslo, 1951).

3. This cycle in the rate of increase and the age structure of the population has been traced back to the middle eighteenth century, with reinforcing influences occurring at various times since. See Gunnar Jahn, "Befolkningsspørsmaal og Familienes Størrelse," *Statistiske Meldinger*, no. 7, p. 166.

4. See Petter Jakob Bjerve, "Sysselsettingsproblemet i de Naermeste aarene Framover," *Arbeidsmarkedet* (saerutredning Nr. 2, 1946), pp. 13–15.

5. Arne Haarr, *Full Sysselsetting: Kan Vi Garantere Retter til Arbeid?* (Oslo, 1952), pp. 41–42.

6. Aukrust and Bjerve, *Hva Krigen Kostet Norge*, p. 119.

7. Arne Haarr, "Arbeidsmarkedet i Etterkrigstiden," *Arbeidsmarkedet*, no. 10 (1948), p. 341. Haarr estimated these reserves amounted to roughly 70,000–80,000 persons, over 5 per cent of the total labor force.

8. Details of these wage negotiations will be considered in Chapter 4.

9. *St. meld. nr. 3 (1945), Om Fastsettelse av Valutakursene*, pp. 2–3.

10. *Nasjonalregnskapet og Nasjonalbudsjettet: Saerskilt vedlegg Nr. 1 til Statsbudsjettet (1945–46)*.

11. *Ibid.*, p. 34.

12. Budget speech in the Storting by Finance Minister Brofoss (February, 1946), published in pamphlet form by Arbeidernes Oppkysningsforbund under title of *Norges Økonomiske og Finansielle Stilling*, p. 19.

13. Organization for European Economic Coöperation, *Interim Report on the European Recovery Program*, 2:635–721 (Paris, 1948).

14. *Ibid.*, pp. 648, 689–90.

15. Speech of Finance Minister Brofoss in the Storting, February 19, 1946.

16. *Ot. prp. nr. 25 (1945–46), Om Utferdigelse av Lov om Engangsskatt på Formuestigning*, p. 4.

17. *Ibid.*, p. 5.

18. *Ot. prp. no. 25 (1945–46)*, pp. 4–5.

19. Cf. Arne Haarr, *Full Sysselsetting*, p. 153.

20. J. K. Galbraith, "The Disequilibrium System," *American Economic Review* (June 1947).

21. See Petersen, *Norsk Arbeidsgiverforening 1900–1950*, pp. 141–155 and Galenson, *Labor in Norway*, pp. 31–33.

22. Quoted in Galenson, *Labor in Norway*, p. 285.

23. Arbeidernes Faglige Landsorganisasjon, *Protokoll over Kongressen 1949* (Oslo, 1949), p. 97.

24. Morten Magnus, "An Analysis of Company Taxation in Norway." Commercial

translation by ECA Mission to Norway of an article prepared for Naeringsokønomisk Forskningsinstitutt (mimeographed), p. 9.

25. Økonomisk Utsyn over Året 1950, nos. XI, 47 (Oslo, 1951), p. 103. A law in December 1950 also provided that 10 per cent of all depreciation allowances permitted under the tax laws were to be placed in special accounts and blocked until further notice.

26. Morten Magnus, "An Analysis of Company Taxation in Norway," pp. 18–20. Magnus does not himself draw this conclusion, although it seems clearly implied in his calculations. For example, his figures indicate that for a company with capital of 1,000,000 kroner and other reserves and surplus of 500,000 kroner to distribute a 6 per cent dividend would require profits before taxes almost 25 per cent higher than if no dividend were declared and all earnings simply retained.

27. Lov av 26. juni 1953 om kontroll og regulering av priser, utbytte og konkurranseforhold, chapter V, paragraph 25.

28. Gøsta Rehn, "The Problem of Stability: An Analysis and Some Policy Proposals" in Turvey (ed.), Wages Policy under Full Employment (London: Wm. Hodge and Co., 1952), pp. 30–54.

Chapter 4

Wage Stabilization and Controlled Inflation, 1939–1952

1. The chronicle of postwar wage negotiations provided in this and the following chapter is necessarily restricted to the highlights of the major settlements. Details of the negotiations and their outcomes may be found in the annual economic surveys of the Central Bureau of Statistics (Økonomisk Utsyn) for the years involved; the official journal of the LO, Fri Fagbevegelse; the journal of the NAF, Arbeidsgiveren; Odd Gøthe, Lønnspolitikken etter Krigen (Oslo, 1951); and Lars Aarvig, Lønnsutvikling og Lønnspolitikk i Norge etter Krigen (Oslo, 1957).

2. Odd Gøthe, Lønnspolitikken etter Krigen (Oslo: Arbeidernes Opplysningsforbund, 1951), p. 7.

3. Gøthe, Lønnspolitikken, p. 8.

4. Contract revisions of the Forestry and Agricultural Workers Union provided about a 20 per cent increase in contract wage rates over the whole period. Other wage adjustments were instituted by the occupation authorities affecting the mine, construction, and clock workers. Norwegian seamen in service with the Allies received rate increases of more than 300 per cent, but this included war risk supplements.

5. St. meld. nr. 1 (1951): Nasjonalbudsjettet 1951, Vedlegg B, p. 137.

6. Statistisk Sentralbyrå, Statistisk Økonomisk Utsyn over krigsårene, p. 239.

7. Gøthe, Lønnspolitikken etter Krigen, p. 12.

8. See Chapter 3.

9. Provisorisk Anordning om Midlertidig Ordning av Lønns- og Arbeidsvilkår i Befridde Distrikter, vedtatti statsråd 15. September 1944, chapter 1, section 1.

10. Ibid., section 2. Wages in private enterprises where no collective agreement existed were to be determined in accordance with regulations established by the state mediator (chapter 2, section 8).

11. Ibid., section 2.

12. Arbeidernes Faglige Landsorganisasjon, Protokoll over forhandlingene ved Representantskapets Møte i Oslo, 18–21 June 1945, p. 169.

13. Fri Fagbevegelse, no. 2 (September 1945), p. 5.

14. For adult males the board's calculations were as follows:

Full compensation	97 øre
Three-quarters compensation	73 øre
Cost of living supplements being paid	38 øre
"Wage drift"	15 øre
Board's award	20 øre

15. See above.
16. Speech of Finance Minister Brofoss to Trade Union Congress 1946, Arbeidernes Faglige Landsorganisasjon, *Protokoll over Kongressen* (1946), pp. 239, 243, and 249.
17. *St. meld. nr. 43 (1947): Om saerlige tiltak til trygging av landets økonomi.*
18. *Ibid.*, p. 6.
19. *Ibid.*, p. 18.
20. See also Gøthe, *Lønnspolitikken etter Krigen*, p. 19.
21. Arbeidernes Faglige Landsorganisasjon, *Protokoll over Forhandlingene ved Representantskapets Møte i Oslo den 27–29 November 1947*, p. 21.
22. Gøthe, *Lønnspolitikken etter Krigen*, p. 20. (Emphasis in the original.)
23. Arbeidernes Faglige Landsorganisasjon, *Protokoll over Forhandlingene ved Representantskapets Møte i Oslo, 14. April 1948*, p. 9.
24. Gøthe, *Lønnspolitikken etter Krigen*, pp. 21–22.
25. Gøthe, *Ibid.*, p. 22.
26. *St. meld. nr. 1 (1950), Nasjonalbudsjettet 1950*, p. 33.
27. *St. meld. nr. 43 (1950), Tillegg til nasjonalbudsjettet 1950, om tiltak til a trygge stabilitcten i landets økonomi* (April 2, 1950). Appendix A.
28. *Ibid.*, p. 46.
29. Statement of Konrad Nordahl, chairman of the LO, reported in Arbeidernes Faglige Landsorganisasjon, *Beretning* (1950), p. 107.
30. Konrad Nordahl, chairman of the LO, in a speech to LO Representative Council Meeting, October 30, 1951, *Protokoll over forhandlingene ved Representantskapets møte i Oslo, 30–31 Oktober 1951*, p. 10.
31. Report of the Monetary and Financial Council, October 15, 1951, quoted in Wage Board Decision of December 7, 1951. Lønnsnemnda, Sak Nr. 205, Kjennelse avsagt 7. desember 1951 (mimeographed), p. 42.
32. *Ibid.*, p. 55.
33. "Uttalelse fra det økonomiske samordningsråd," *St. meld. nr. 1, 1952, Nasjonalbudsjettet 1952,* Vedlegg 11, p. 138.
34. Odd Gøthe, "Nå bør prisene stabiliseres," *Fri Fagbevegelse* (January 15, 1952), pp. 8–10.
35. Lønnsnemnda, Sak Nr. 205, p. 47.

Chapter 5

The Struggle for Wage-Price Stability, 1952–1958

1. Konrad Nordahl in a speech to the Representative Council of the LO, October 30, 1951. *Protokoll over forhandlingene ved Representantskapets møte i Oslo, 30–31 Oktober 1951*, pp. 22–23.
2. Speech by Prime Minister Oscar Torp in the Storting, February 16, 1952.
3. Speech of P. Mentsen to the Representative Council Meeting in May, 1952, *Protokoll*, pp. 36–37.
4. *Arbeidsgiveren*, no. 6 (March, 1952), pp. 52–53; no. 7 (March 14, 1952), pp. 59–60.

5. "Jernindustrien til Lønnsnemnda," *Fri Fagbevegelse,* no. 4 (April 15, 1952), p. 114.

6. Lønnsnemnda Sak, nr. 214 (April 4, 1952); reprinted in *Arbeidsgiveren,* no. 10 (April 18, 1952), pp. 89–92.

7. *Økonomisk Utsyn over året 1952,* N.O.S. XI, 119 (Oslo, 1951), p. 91.

8. Interview with Kjell Holler, Chief Economist of the LO, July 6, 1956.

9. *Økonomisk Utsyn over året 1952,* pp. 85ff.

10. "Krav om effektive tiltak mot prisstigningen," *Fri Fagbevegelse* (October 15, 1952), p. 293.

11. *St. meld. nr. 1 (1953): Nasjonalbudsjettet 1953,* p. 32.

12. Speech of Finance Minister Trygve Bratteli before Representative Council of the LO, *Protokoll 1953,* pp. 17–31.

13. *Protokoll over forhandlingene ved Representantskapets møte i Oslo 19–20 January 1953,* p. 34.

14. Arbeidernes Faglige Landsorganisasjon, *Protokoll over Kongressen 1953* (Oslo), p. 285.

15. Finance Minister Bratteli's address to the Representative Council of the LO, November 1953. Arbeidernes Faglige Landsorganisasjon, *Protokoll over forhandlingene ved Representantskapets møte i Oslo, 26. November 1953,* p. 18.

16. *Ibid.,* p. 22.

17. Nordahl in address to the Representative Council (November 1953), *Protokoll,* p. 32.

18. Statistisk Sentralbyrå, *Økonomisk Utsyn over året 1954* (Oslo, 1955), p. 88.

19. Arbeidernes Faglige Landsorganisasjon, *Trade Union News Bulletin from Norway,* no. 4, 9:26 (April 1954).

20. "Politiske Direktiver til de fagorganiserte," *Fri Fagbevegelse* (May 15, 1954), p. 131.

21. Arbeidernes Faglige Landsorganisasjon, *Beretning 1954* (Oslo, 1955), p. 84.

22. *Fri Fagbevegelse,* no. 10 (Oktober 1954), p. 292.

23. "Price control according to the terms of the proposed law does not imply that comprehensive and detailed regulations by the government, which might be necessary in certain economic situations, will be introduced or maintained as permanent measures." *Ot. prop. nr. 60 (1952) Lov om priser og konkurranse-reguleringer m.v.,* p. 53.

24. Lov av 26, juni, 1953, om kontroll og regulering av priser, utbytte, og konkurranseforhold.

25. See *St. meld. nr. 27 (1955), Prisreguleringsoverenskomsten 1953–54,* pp. 11–15.

26. Jordbruksavtalen av 16, april 1956 (Reprinted in Landbrukets Sentralforbund, *Landbruksøkonomiske Oversikter,* May 1956).

27. Action of the Representative Council Meeting of the LO, January 16, 1956, reported in *Fri Fagbevegelse,* Nr. 2 (February 1956), p. 45.

Chapter 6
The Evolution of General Wage Changes

1. Some econometric research to investigate the strength and character of the influences operating on wages outside the contractual agreements is being planned by Mr. Hermod Skånland of the Norwegian Ministry of Finance. I am indebted to him for several valuable discussions of these problems and for the opportunity to read the preliminary outline of his study which presents, in important respects, an analysis similar to the one given here.

2. See, for example, Odd Gøthe, *Lønnspolitikken etter Krigen* (Oslo, 1951), pp. 75–77; The Swedish Confederation of Trade Unions, *Trade Unions and Full Employment* (Stockholm, 1953), pp. 55–56; A. Lund, "Spontan og autonom lønstigning" in *Festskrift til Jørgen Pedersen* (Copenhagen, 1951); H. A. Turner, "Wages: Industry Rates, Workplace Rates, and the Wage Drift," *The Manchester School of Economic and Social Studies*, 24:95–123, no. 2 (May 1956).

3. Statistisk Sentralbyrå, *Lønnsstatistikk 1951*, p. 22.

4. See also the report of the Secretariat to LO Congress 1946. *Protokoll over Kongressen 1946*, pp. 396–97.

5. Statistisk Sentralbyrå, *Arbeidslønninger 1949*, N.O.S. 11:23, no. 54; *Lønnsstatistikk 1952*, N.O.S. 11:32, no. 163.

6. See also Lars Aarvig, "Lønnsutvikling og Lønnspolitikk i Norge etter Krigen," *Økonomi, Mai* 1957, no. 31, p. 93.

7. Statistisk Sentralbyrå, *Lønnsstatistikk 1951*, N.O.S. 11:22, no. 126.

8. Reported in Swedish Conferation of Trade Unions, *Trade Unions and Full Employment* (Stockholm, 1953), p. 56.

9. Bent Hansen and Gösta Rehn, "On Wage Drift: A Problem in Money-Wage Dynamics," in *25 Essays in Honour of Erik Lindahl*. Stockholm: Ekonomisk Tidskrift, 1956.

10. The counterparts to these problems which wage drifting posed for national wage policy in Norway have also been recognized and emphasized in essentially similar situations in other countries. See, for example, H. A. Turner, "Wages: Industry Rates, Workplace Rates and the Wage Drift," *The Manchester School of Social Studies*, 24:117ff., no. 2 (May 1956), and The Swedish Confederation of Trade Unions, *Trade Unions and Full Employment*, pp. 86ff.

Chapter 7

Wages, Prices, and Labor Costs

1. On the construction of the cost-of-living index, see Statistisk Sentralbyrå, *Statistiske Oversikter 1948*, N.O.S. 10:330–331, no. 178 (Oslo, 1949), and article in *Statistiske Meldinger*, no. 6 (1953), pp. 129–142. On consumption price index, see Statistisk Sentralbyrå, *Nasjonalregnskap 1930–1939 og 1946–1951*, N.O.S. 11:67–70, no. 109 (Oslo, 1952).

2. It should be mentioned that the average annual income figures are average income per full-time equivalent employed and not an average per worker. This restricts the use of the figures as an indicator of worker income since "man-year" is defined as the normal working year and varies from as little as 26 weeks in whaling to the legal maximum of 49 weeks. See *Nasjonalregnskap 1930–1939 og 1946–1951*, p. 329 note 2, table 39.

3. Konrad Nordahl, in a speech to the Representative Council of the LO, May 1952. Arbeidernes Faglige Landsorganisasjon, *Protokoll over forhandlingene ved Representantskapets møte in Oslo* (May 1952), pp. 35–36.

4. See *Jamstilling Komitteens Instilling* (Komitteen Oppnevnt ved Kongelig Resolusjon av 7. juni 1946) (Oslo, 1951).

5. "Prisutviklingen i Norge etter Krigen," *Statistiske Meldinger*, Nr. 10, 1956, pp. 346–64.

6. Lars Aarvig, *Lønnsutvikling og Lønnspolitikk i Norge etter Krigen*, p. 97.

7. Lars Aarvig, *Lønnsutvikling og Lønnspolitikk i Norge etter Krigen*, p. 121.

Chapter 8

Wages, Incomes, and The Financing of Investment

1. "The assistance given under the Marshall Plan made it possible to carry on with the reconstruction programme of 1946. I would stress the fact that this programme has at all times formed the fundamental basis for our policy and actions." Erik Brofoss, *Norway's Economic and Financial Problems: Two Lectures by the Norwegian Minister of Commerce at the University of Oslo Summer School for American Students* (July 1952) (mimeographed), p. 22.

2. *St. meld. nr. 62 (1953). Om et langtidsprogram for 1954–1957; St. meld. nr. 67 (1957). Om langtidsprogrammet for 1958–1961.*

3. An analysis of the Norwegian postwar economic programs which does attempt some evaluation of the planning compared to actual developments has been made by Miss Alice Bourneuf in *Norway: The Planned Revival* (Cambridge: Harvard University Press, 1958). Miss Bourneuf's study covers in more detail for the period 1945 to 1952 the fiscal and monetary aspects of Norwegian policy which are touched upon in this chapter.

4. Brofoss, *Norway's Economic and Financial Problems: Two Lectures*, p. 22. The dry summer of 1947 which adversely affected agriculture output and the supply of electric power was also a contributing factor in the 1947 decision to cut back.

5. Note should be made that the national accounts figures used here are based on Norwegian definitions which differ significantly from those of the United States and United Kingdom, for example. In particular, gross investment in Norway includes ordinary repairs and maintenance as well as a certain amount of government investment which in the United States would be excluded from the investment category. The conclusion in the text holds, however, even when allowance is made for these differences. See "Enkelte Trekk ved Investieringsvirksomhet i Norge," *Statistiske Meldinger* no. 12 (1954), p. 425, based on OEEC statistics.

6. See also Storting Melding Nr. 1 (1951), *Nasjonalbudsjettet 1951*, Vedlegg, p. 137.

7. This follows from the accounting identity

Net Domestic Investment + Net Foreign Investment = Public Saving + Private Saving

Subtracting net public investment and net transfers received from abroad from both sides we have

Net Private Domestic Investment − Import Surplus = Government Surplus + Private Domestic Saving

The import surplus as here defined is the concept used in U. S. national accounting and differs from the Norwegian definition in that it includes net interest and dividend expenditures abroad. The government "surplus" obtained by subtracting net public investment from public saving can be considered only an approximation to the concept employed in the U. S. national accounts.

8. See *St. meld. nr. 1 (1953): Nasjonalbudsjettet 1953*, p. 19 and pp. 31–32.

9. Odd Aukrust, "Trends and Cycles in Norwegian National Income Shares," in *Income and Wealth Series VI* (1957) published by the International Association for Research in Income and Wealth.

10. *St. meld. nr. 75 (1952), Retningslinjer for Penge- og kredittpolitikken*, p. 4.

11. See *St. meld. nr. 75 (1952). Retningslinjer for Penge- og kredittpolitikken* in which the guidelines for monetary policy during this period were laid down.

12. *Ot. prp. nr. 55 (1953)*: *Om midlertidig lov om adgang til regulering av renter og provisjon* (passed July 17, 1953, and made effective as of September 15, 1953).

13. *Ot. prp. nr. 80 (1952)*: *Lov om kontroll og regulering av priser, utbytter og konkurranseforhold* (passed July 26, 1953 and made effective as of January 1, 1954).

14. See Chapter 5 above.

15. *Norges Bank: Report and Accounts for the Year 1956* (Oslo, 1957) p. 5.

Chapter 9

Wage Structure and Employment

1. See Gunnar Braathen, "Sysselsettingsproblemene i Norske Naeringsliv," *Arbeidsmarkedet*, no. 10 (1953), pp. 426–431.

2. For description in English of Norwegian employment service activities, see *Employment Policy in Norway: A Survey* published by the Norwegian Joint Committee on International Social Policy (Oslo, May 1950) and "An Outline of Social Legislation," *Norges Bank Bulletin*, no. 3 1953, pp. 5–8. Also, Galenson, *Labor in Norway*, pp. 268–271.

3. Galenson, *Labor in Norway*, p. 2.

4. Odd Gøthe, *Lønns-politikk etter Krigen*, pp. 27–28. See also Galenson, *ibid.*, pp. 175–176 and p. 295.

5. Gøthe, *ibid.*, pp. 38–39. (Emphasis supplied).

6. Konrad Nordahl, Chairman of the LO, in the Representative Council meeting, October 30, 1950, *Protokoll over forhandlingene ved Representantskapets Møte 30–31 October, 1951*, p. 11.

7. Gøthe, *Labor in Norway*, pp. 55–56 (Emphasis in the original).

8. "Lønnsdifferensieringen mellom faglaerte og ufaglaerte arbeidskraft," *Fri Fagbevegelse*, no. 10 (October 15, 1953), p. 325.

9. Konrad Nordahl in an address to the 1949 Congress of the LO, *Protokoll over Kongressen 1949*, pp. 213–214.

10. *Fri Fagbevegelse* no. 10 (1953), p. 325.

11. P. Mentsen, vice-chairman of the LO in a report to the Representative Council on the 1952 negotiations, *Protokoll over forhandlingene ved Representantskapets møte i Oslo, 19 og 20 Mai 1952*, p. 37.

12. See also Norwegian Joint Committee on International Social Policy, *Employment Policy in Norway*, p. 45.

13. Braathen, "Sysselsettingsproblemene i Norske Naeringsliv," *Arbeidsmarkedet*, p. 427. These are rough estimates; unfortunately the statistics are not sufficiently detailed to permit any analysis of what population groups (by age, sex, industry, etc.) were most important in increasing labor force participation.

14. *St. meld. nr. 62 (1953)* p. 119. In part, the problem is being attacked from the opposite side, so to speak, through measures designed to direct new and expanding industries to locations outside of the present industrial areas. See also *ibid.*, Chapter XV.

15. See Reynolds and Taft, *The Evolution of Wage Structure* and Rothbaun, "National Wage-Structure Comparisons" in Taylor and Pierson (eds.) *New Concepts of Wage-Determination*, pp. 299–327.

16. See also John T. Dunlop, "Wage-Price Relations at High Level Employment," *The American Economic Review* (May 1947), pp. 243–253.

17. In the 1949 negotiations the LO proposed, without success, an addition to the master agreement with the Employers' Association providing that no reduction in piece rates could be instituted except when "the production increases are due to new

machines or other technical rationalization measures." According to Gøthe the object was to remove the fear of piece rate cutting so as to make possible greater use of incentive systems and "greater effort on the part of the individual worker." Gøthe, *Lønns-politikk etter Krigen*, p. 82.

18. *Lønnsstatistikk*, 1952, p. 40.

Chapter 10
Trade Unions and Wages in A Controlled Economy

1. Galenson, *Labor in Norway*, p. 339.

2. Konrad Nordahl in remarks before the 1953 LO congress, *Protokoll over Kongressen* 1953, p. 71.

3. Arbeidernes Faglige Landsorganisasjon, *Protokoll over Kongressen* (1953), pp. 359–60.

4. Melvin Reder, "The General Level of Money Wages," Industrial Relations *Research Association: Proceedings of the Third Annual Meeting 1950*, p. 192.

5. See, for example, A. M. Ross, *Trade Union Wage Policy*, p. 4.

6. J. R. Hicks, "Economic Foundations of Wage Policy," *Economic Journal*, 65:391, no. 259 (September 1955).

7. John T. Dunlop, "The Task of Contemporary Wage Theory" in Dunlop (ed.), *The Theory of Wage Determination*.

8. T. Haavelmo, *The Probability Approach in Econometrics*, Cowles Commission Papers, New Series, no. 4 (1944), Chapter II, Section 8.

9. Cf. Lindblom, *Unions and Capitalism*, p. 138: "The first or immediate consequence of unionism's new power will be unemployment or inflation."

10. Walter A. Morton, "Trade Unionism, Full Employment and Inflation," *American Economic Review*, 60:26, no. 1 (March 1950).

11. William H. Beveridge, *Full Employment in a Free Society* (New York: W. W. Norton & Co., Inc., 1945), p. 200.

12. Martin Tranmael, quoted in Galenson, *Labor in Norway*, p. 338.

13. See Sverre Sultuvedt, "Tanken om industrielt demokrati," *Fri Fagbevegelse*, December 15, 1952, pp. 356–57 and series of comments and replies in succeeding issues.

14. Beveridge, *Full Employment in a Free Society*, p. 199. Since our interest here is with the problem of economic stability under full employment, we shall not be concerned with the corollary conclusion that there is no inherent mechanism which can assure full employment at any freely determined wage level. But we may note that the implication of challenging the extra-economic nature of wage determination is not that under-employment equilibrium cannot exist but that, if it does, it will not be simply because of non-economic behavior in the labor market and that government efforts to reach full employment cannot be confined to fiscal policy measures which neglect any impact on the wage level.

15. Ross, *Trade Union Wage Policy*, p. 97.

16. Galenson, *Labor in Norway*, pp. 320–21.

17. In this respect Norwegian experience parallels that of Sweden. See also Swedish Confederation of Trade Unions, *Trade Unions and Full Employment* (Stockholm, 1953).

18. See also the essay by H. G. Johnson, "The Determination of the General Level of Wage Rates," in Dunlop (ed.) *The Theory of Wage Determination*. Essentially

the same point lies at the heart of R. G. Hawtrey's analysis of Great Britain's economic problems in his book *Cross Purposes in Wage Policy*.

19. See also C. E. Lindblom, "Labor Policy, Full Employment, and Inflation" in Max F. Millikan (ed.), *Income Stabilization for a Developing Democracy,* pp. 536–37 and Henri Anjac, "Inflation as the Monetary Consequence of the Behavior of Social Groups," *International Economic Papers,* no. 4 (1954), pp. 109–123.

20. Sir Douglas Copeland, "The Full Employment Economy with Special Reference to Wages Policy," *Oxford Economic Papers* (*New Series*), 5:221–234 (October, 1953).

21. Kenneth Arrow, *Social Choice and Individual Values,* Cowles Commission Monograph no. 12 (1951).

22. Cf. Arrow, *Social Choice,* pp. 89–91.

23. See Robert K. Merton, *Social Theory and Social Structure* (Glencoe, Ill., 1949), p. 134. "To the extent that a society is stable . . . conformity to both cultural goals and institutionalized means . . . is the most common and widely diffused [type of individual adaptation]. Were this not so the stability and conformity of the society could not be maintained."

24. Paul Samuelson, "Principles and Rules in Modern Fiscal Policy," in *Money, Trade and Economic Growth: In Honor of John H. Williams* (New York: Macmillan, 1951), pp. 157–176.

25. Herbert A. Simon, *Models of Man: Social and Rational* (New York: John Wiley and Sons, Inc., 1957), p. 199.

Index of Names

The Library of Congress has cataloged this book as follows:

Leiserson, Mark Whittlesey.
    Wages and economic control in Norway, 1945–1957. Cambridge, Harvard University Press, 1959.

    174 p.   24 cm.   (Wertheim publications in industrial relations)

    1. Norway—Economic policy.   2. Wages—Norway.   i. Title.

HC365.L4   331.29481   59–5565 ‡

Library of Congress